STORIES FROM GAELIC IRELAND

Stories from Gaelic Ireland

Microhistories from the
sixteenth-century Irish annals

BERNADETTE CUNNINGHAM AND
RAYMOND GILLESPIE

FOUR COURTS PRESS

Set in 11.5 on 14 point Centaur for
FOUR COURTS PRESS
7 Malpas Street, Dublin 8, Ireland
e-mail: info@four-courts-press.ie
http://www.four-courts-press.ie
and in North America
FOUR COURTS PRESS
c/o ISBS, 920 N.E. 58th Street, Suite 300, Portland, OR 97213.

A catalogue record for this title
is available from the British Library.

ISBN 1–85182–747–1

Printed in Great Britain
by MPG Books, Bodmin, Cornwall.

Contents

Illustrations

Abbreviations

AConn	A.M. Freeman (ed.), *Annála Connacht: the annals of Connacht, 1224–1544* (Dublin, 1944, reprint Dublin, 1970)
AFM	John O'Donovan (ed.), *Annála ríoghachta Éireann: annals of the kingdom of Ireland by the Four Masters* (7 vols, Dublin, 1854, reprint New York, 1966)
ALC	W.M. Hennessy (ed.), *The annals of Loch Cé* (2 vols, London, 1871, reprint Dublin, 1939)
AU	W.M. Hennessy and B. MacCarthy (eds), *Annála Uladh, Annals of Ulster; otherwise Annála Senait, Annals of Senat: a chronicle of Irish affairs, 431-1131, 1155-1541* (4 vols, Dublin, 1887-1901, reprint Dublin, 1998).
BL	British Library
Cal. Carew MSS	*Calendar of the Carew manuscripts preserved in the archiepiscopal library at Lambeth,* (6 vols, London, 1867-73)
Cal. pat. rolls Ire., Jas I	*Irish patent rolls of James I: facsimile of the Irish record commissioners' calendar prepared prior to 1830,* with foreword by M.C. Griffith (Dublin, 1966)
Cal. S.P. Ire.,	*Calendar of the state papers relating to Ireland* (24 vols, London, 1860-1911)
DIL	*Dictionary of the Irish language based mainly on Old and Middle Irish materials* (Dublin, 1983)
Fiants Ire.,	*The Irish fiants of the Tudor sovereigns* (4 vols, Dublin, 1994), reprinted from *Reports of the Deputy Keeper of the Public Records in Ireland, 1875-1890*)
NA	National Archives, Dublin
NLI	National Library of Ireland
PRO	Public Records Office, London
RIA	Royal Irish Academy, Dublin
TCD	Trinity College, Dublin

Note on editorial style

Quotations from Irish language texts have not been normalised and follow the forms of the published editions cited. Where published translations into English are available of texts in Latin or Irish we have used those translations in quotations, making amendments only where the existing translation is misleading.

Personal names of individuals of Gaelic origin are given in Irish in the text unless they are better known under the English form of the name. Names of families and individuals of Anglo-Norman origin are given in English throughout. Place-names are given in anglicised form.

Dates are given old-style with the year beginning on 1 January which was the normal annalistic practice in the sixteenth century.

Preface

In the 1760s the Dublin antiquarian Walter Harris prepared for publication a translation of the works of one of his distinguished seventeenth-century relatives, Sir James Ware. Harris explained to his readers that 'a mere amusement, however odd it may seem, first led me into this laborious undertaking'. While we have not had the benefit of what Harris describes as 'a country retirement' to carry on this work we think we understand something of his motivation. The essays which make up this volume were also written for 'amusement', as a result of encountering what we thought were strange episodes which featured in the annalistic records of the sixteenth century. While Ware and many others have plundered the Irish annals for information on subjects relevant to specific research topics this book exploits the annals in a different way. Rather than quarrying the text for facts we have focused on the annalists as storytellers. The stories they told are not literary creations which, in the modern sense, make a virtue of originality. Rather the stories reflect the familiar codes and conventions of other early modern prose writing in Irish. Identifying such conventions and codes helps us to understand something of the historical and cultural worlds which shaped the stories discussed here. We believe that our focus on these stories sheds light on the hopes, fears and beliefs of those who told the stories, and of the peoples and societies about whom these stories were originally told.

As the narrator of the late twelfth- or early thirteenth-century text *Acallam na Senórach* observed 'storytelling is a complicated matter' [gablánach in rét an scéluighecht] and the stories told here are no different from their medieval predecessors. It would not have been possible to relate them if it were not for generations of scholars who prepared the editions of the texts on which we have relied and so made them accessible to non-specialists.

More recently a number of people have assisted us in a variety of ways. We have presented versions of some of these stories to seminar audiences throughout Ireland including Tuam, Roscrea, Dublin and Maynooth and we have benefited from the informed comments of listeners. Pádraig Ó Riain advised us on the use of hagiographical source material and Salvador Ryan on late medieval religion. Heather King lent us her drawing of the Fitton brass which is reproduced as figure 16 below. We are particularly grateful to Caoimhín Breatnach and to Edel Bhreathnach who each read and commented on drafts of all the essays in this collection. We are very grateful for their advice and corrections.

When the Church of Ireland dean of Elphin, Francis Burke, reported on his first encounter with the Annals of Loch Cé in his *Loch Cé and its annals* (Dublin, 1895) he observed

> the details of the Annals are set before us in such an abrupt, discon-
> nected and unattractive form that we cannot wonder at the general
> ignorance which prevails of their contents. Any effort, then, made to
> put the facts of this narrative into a readable shape and which makes
> accessible to all a valuable source of knowledge, which hardly one in
> five thousand would otherwise care to investigate, is not altogether
> devoid of credit.

We hope that this book would have been acceptable to Francis Burke.

B.C.
R.G.

Introduction: sources and methods

This is a book about the private lives of public events. The stories discussed in this volume are all public events, well known and easily accessible. They were recorded by the learned class of Gaelic Ireland in their historical annals of notable persons and events. The private lives behind those well-known stories are less easy to reconstruct. The modern historian's interpretative methodology of weaving motives around actions is constrained by the relative scarcity of evidence from a society which lacked a centralised mechanism for record keeping. The political structures within that society were highly fragmented and the particular focus of texts such as the annals does not readily facilitate historians' attempts to describe them. Those who compiled the various annals concentrated on immediate events and personalities rather than on descriptions of polities or territories. Their mental geographies served to emphasise the specific power relationships of individual leaders rather than the underlying structure of lordship. The annals also reflect local societies in which there were significant differences in social organisation between one lordship and the next. The extent of this local variation makes it vital for the historian to situate descriptions of the social order in specific times and places. That is why these stories of lordship, church, learning, lineage, life and death, are important. The narratives of particular events discussed in these essays, selected from among those that have survived in the annals, help to delineate the framework of social relations in particular places in sixteenth-century Ireland. Set in specific locations, and telling stories of the exploits of particular people in those places, the stories lay bare some of the assumptions, spoken and unspoken, that informed social interaction. Historians who have attempted to understand Gaelic society on these terms in the past have highlighted two main difficulties: the sparseness of the evidence and the intractable nature of that evidence. Using the existing evidence and the techniques of microhistory, this book of essays seeks to turn these two perceived problems into strengths.

I

By comparison with other western European societies sixteenth-century Gaelic
Ireland is an underdocumented world. The reasons for this are complex. One
reason is certainly that some records emanating from within that society have
been destroyed through war or poor record-keeping. A second is that certain
kinds of records never existed. For example, unlike other western European
societies, Gaelic Ireland never developed a centralised legal authority or chancery-
like body. A third explanation is that the socially prescribed rules for writing
meant that before the sixteenth century relatively few documents of the kind
associated with administrative government were generated in Gaelic Ireland,
remembering being carried on through oral tradition. The kinds of written
sources that survive from Gaelic Ireland are those appropriate to a kin-based
lordship society, most commonly comprising genealogies and political poetry.

Within this context the four major sets of Irish historical annals that contain substantial entries relating to the sixteenth century are of exceptional significance. Three of these compilations, the Annals of Ulster, the Annals of
Connacht, and the Annals of Loch Cé may be regarded as roughly contemporary with the events they record for the sixteenth century, in so far as the manuscripts reached their extant form in the course of that century. The Ulster
annals open with the year 431, and the text as it is now known survives in two
manuscripts, Trinity College, Dublin MS 1282 and Bodleian Library MS
Rawlinson B 489. A significant portion of both manuscripts was written by
one scribe, Ruaidhrí Ó Luinín. He completed the text as far as AD 1489 in the
Trinity College, Dublin manuscript. The manuscript was then continued by
two scribes, and it probably extended to the year 1532, though it is now incomplete and ends at the year 1504. The manuscript was prepared under the direction of Cathal Óg Mac Maghnusa 'one that projected and collected and compiled this book from very many other books' [nech ro chumdaigh 7 ro th f eglaim
7 ro thinoil an leabur sa a leabhraibh ilímdai[bh] ailibh.][1] Ó Luinín then col-
laborated with Ruaidhrí Ua Caiside in transcribing a second copy of the Annals
of Ulster, now Bodleian manuscript Rawlinson B 489, for the use of Ruaidhrí
Mac Craith of Termonmagrath. This manuscript has numerous sixteenth-cen-

---

1 *AU*, iii, pp 430–1; TCD, MS 1282 was the manuscript known to the Four Masters as 'The book of
Seanadh Mhic Mhaghnusa on Lough Erne' [*Leabhar Seanaidh Mec Maghnusa for Loch Érne*]; the title relates
to the place where the annals were compiled in County Fermanagh (*AFM*, i, p. lxiv); Nollaig Ó Muraíle,
'*Annála Uladh*: the Annals of Ulster: introduction to the 1998 reprint' *AU* (repr. Dublin, 1998), p. 6.

tury additions by unidentified scribes that are unique to this copy of the Ulster annals. Gearóid Mac Niocaill's assessment of the early sixteenth-century portion of the Rawlinson B 489 text of the Annals of Ulster is that 'it ranks as a contemporary source in its own right'.[2] The most recent analysis of the scribal hands in Rawlinson B 489, published in the catalogue of Irish manuscripts in the Bodleian Library prepared by Brian Ó Cuív, has revised earlier findings as to the identity of the scribes involved. Ó Cuív concludes that Ruaidhrí Ua Caiside wrote the text of Rawlinson B 489 to the beginning of 952, followed by Ruaidhrí Ó Luinín who wrote the section for the years 952 to 1506. An unidentified 'scribe 3' then took over and assisted by 'scribe 4' wrote the section 1507 to 1535 which contains the two stories from the Annals of Ulster discussed here.[3] The stories of 'The burning of Domnach Magh da Claine (1508)', and 'The murder of a historian (1534)' are recorded in the Rawlinson B 489 manuscript only, and in Ó Cuív's view are the work of 'scribe 3'. As many as ten scribes added further sixteenth-century material to the manuscript, including Matha Ó Luinín, grandson of one of the original scribes, who lamented the untidy contributions other scribes had made to his grandfather's exemplary manuscript.[4]

The Annals of Connacht were ultimately the product of the Ó Maoil Chonaire school of *seanchas*.[5] The unique surviving manuscript of the Annals of Connacht, Royal Irish Academy MS C iii 1, covers the years 1224 to 1544 with one later entry dated 1562. Although there is still doubt as to the identity of the scribes, this sixteenth-century vellum manuscript is thought to be the work of Paitín Ó Duibhgeannáin, Seán Riabhach Ó Duibhgeannáin and a third, unnamed, scribe who was probably also a member of the Ó Duibhgeannáin family.[6] The text is believed to derive from a mid-fifteenth century Ó Maoil Chonaire compilation, an origin it shares with the more extensive Annals of Loch Cé.[7] It has been suggested that the Annals of Connacht may possibly be the source known to the Four Masters as '*Lebhar Muintere*

2 Gearóid Mac Niocaill, *The medieval Irish annals* (Dublin, 1975), p. 37; Ó Muraíle, 'Annála Uladh' in *AU* reprint, pp 18–19. 3 Brian Ó Cuív, *Catalogue of Irish language manuscripts in the Bodleian Library at Oxford and Oxford College libraries, part 1* (Dublin, 2001), pp 156–61; Ó Cuív's analysis of the scribal hands in the Rawlinson B 489 manuscript substantially revises the findings of Aubrey Gwynn cited in Ó Muraíle, 'Annála Uladh', in *AU* reprint, p. 19. 4 Mac Niocaill, *The medieval Irish annals*, p. 37; Ó Muraíle, 'Annála Uladh' in *AU* reprint, pp 18–19. 5 Mac Niocaill, *The medieval Irish annals*, pp 32–3; *AConn*, pp x–xiv. 6 *Catalogue of Irish manuscripts in the Royal Irish Academy* (Dublin, 1926–70), pp 3274–5; but see also *AConn*, pp x–xiv; in a footnote to his discussion of the scribes of Annals of Connacht, Freeman seems keen to accept the suggestion that the Annals of Connacht should be identified as the 'Annals of Kilronan', *AConn*, p. xiv, n. 2. 7 Mac Niocaill, *The medieval Irish annals*, p. 32.

Duibgeandáin chille Rónáin' [Book of the O'Duigenans of Kilronan], though this
identification is not certain.[8]

The third major collection of sixteenth-century annals, the Annals of Loch
Cé, were compiled under the direction of Brian Mac Diarmada in the years
1588-9. The Mac Diarmada family of Moylurg traditionally had their chief residence at Carraig Mhic Diarmada, situated in Lough Key, in north Roscommon.
The principal surviving manuscript of the Loch Cé annals containing entries
for years between 1014 and 1577 (with major lacunae) is now Trinity College
Dublin MS 1293. The manuscript is the work of various scribes, principally
Pilib Ballach Ó Duibhgeannáin but also including Brian Mac Diarmada himself. Another section of the Annals of Loch Cé, covering the years 1568 to 1590
can be found in British Library Additional MS 4792, a manuscript contemporary with the events it describes.[9] It is unclear whether British Library
Additional MS 4792 was originally intended as an integral part of the Annals
of Loch Cé,[10] but this latter source is important as it is the only extant near
contemporary annalistic source for the later sixteenth century, the Annals of
the Four Masters being compiled more than a generation later. The older sections of the Annals of Loch Cé, like the Annals of Connacht, are thought to
derive from a mid-fifteenth century Ó Maoil Chonaire source and there is a

---

8 *AFM*, i, p. lxv; Mac Niocaill, *The medieval Irish annals*, pp 32-5; O Muraíle, '*Annála Uladh*' in *AU* reprint, p.
27. There may, of course, have been more than one manuscript of this title, with place identifiers used to
distinguish between separate manuscripts associated with different branches of the Ó Duibhgeannáin
family. The extent of the correspondence between the fifteenth- and sixteenth-century entries in the Annals
of Connacht and the Annals of the Four Masters appears to justify the conclusion that the manuscript
now known as the Annals of Connacht derives from an annalistic source that was available to the Four
Masters and probably known to them as '*Lebhar Muintere Duibgeandáin Chille Rónáin*'. Other manuscripts used
by Mícheál Ó Cléirigh in the early seventeenth century were also linked to the Ó Duibhgeannáin family
(Paul Walsh, *Irish men of learning* (Dublin, 1947) pp 13-14), but it is clear that the Ó Duibhgeannáin manu-
script that contained the text of the Leabhar Gabhála was not the manuscript described as '*Lebhar Muintere
Duibgeandáin Chille Rónáin*'. Elsewhere Ó Cléirigh described the Book of Glendalough as '*Leabhar Muintire
Duibhgeandáin ó Seanchuaich Ua nOilealla*' (Seamus Pender (ed.), 'The O'Clery book of genealogies' in *Analecta
Hibernica*, no. 18 (1951), p. 64). It has also been suggested that Bodleian Rawlinson MS B 502, was known
as the Book of the O'Duigenans (Anne O'Sullivan, 'Verses on honorific portions' in James Carney and
David Greene (eds), *Celtic studies: essays in memory of Angus Matheson* (London, 1968), p. 119). For ongoing dis-
cussion of these identifications see Pádraig Ó Riain, 'The book of Glendalough or Rawlinson B 502' in
Éigse, xviii (1981), 161–76 at pp 166–7; Caoimhín Breatnach, 'Rawlinson B 502, Lebar Glinne dá Locha and
Saltair na Rann' in *Éigse*, xxx (1997), 109–32; the most recent analysis is Ó Cuív, *Catalogue of Irish language manuscripts in the Bodleian Library*, i, pp 163–200, which does not support the identification of Rawlinson MS B
502 with the Book of the O'Duigenans.   9 *ALC*; Paul Walsh, 'The annals of Loch Cé' in *Irish Ecclesiastical
Record*, 5th ser, lvi (1940), pp 113–22.   10 A.M. Freeman asserted that BL, Add. MS 4792 'could never have
belonged to the original compilation' of the Loch Cé annals, *AConn*, p. 21.

close correspondence between the older sections of the Annals of Connacht and the Annals of Loch Cé. Again, like the Annals of Connacht, the Loch Cé annals owe their extant form primarily to the work of the learned family of Ó Duibhgeannáin.[11] For the historian of sixteenth-century Gaelic Ireland, the fact that the record of events in the Annals of Loch Cé extends almost to the end of the century gives them a particular significance since the compilers evidently had access to eyewitness accounts or very recent traditions about the events they were describing. Five of the stories in this volume are drawn from the Loch Cé annals, two of them preserved only in the fragment of those annals preserved in British Library Additional MS 4792.

Brian Mac Diarmada's role as patron of the work was important in shaping the sixteenth-century entries in these annals. It is no mere coincidence that three of the sixteenth-century stories from the annals explored in these essays relate to activities of the Mac Diarmada family as recorded in the Annals of Loch Cé. The manner in which Clann Diarmada feature in the Annals of Loch Cé is not straightforward. Some branches of the family merited more attention than others. A case in point is the treatment of the death of Eoghan Mac Diarmada in 1534. Although he merits a fulsome obituary in the Annals of Connacht, the Annals of Loch Cé simply note his death, which seems to be an instance of Brian giving less prominence to a branch of the Mac Diarmada family that was not his own.[12] Again in 1465 the Annals of Connacht record the election of Conchobhar Óg Mac Diarmada as lord of Moylurg, an event ignored by the Loch Cé annals probably for similar motives.[13]

This corpus of sixteenth-century Irish annalistic material is not without its problems of interpretation. It presents a record of selected local events, rather than a comprehensive overview of Gaelic Ireland. As the essay below on Sir Nicholas Malby demonstrates, the annalists were much less interested in national than in local events and in many cases they got even basic information about external events spectacularly wrong. This is not to say that the annalistic evidence was insular. The texts reveal evidence of knowledge about events across Europe. For example, the Annals of Loch Cé record the battle of Flodden in 1516, the General Chapter of the Franciscans in Rome in 1517, the taking of Antwerp in 1585, the campaigns of the king of Persia against the Turks, and the execution of Mary, queen of Scots. This sort of material was not collected systematically and it probably represents what came to hand locally

11 Mac Niocaill, *The medieval Irish annals*, pp 32–3.   12 *AConn*, pp 684–5; *ALC*, ii, pp 282–3.   13 *AConn*, pp 528–9; *ALC*, ii, pp 166–7.

through the movements of clergy, merchants or other casual means such as 'the folk who spread news and frequent ports' [lucht sgailti na scél ₇ chuartaighthi na cuan].¹⁴ Despite the inclusion of these external references, however, the main focus of the annals was local. Almost half of the sixteenth-century obituaries in the Annals of Loch Cé relate to Connacht families and most of these pertain to families in north Connacht. The next largest proportion relates to families from west and south-west Ulster, which traditionally had close connections with north Connacht, reflecting the geographical association between the contents of the compilation and the Mac Diarmada family of Moylurg in Roscommon. It follows from this that the concerns in the annalists' minds were local and it was local dynastic priorities that shaped the content of most entries.

The final collection of Irish annals to contain a significant number of entries relating to the sixteenth century is the Annals of the Four Masters. These annals were compiled in the 1630s in a world that was politically and culturally very different from that of the sixteenth century. Although they enjoyed the patronage of Fearghal Ó Gadhra of Sligo, they were essentially the outcome of a research project conceived and masterminded by the Irish Franciscan scholars at St Anthony's College, Louvain. Generally writing from a more national than a local perspective, and drawing on a range of earlier annals, they present a history of Ireland from Old Testament times to the year 1616. Two sets of the Annals were prepared by Mícheál Ó Cléirigh and his fellow scribes between 1632 and 1636, one set for their patron and the other set to be taken to Louvain with a view to publication perhaps in a Latin translation.¹⁵

For historians, the interpretative challenges posed by the Annals of the Four Masters as a source are rather different to those associated with the annals compiled in the sixteenth century. The first issue is simply a stylistic one. In some cases, such as the burning of the church at Domnach Magh Da Claine, which will be considered in the fourth essay in this volume, the Four Masters appear to have faithfully reproduced their source text in the Annals of Ulster with few changes. In other cases they seem to have modified their original source

---

14 *AU*, iii, pp 538-9. The same phrase occurs in *ALC*, ii, pp 236-7 and *AC*, pp 640-1 suggesting it may have a common source. 15 These two sets are now represented by five manuscripts: RIA, MSS 23 P 6; 23 P 7; C iii 3; TCD, MS 1301; University College Dublin, Franciscan MS A 13. For discussion of the relationships between these manuscripts see Nollaig Ó Muraíle, 'The autograph manuscripts of the Annals of the Four Masters' in *Celtica*, xix (1987), pp 75-95. For discussion of the background to the publication plans see Bernadette Cunningham, 'The culture and ideology of Irish Franciscan historians at Louvain, 1607-1650' in Ciarán Brady (ed.), *Ideology and the historians: Historical Studies, xvii* (Dublin, 1991), 11-30, 223-7; Pádraig A. Breatnach, 'An Irish Bollandus: Fr Hugh Ward and the Louvain hagiographical enterprise' in *Éigse*, xxxi (1999), pp 1-30, esp. p. 6.

very considerably. A case in point is the description of Ó Domhnaill's 1527 capture of Castlemore, a place we shall explore in the second essay in this volume. According to the list of sources named by the Four Masters them-selves, the Book of the Uí Duibhgeannáin of Kilronan [*Lebhar Muintere Duibgeandáin chille Rónáin*], now thought to be substantially represented by the Annals of Connacht, was their main source for this period. They also drew on material from the Annals of Ulster. In each of these sources the taking of Castlemore in 1527 is mentioned only in passing. The Annals of Connacht noted that 'O'Donnell led an army into Moylurg and destroyed the corn and buildings of the country. He took Castlemore and Bannady ...' [Sloiged leis O nDomhnaill a Moigh Luirg 7 an tir do milled idir arbar 7 fhoirgnem et an Caislen Mor 7 an Bennada do ghabail].[16] In contrast, the Annals of the Four Masters described the event in rather more detail.

> An army was mustered by O'Donnell ... and they marched on, with-out halting, until they reached Moylurg. They destroyed the whole country, both corn and buildings. They afterwards proceeded to Castlemore-Costello, for the purpose of taking it. This was an impreg-nable fortress, for it contained provisions, and every kind of engines, the best to be found at that time in Ireland for resisting enemies, such as cannon, and all sorts of weapons. These chieftains, nevertheless, proceeded to besiege the castle, and they placed their army in order all around it, so that they did not permit any person to pass from it or towards it, until they at last took it.

> [Sloicheadh lá hua ndomhnaill ... 7 ní ro hairiseadh leó co riachtat-tar Magh Luircc. Ro milleadh an tír co leair leó etir arbhar 7 foircc-neamh. Aseadh lotar iaramh co caislén mór mic Goisdealbhaigh dia ghabháil. Bá daingean díothoghlaighi eisidhé ar ro bhádar an uile aidhme gabhála fri naimhdibh feibh is deach baoí in erinn an tan sin isin mbaile ísin etir bhiudh 7 ordanás 7 gach aidhme archeana, ara aoi tra ro ghabhsat na maithe sin acc iomshuidhe imon mbaile, 7 Ro sreathnaighseat a slógha ina uirthimcheall conár leaiccseat neach anonn nó anall dia shaicchidh go ro gabhadh an caislén leó go dheóidh].[17]

The story in the Four Masters' account is longer and has more circumstantial detail than in the earlier annals, but is improbable from a sixteenth-century per-

16 *AConn*, pp 664–5.   17 *AFM*, v, pp 1390–1.

spective. Despite the annalists' attempt to expand its importance, Castlemore was not a significant fortification and it features infrequently in both English and Irish sources. It is also unlikely that the defences of the castle had cannon since these were in short supply in early sixteenth-century Ireland. Most of the ordnance was under the control of the Dublin administration although Ó Domhnaill may have acquired some cannon from France by 1516, and more ord-nance arrived by 1536.[18] It seems that, primarily to exalt the achievements of Ó Domhnaill, and perhaps also for stylistic reasons, the Four Masters enhanced their annalistic sources by interpolating other narrative prose material of dubi-ous historical accuracy. This may particularly be the case for the mid-sixteenth-century entries. The two main sources which the Four Masters claim to have used for the sixteenth century, the Annals of Ulster and the source from which the Annals of Connacht are probably derived, end in 1541 and 1544 respectively. The late sixteenth-century sources which are identifiable, *Beatha Aodha Ruaidh Uí Dhomhnaill* and, tentatively, the annals of Maoilín Óg Mac Bruaideadha, do not begin until the late 1580s.[19] For these years in the middle of the sixteenth cen-tury the Four Masters were clearly drawing on sources now lost and possibly on oral evidence. As they note in the obituary of Maghnus Ó Domhnaill under the 1563, he was well disposed to the church, poets and learned men 'as is evident from the [accounts of] old people and historians' [amhail as reil acc senaibh 7 acc seanchaidhibh].[20] The entries are certainly qualitatively different to what had gone before with longer entries than normal and on some occasions the narra-tives resort to direct speech. It has more the feel of a saga than an annalistic com-pilation.[21] At one level this makes these annals of less value as reliable accounts of sixteenth-century events than the more strictly contemporary versions.

A second distinctive feature of the Annals of the Four Masters is that they were created within a very different political and social context from the events that they describe. Predictably, the Four Masters sometimes reflect seventeenth-rather than late sixteenth-century perceptions and concerns. One of the most graphic examples of the changed perspective of the seventeenth-century annal-ists relates to their description of the religious changes of the 1530s. The entry in the contemporary Annals of Connacht for the year 1538 provides a matter-of-fact description of the destruction of images and relics and a reference to the dissolution of the religious orders. The passage ends with the brief causal

18 *AConn*, pp 630–1, 694–5; *ALC*, ii, pp 296–9.   19 Bernadette Cunningham, 'The historical annals of Maoilín Óg Mac Bruaideadha, 1588–1603' in *The Other Clare*, xiii (1989), pp 21–4; Paul Walsh (ed.), *Beatha Aodha Ruaidh Uí Dhomhnaill* (2 vols, London, 1948–57).   20 *AFM*, v, pp 1596–7.   21 For direct speech see *AFM*, v, pp 1614–5, 1670–1.

comment 'and on that account the pope and the Church both here and in the east were excommunicating the English' [7 an Papa 7 an Eclais abus 7 toir ac coinnelbhathad na Saxanach trid sin].[22] The Annals of Ulster record the destruction of these and other images in a similarly matter-of-fact way. However, rather than adding a reference to the pope the episode ends in the style of a medieval *exemplum*, where the unnamed Saxon captain deemed to be responsible for a particular act of desecration met his death 'through miracles of God and Catherine' [trid mhirbhuile De 7 Catrina].[23]

The description of the same events provided by the Annals of the Four Masters under the year 1537 displays a deeper understanding, from the perspective of continental Europe in the 1630s, of the motives for and wider context of the Reformation through which the accounts of the destruction of religious images and of monasteries could be contextualised.

> A heresy and a new error [sprang up] in England, through pride, vainglory, avarice, and lust, and through many strange sciences, so that the men of England went into opposition to the Pope and to Rome. They at the same time adopted various opinions, and [among others] the old law of Moses, in imitation of the Jewish people; and they styled the King the Chief Head of the Church of God in his own kingdom. New laws and statutes were enacted by the King and Council [parliament] according to their own will. They destroyed the orders to whom worldly possessions were allowed, namely, the Monks, Canons, Nuns, Brethren of the Cross, and the four poor orders, i.e. the orders of the Minors, Preachers, Carmelites, and Augustinians; and the lordships and livings of all these were taken up for the King. They broke down the monasteries, and sold their roofs and bells, so that from Aran of the Saints to the Iccian Sea there was not one monastery that was not broken and shattered, with the exception of a few in Ireland, of which the English took no notice or heed. They afterwards burned the images, shrines, and relics, of the saints of Ireland and England ...

> [Eithriticceacht, 7 Seachrán nua hi saxaibh tri dhiumas, 7 ionnoccbháil tria accobhar, 7 antoil, 7 tré iomatt ealadhan néccsamhail co ndeachattar fir saxan i nacchaidh an Phapa 7 na rómha acht atá ní cheana so adhrattar do bharamhlaibh examhlaibh, 7 do sheanreacht maoísi ar aithris an cinidh iudaighe, 7 ro ghairsiot áirdcheann eacclaisi

22 *AConn*, pp 710–11. 23 *AU*, iii, pp 624–5.

dé ina flaitheas feain don righ. Do rónadh las an righ ⁊ las an ccomhairle dlighthe ⁊ statuiti nuaidhe iar na ttoil feain. Ro scriosadh leó na huird diar bó ceadaighthech sealbh saoghalta do beaith occa .i. manaigh, cananaigh cailleacha dubha, ⁊ braithri croisi, ⁊ na ceaithre huird bhochta .i. an tord minúr, presidiur, carmuliti, ⁊ augustiniani. Ro tóccbhadh a tticchearnus ⁊ a mbeatha so uile gus an rígh. Ro briseadh leód na na mainistrecha. Re Reacsat a ccinn ⁊ a cclucca cona baoí aon mhainistir ó arainn na naomh co muir niocht gan briseadh, gan buansebadh acht madh beaccan namá i nérinn ná tuccsat goill dia nuí nach dia naire. Ro loiscseat bheos, ⁊ ro brisseatt iomáighe oird-earca scrine ⁊ taisi naemh Ereann ⁊ Shaxan . . .]

The Four Masters then noted the destruction of relics at Trim and Dublin before concluding

> They also appointed archbishops and sub-bishops for themselves; and, though great was the persecution of the Roman emperors against the Church, scarcely had there ever come so great a persecution from Rome as this; so that it is impossible to narrate or tell its description, unless it should be narrated by one who saw it.

> [Do rónadh leó tra airdepscoip, ⁊ suib epscoip aca feain, ⁊ ger mhor inghreaim na nimpireadh Rómhanach i nacchaidh na heaccailsi as suaill iná tainic a chomhmór so on róimh anoir riamh conách eaittir a tuaruscbháil dfhaisneais ná dinnisin muna nairneaideadh an tí do chonnairc í].[24]

This extreme example provides vivid evidence of how hindsight allowed the Four Masters write about the sixteenth century from a broader perspective than was possible for the earlier annalists who had experienced the same events at first hand.

In addition to the four major collections of annals which throw light on sixteenth-century developments in Gaelic Ireland, there are also a number of minor annals which contain further entries on sixteenth-century people and events. Historical material in the form of annals relating to Breifne for the period 1161 to 1583 survive in a unique copy in a late eighteenth-century manuscript transcribed by Philip O'Connell.[25] These annals contain entries for a total

24 *AFM*, v, pp 1444–9. 25 RIA, MS 23 F 12. The manuscript also includes an English translation of

of ninety-three years, mostly in the fifteenth and sixteenth centuries and, in the assessment of their modern editor, include 'a considerable amount of local information not known from other sources'.[26] A fragmentary historical and genealogical manuscript transcribed in part by Eoghan Carrach Mac Conmhaíl in 1668 includes miscellaneous short annals with sixteenth-century entries of both Leinster and Ulster interest.[27] A collection of short annals relating to Fermanagh in the period 1566 to 1625 form part of a manuscript transcribed in 1718 for Captain Brian Mac Conchobhair Modartha Méig Uidhir, copied from the 'Book of Knockninny' compiled in the 1630s. Though many of the entries in this compilation relate to the Mág Uidhir family, the Fermanagh annals also mention more distant events and personalities such as the building of the bridge at Athlone and the deaths of members of a variety of Ulster families including Ó Domhnaill, Ó Néill, Ó Raghallaigh, Ó Ruairc, Ó Dochartaigh and Mac Mathghamhna. As in other cases, these annals of Fermanagh record of some events not noticed in any other extant annals.[28]

II

Given the nature of the evidence that has survived from sixteenth-century Ireland reconstructing almost any aspect of its history is not straightforward. It is clear, however, that the surviving evidence for such a reconstruction is much richer that it might seem at first glance. The annals, in particular, provide a wealth of underused source material, even if the nature of the annalistic evidence is challenging. None of the annals provide a coherent narrative of sixteenth-century Irish history. Rather they present a sequence of episodic accounts of specific events arranged in annual entries. These preserve a record of the origin of social and political arrangements in their descriptions of warfare and

the annals in the hand of Theophilus O'Flanagan. The Irish text has been published, with indexes, in Éamonn de hÓir (ed.), 'Annála as Breifne' in *Breifne*, iv, no. 13 (1970), pp 59–86. **26** James Carney (ed.), *A genealogical history of the O'Reillys* (Cavan and Dublin, 1959), p. 19. **27** Annalistic extracts from TCD MS 1372 (H iv 31) are printed in Paul Walsh (ed.), 'Memoranda Gadelica' in *Irish Book Lover*, xix (1931), pp 166–71; xxii, pp 104–9; xxiii, p. 7-10; Paul Walsh (ed.), 'Short annals of Leinster' in *Irish Book Lover*, xxiv (1936), pp 58–60. **28** RIA, MS C vi 1, pp 480–4, printed with an English translation in 'Annála beaga Fear Manach: short annals of Fermanagh' in Paul Walsh, *Irish chiefs and leaders* (Dublin, 1960), pp 58–66. On the history of the Maguire manuscript known as the 'Book of Knockninny' see Bernadette Cunningham and Raymond Gillespie, 'The purposes of patronage: Brian Maguire of Knockninny and his manuscripts' in *Clogher Record*, xiii, no. 1 (1988), pp 38–49; Paul Walsh, *Irish men of learning* (Dublin, 1947), pp 241–5.

their recording of agreements on the division of territory and influence. In short they are a form of social memory. All annalistic stories are, broadly speaking, regarded as of equal importance and are recounted independently of related events noted for other years. Connections are not normally made by the annalists between events occurring in the same year which may have had a bearing on one another. At times, more than one episode relating to a named individual will be recorded in a given year without any indication of a connection between them. Thus the sort of words that narrative historians use to link events and create a large-scale history such as 'after this' or 'at the same time' are conspicuously absent from most annalistic entries.

The origins of annals, deriving ultimately from the practice of recording obituaries on Easter tables, had a lasting influence on annalistic prose style.[29] Short staccato sentences, recording essential information in the minimum of words were the norm in the early annals. The later medieval compilations regularly retained this same style but showed a growing tendency to include more discursive entries and adopt a more engaging narrative style. Causal explanations were occasionally incorporated into these longer narratives which were sometimes moral in tone. The use of direct speech, common in the narrative prose literature, is rare in the annals. Instances do, however, occur in the Annals of Connacht, as in the description of the military exploits of Murchadh Ó Conchobhair, king of Offaly, in 1406.[30] In the later sections of the Annals of the Four Masters, and particularly in the lengthy passages adapted from the writings of Lughaidh Ó Cléirigh, this story-telling device of using direct speech to enliven the narrative is particularly prominent. Thus the later sections of these annals have little in common with the concise condensed style of the earlier annalistic tradition.

Within the annals, events within a given year are not necessarily recorded in chronological order. In the Annals of Ulster for 1491, for example, the first dateable entry is probably in January while the second refers to the Christmas of the previous year. The next entry is for May and then the action moves to September and November before returning to the feast of the exaltation of the Cross in September.[31] There is much less internal evidence for dating in the Annals of Connacht but in the case of the year 1527 the action moves from March to September and back to May.[32] The sixteenth-century entries in the Annals of Loch Cé are in many cases even more haphazard. Entries such as

---

29 Dáibhí Ó Cróinín, 'Early Irish annals from Easter-tables: a case restated' in *Peritia*, ii (1983), pp 74–86. 30 *AConn*, pp 396–7. 31 *AU*, iii, pp 351–9. 32 *AConn*, pp 662–6.

that for the giving away of Castlemore to Theobald Dillon, discussed in the second essay below, are placed in the text where there was some blank parchment rather than necessarily in their chronologically correct place. Events were occasionally entered under the wrong year, a fact sometimes realised only later. Thus the entry for the death of Henry VIII was placed in 1547 by the annalist of Loch Cé with a later scribal note by one of the compilers, Brian Mac Diarmada, 'It is in the other kalend yonder the death of the king should be.' [Is andsa challaind sin thall is coir bas a[n] righ.][33]

The sixteenth-century Irish annals need to be understood not as a grand narrative sweep of the period but rather as a series of stories often selected from earlier sources and often rather haphazardly arranged under the year in which they occurred. Sometimes the stories are very brief, noting a death in a few words and sometimes, like the stories on which this book is based, they are much longer. In general, the earlier annals, Ulster and Connacht, tend to have shorter stories while the stories in the later sections of the Loch Cé annals tend to be longer reflecting a move towards the creation of a larger-scale historical narrative. These stories are important for what they tell us of the reality of the sixteenth-century world. They are not necessarily the 'what happened' of objective history nor are they fiction. They occupy a middle ground between fact and fabrication. Their importance derives in part from the fact that they are literary constructs and therefore reflect the attitudes and values of those who wrote them and embody the literary forms of their milieu. Elements of the influence of hagiographical tradition, for example, can often be discerned. However, the stories in the annals are not merely literary creations since they are rooted in real events. Their literary form and their grounding in reality together give these stories their narrative force and make them the smallest unit of historiographical fact. It is in this that their importance lies.

Given the survival of such stories within the text of the annals, the challenge facing modern historians is how to interpret them so as to cast light on Gaelic society in sixteenth-century Ireland. As Clifford Geertz has noted 'the trick is to figure out what the devil they think they are up to'.[34] This book adopts the techniques of microhistory to try and elucidate what some of these stories might tell us about that late medieval world. Microhistory as a technique is essentially a reduction in the scale of historical study and the intensive study of the documentary material available at micro level.[35] It is not an

33 *ALC*, ii, p. 351, n. 6. For other examples see *AConn*, pp 639, 711.   34 Clifford Geertz, *Local knowledge: further essays in interpretative anthropology* (London, 1993), p. 58.   35 For overviews of this historical practice see Giovanni

attempt to propose a particular series of theoretical questions but rather to use small-scale studies to test much wider propositions about social systems and political arrangements. The reduced scale of microhistory allows historians to observe more finely focused face-to-face interactions in the past. Stories, such as those preserved in the annals, provide the raw data for this approach to the past. Such stories have the advantage that they record events within the past without the framing events of the wider interpretative sweep, yet the episodes both comprise and refract that wider sweep. These short narratives therefore provide openings, although sometimes ill-defined ones, into the past. The significance of these stories can be illuminated when the singular events they recount are inserted into a wider social web of significances. By using context and elucidating parallels to the events described in the stories recorded by the annalists it is possible to 'thicken' the description and allow us to see something of the society that produced those stories.

These essays try to use a number of stories from the sixteenth-century Irish annals to recreate the relationships, decisions, restraints and freedoms which applied to real situations and actual people in the past. By contextualising the stories from other episodes in the annals themselves and from other contemporary, often literary, sources it is possible to reconstruct some aspects of what the stories related here meant to those who were involved in them. The importance of genealogical context, for instance, was so commonplace to the contemporary annalists and to the readers or hearers of the annalistic record that they did not always consider it necessary to record this context in their narrative. Such evidence has to be drawn from external genealogical sources.

The methodology of microhistory raises two problems, first of the representativeness of these stories of the collective mentality of the society at the point of time where they occur, and secondly of whether these stories can reveal anything about the process of historical change over time. By definition these stories, since they were recorded at all, are exceptional. Most were recorded for a purpose, and this dimension is discussed in each of the essays below. The deliberate burning of a church while Mass was in progress, as recorded in 'The burning of Domnach Magh de Claine' below, was hardly a typical event in Gaelic Ireland but its untypicality tells us a good deal about the boundaries between what was held acceptable and what was unacceptable in past worlds. The integration of St Patrick into this story points to the sort of social and

Levi, 'On microhistory' in Peter Burke (ed.), *New perspectives on historical writing* (Oxford, 1991), pp 93–113; Edward Muir, 'Introduction: observing trifles' in Edward Muir and Guido Ruggiero (eds), *Microhistory and the lost peoples of Europe* (Baltimore, 1991), pp vii–xxvii.

religious authority that prevented such violent episodes becoming a normal event. Similarly the way in which the annalists chose to memorialise Sir Nicholas Malby in the 1580s was not an honour accorded to all the New English administrators in sixteenth-century Connacht. However, it does illustrate the negotiation process through which some individuals on the ground attempted to deal with the contingent situation which the changing power politics of informal colonisation brought to Connacht. Perhaps more typical of the world of Gaelic Ireland in the sixteenth century was the enforcement of the claims of an overlord and his attempt to build cultural capital from that experience, explored in the first essay here, and the death of the same lord examined in the penultimate essay.

It is certainly true that snapshots at one point in time can tell us little about change over time. These stories are thus unlike the sort of serial social history that charts the changing positions and relations of different groups over time and how they related to large-scale historical processes such as urbanisation, industrialisation and modernisation. That is not to say that such stories are not valid within a significant chronological range. Many of the subjects discussed in these essays touch on fundamental ideas of social organisation which tended to change only slowly. The stories discussed in this book have been deliberately selected to reflect the period before the Nine Years' War after which extensive colonisation and shifts in local perceptions of authority initiated significant social changes in provincial Ireland. These stories deal not with social groups but rather with values and patterns of behaviour, that is, how that society wished to present itself to the world. Thus, rather than reflecting changing relationships over time they provided the matrix which allowed contemporaries to make sense of the world around them. In short they depicted and reinforced social values in a world where tradition, order, and consensus vied with the countervailing tendencies of discord and dissension and in which innovation was presented in strongly traditional forms.[36]

Despite the fragmented nature of authority in Gaelic Ireland and the haphazard geographical spread of the stories discussed here it seems to us that, taken together, these narratives go some way to describing what might be termed a culture of lordship which permeated Gaelic society. The shared attitudes to authority, both civil and religious, together with common perceptions of the roles appropriate to particular groups, such as poets or genealogists, and the

36 For example, Nerys Patterson, 'Gaelic law and the Tudor conquest of Ireland: the social background of the sixteenth-century recensions of the pseudo-historical Prologue to the *Seanchas már*' in *Irish Historical Studies*, xxvii, no. 107 (May 1991), pp 193–215.

importance of lordship over landownership which appear in these stories all go a long way to explaining what held this politically fragmented world together. Although in the final analysis these narratives are not representative of anything except themselves they do have a wider significance. They recall concrete events that refract what were widespread social values and, in particular, the matrix of assumptions that conditioned the way in which the participants in those events viewed the world. The essays do not seek to present a wide-ranging history of Gaelic Ireland in the sixteenth century but rather to elucidate historical causation on the level of individuals or small elite groups. This micro scale reflects something of the reality of life as it was lived in Gaelic Ireland. It allows us tell the stories of real people who in large scale studies of Gaelic lordship, economy, or society might be left out.

III

In his 1958 assessment of the sixteenth-century entries in the Annals of Ulster Aubrey Gwynn commented that

> the main interest of the last and most detailed section of these Annals is indeed that they give us an astonishingly complete and vivid picture of life in this whole area in the last phase of a native Irish tradition which was so soon to be challenged by the new forces of Henry VIII and Elizabeth I of England.[37]

Just how rich that material might prove to be when the details have been more fully examined might have surprised even Gwynn. The studies which comprise this book illustrate the possibilities which the annalistic record presents for the reconstruction of many dimensions of sixteenth-century Gaelic society in Ireland. Together the essays show the importance of using annalistic entries not simply as building blocks in a meta-narrative of the early sixteenth century but also as episodes of social interaction which deserve to be contextualised and analysed in their own right as microhistories of sixteenth-century Ireland.

37 Aubrey Gwynn, 'Cathal Mac Maghnusa and the annals of Ulster: part I' in *Clogher Record*, ii, no. 2 (1958), p. 231.

Getting and spending: the political economy of the Mac Diarmada lordship, 1549

Aodh son of Cormac, son of Ruaidhrí Mac Diarmada died in 1549. He had many claims to fame, including being abbot of the Cistercian house of Boyle, but the most significant was that he had been lord of the Mac Diarmada lordship for the previous fifteen years. It had not been a particularly successful rule. From the beginning it had been marked by dissension within the lordship and two of the contenders, Ruaidhrí and Tomaltach had gone as far as to seize the lord's residence. It is hardly surprising that his obituary in the Annals of Loch Cé recorded that he had died 'after suffering numerous dangers from his own kindred, and from other enemies.' [iar nguasachtaibh iomdha on fhine féin ocus ó esgcairdib eli.][1] The same annalist was considerably more effusive in his portrayal of Aodh's successor, Ruaidhrí son of Tadhg son of Ruaidhrí Óg Mac Diarmada, and even offered a guarded comparison between the two men. The annalist was Ruaidhrí's son, Brian, and he placed particular emphasis on the positive manner in which his father as new lord of Moylurg had inaugurated his lordship in 1549.

> A school invitation was given by Mac Diarmada, i.e. Ruaidhri, at Christmas of this year; and it is not possible to count or over-reckon all that he gave to the poets, and professors, and learned men of Erinn, and to all men besides. A good son of Mac Diarmada, i.e. Maelruanaidh, the son of Ruaidhri Mac Diarmada, gave the like invitation, and distributed much of the world's riches to the men of Erinn, after the example of his father. This Ruaidhri Mac Diarmada secured, and firmly established, many of the neighbouring and distant territories under his government and heavy tribute, for he exacted two hundred cows the two Mag Raghnaills, and one hundred cows from Mac

1 ALC, ii, pp 283, 313, 353.

Donnchadha of the Corann, and sixty cows from O Gadhra; forty-eight cows from O hAinlighe, and forty-eight cows from Mac Branáin; and twenty-four cows from O Flannagáin, and twenty-four cows from Cruthon-O Maine; and twenty-four cows from the descendants of Toirdhelbhach Carrach O Conchobhair, and twenty pair of bonaght-men from the descendants of Tadhg, son of Brian Mac Donnchadha, and twenty shillings rent every year therewith. And he imposed a trib-ute on the descendants of Ruaidhri Mac Donnchadha, in Cúil-Degha, and a tribute on the descendants of Aedh Buidhe, and on the Slicht Muirghesa, and a tribute on the descendants of Dubhgall Gruama. Great depredations were committed by Mac Diarmada on the descen-dants of Donnchadh O Cellaigh; and he burned their portion of country. And he took three score cows from Mac Goisdelbh the same year, and great preys from Clann-Philip, in which were twelve hun-dred cows, and ten saddle horses along with them, and all these were given to the professors and poets of Erinn in one day, i.e. the day of Stephen's festival.

[Gairm sgoile do thabhairt do Mac Diarmada .i. do Ruaidhri a nod-luic na bliadna sa, ocus ni heidir a riomh ina ro áiremh ar thidhluic sé deigsibh ocus dollamnaibh ocus daois ealadna Erenn, ocus da gach duine airchena. Mac maith do Mac Diarmada .i. Maolruanaidh mac Ruaidri Mic Diarmada do thabhairt na garma cedna, ocus ioliomad do maithess ant shaogail do sgaoiled ar feruigh Erenn ar lorg a athar. Ro dhaingnigh ocus ro dheghshocraidh an Ruaidhri sin Mac Diarmada fo an thigerntus ocus fo na troim chios moran do na tirib a gcian ocus a bfhogus, oir do bhen sé da ced bó don da Mhag Raghnaill, ocus ced bó do Mac Donnchada an Choruinn, ocus tri fichit bo dUa Ghadhra; ocht mba ocus dá fhichet dUa Ainlighe, ocus ocht mba ocus dá fhichet o Mac Branáin, ocus cetra ba fiched o Ua Fhlannagáin, ocus cethra ba fichet o Crúthonn O Maine; ocus cethra ba fichet ó tshlicht Toirrdhelbaigh charraigh I Conchobair, ocus fiche bert bhuandachta ó tshlicht Taidhg mic Briain mic Donnchada, ocus fiche sgillinn do chíos gacha bliadna maille risin; ocus cioss ar tshlicht Ruaidri Mic Donnchada a gcúil Degha; ocus cioss ar tshlicht Aodha buidhe ocus ar shlicht Muirghessa; ocus císs ar slicht Dubhghaill gruama. Crecha móra do dhenum do Mac Diarmada ar slicht Donnchada hI Cheallaigh, ocus a gcuid tíre do loscud; ocus trí fichit bo ó Mac Goisdealbh an bliadain cedna. Crecha móra ó chlainn Filip ina raibhe da ced dhec bó

> ocus deich neich díla maille rú; ocus iadsin uile do thindlucad a nen
> lo dollamnaibh ocus degsib Erenn .i. Lá fhel Sdefain].[2]

The events described by the annalist are clearly complex. On the one hand the
core of this description could be read as an instance of the exaction by a lord
of tribute in the form of cattle such as is recorded elsewhere in the annals. That
the description of Ruaidhrí Mac Diarmada's exactions was recorded within
the context of a display of hospitality to poets seems, at first, of secondary
importance given the annalist's attention to detail concerning the achievements
of the raid which paid the poets. In reality, however, both the peaceful exaction of *cíos* [tribute] and the more aggressive *creach* [forced gift], together with
the display of hospitality to the learned class, were integral to the ritual of
inauguration of the new lord of Moylurg. Much of the tribute was collected
without violence. Only the Uí Ceallaigh, Clann Pilib and MacCostello are
explicitly stated to have been raided while in other cases a fixed tribute seems
to have been exacted. The raid and the sharing of hospitality which followed
it are the most dramatic parts of the story.

Cattle raiding was an intrinsic part of life in Gaelic Ireland. At one level it
provided a mechanism for accumulating wealth in an underpopulated society
where the scarcity of human resources severely limited the economic value of
land.[3] In the case of the Mac Diarmada lordship the low level of population in
relation to resources is evident from the unstable pattern of settlement. In 1592
Sir Richard Bingham, the governor of Connacht, observed from personal experience in the former monastic lands around Boyle in north Roscommon

> they [the Irish] have a custom that every May the tenants are at lib-
> erty to remove from one landlord to another to what place they will,
> by which it is commonly seen that he who has ten or six quarters of
> land, more or less inhabited this year … shall not have five or three
> quarters inhabited the next year by reason that the tenants which he
> had are gone from him … Most of my own tenants in the Boyle are
> gone away this May and left the land waste.[4]

In addition land would be kept waste in summer to allow for winter grazing,
another indication that land was plentiful.[5] There are features that appear

---

2 *ALC*, ii, pp 354–7.   3 Katharine Simms, 'Warfare in the medieval Gaelic lordships' in *Irish Sword*, xii
(1975–6), pp 98–108.   4 PRO, SP 63/164, no. 26.   5 In 1572 the lordship was described as waste so that no
one had any benefit from it, PRO, SP63/35, no. 12.

unusual in the story recorded by the Loch Cé annalist for 1549. First, the enforcement of tribute, despite the praise of the annalist, was not particularly spectacular. Less than 500 cattle were collected as tribute in the main expedition with a further 1,200 taken by force in the *creach*. In comparison with other recorded raids this seems a small number. The annals provide some indications of the sort of numbers of cattle which Mac Diarmada might seize during a cattle raid. In 1553 on a raid against Ó Conchobhair Ruadh some 4,000 cattle and 500 stud mares were seized and later that year, in what seems to have been a revenge attack, 1,200 cattle were taken.[6] In 1549 between 900 and 1,000 cattle were seized in a raid. Throughout the 1560s between 1,000 and 5,000 cattle were reported as being taken on the occasion of each of a number of raids.[7]

A second feature of the story is that most of the exactions claimed seem not to have been directed towards seizing large numbers of cattle but at taking very specific numbers of cattle from particular people. The numbers seized were, in the main, multiples of twelve indicating that it was a structured tribute, possibly determined by precedent.[8] Such structuring along lines of precedent is certainly attested in other contexts. The lords' stewards frequently collected tributes due from their followers along lines guided by tradition and precedent, and may even have been cast into legal form in some cases.[9] The listing of the rights of MacWilliam Burke in the 1570s, for instance, was compiled from the 'testimony of the stewards' [d'fhiaghnuisí na maor] or as the compilers of the document put it 'as we have heard and received from the stewards' [mar do chualamar agus mar do fuaireamar ó na maoruibh]. The steward's testimony, in turn, was set by tradition. In the case of MacWilliam rights 'the stewards bear testimony to this accordingly as they received it from their ancestors' [atáid na maoir dá dhéanamh d'fhiaghnuise annso, do réir mar fuaireadar ó na sinnsearuibh táinig rompa.][10] Such tradition could act as a pretext for refusing to pay tribute. A late seventeenth-century text, preserved in the *Genealogical history of the O'Reillys*, records an older story of how Seaán Ó Néill demanded tribute from Ó Raghallaigh but

6 *Cal. Carew MSS, 1515–74* p. 239, *ALC*, ii, pp 360–3. 7 *ALC*, ii, pp 352–3, 384–5, 386–7, 388–9, 404–5, 412–13. 8 The exactions imposed by Mac Diarmada on his inauguration do not, however, correspond to the older description of the rights of Mac Diarmada, probably dating from the fourteenth century and emphasising Mac Diarmada's association with the kingship of Connacht (Nessa Ní Shéaghdha, 'The rights of Mac Diarmada' in *Celtica*, vi (1963), 156–72). 9 For the suggestion of a legal form see Katharine Simms, 'Late medieval Donegal' in William Nolan, Liam Ronayne and Mairead Dunlevy (eds), *Donegal: history and society* (Dublin, 1995), pp 192–3. 10 Tomás Ó Raghallaigh (ed.), 'Seanchus Búrcach' in *Journal of the Galway Archaeological and Historical Society*, xiii (1927), pp 110–11, 116–17. For the date of the text see Art Cosgrove (ed.), *New history of Ireland: ii medieval Ireland, 1169–1534* (Oxford, 1987), pp 814–15.

Maol Mórdha answered that no man in his position had ever paid tribute to O'Neill and asked a stay of a week so that he might take counsel with the nobles of his land.

[Dubhairt Maoilmordha nach ar dhíol fear 'áite árdchíos re O Néill aríamh ⁊ d'iarr cáirde seachtmhuine aire, go ndéanamh a chomhairle re maithe a thíre].[11]

The consistency of treatment of the dues in the 1549 annal entry may suggest a recent origin for the tribute. Other tracts recording duties paid by one lord to another, such as the *Ceart Uí Néill* or *Cíos Mhic Mhathghamhna*, are far more complex texts. They are evidently composed of layers built up over time, with differing dues and distinctive vocabularies for the rights and duties in a manner that is not found in this case.[12]

Finally, and crucially, the 1549 Mac Diarmada story of obtaining wealth is set in a wider context, that of a poetic assembly at which the entire profits of the *creach*, as distinct from the more formal *cíos*, were distributed to the poets on St Stephen's day. There are other annalistic parallels for this connection between getting and spending. Maolruanaigh Ó Cearbhaill, who died in 1532, was remembered by the Ulster annalists as 'the one who most collected and bestowed from the time of Brian Boruma downwards' [an t-é is mo do thinóil ⁊ do thidhlaic o aimsir Briain Bhórama anuas].[13] The obituary of Eoghan Mac Diarmada, who died in 1534 after only one year as lord of Moylurg, explicitly linked cattle raiding and generosity to the learned class when it noted he was

an exultant plundering captain, one who never went to sleep without having taken a prey or enforced a concession from his reluctant foes, who bestowed wealth and high honour on the men of every art in proper measure.

[cenn fedhna crechach conghairech et fer nar chodoil gan crech no comaidh co hainndeónach ona escaraid et fer maoínedh ⁊ moronora do thabairt d'aos gacu dána co deghordaighthi].[14]

Such generosity cannot have characterised every raid since it would have negated the function of the raid as a way of forming capital. In the case of Ruaidhrí

11 James Carney (ed.), *A genealogical history of the O'Reillys* (Cavan and Dublin, 1959), pp 39, 88.   12 Éamon Ó Doilbhín, '*Ceart Uí Néill*: a discussion and translation of the document' in *Seanchas Ard Mhacha*, v (1969–70), pp 324–58; Seosamh Ó Dufaigh (ed. & trans.), '*Cíos Mhic Mhathghamhna*' in *Clogher Record*, iv (1961–2), pp 125–34.   13 *AU*, iii, pp 582–3.   14 *AConn*, pp 684–5.

Mac Diarmada's activities to mark the inauguration of his lordship, however, extracting wealth from neighbouring lordships, in the form of both *cíos* and *creach*, is inextricably linked with the new lord's display of hospitality to the poets. The annalist makes this clear by beginning with mention of the poetic gathering hosted by Mac Diarmada and returning to the same matter as the conclusion of his story. Since the episode was clearly more than just a cattle raid, the context of the raid and the reasons for the disposal of the prey in the generous manner reported merit more detailed exploration.

I

To understand the significance of that part of the story which deals with the cattle raid it is important to place it in its immediate political context. It was the first raid of Ruaidhrí Mac Diarmada since becoming lord of Moylurg earlier that year. Thus it was not simply a military occasion but an event charged with considerable political and social significance. The story illustrated how a newly chosen Gaelic lord should behave. Within Gaelic society, the first raid conducted by a new lord was an important event which served as a measure of his strength and an omen for the future.[15] Similarly the voluntary payment of tribute from lesser families was a sign respect for the new lord's power. The sort of raiding which the annalist described in this story was not aimed primarily at generating wealth. Little was taken in cash or even precious metals which could have been recirculated as gifts. The Annals of Connacht for 1536 describe a raid on the MacCostellos by 'the new O'Connor' [Ua Conchobair nua] which did not yield much prey but Kilcolman castle was surrounded and MacCostello was forced to yield up 'an engraved(?) mailcoat(?) which he possessed, the mailcoat of Mac Feorais' [luirech comhradhach do bi aige .i. luirech Meic Feorais].[16] Wealth was not at issue here, but the symbolic importance of taking the mailcoat was considerable. Again in 1592 when Aodh Ruadh Ó Domhnaill was inaugurated his 'first feat of arms' [chédgaisgidh] was directed against some of the Uí Néill

> as he had a great grudge against them at that time, for they used to
> invade his territory ever since his father had grown weak and infirm

15 For an examination of this see Pádraig Ó Riain, 'The *"crech ríg"* or "regal prey"' in *Éigse*, xv (1973–7), pp 24–30. 16 *AConn*, pp 690–3. '*Luirech*' might also be translated as 'breastplate'.

and he himself had been captured by the English. There was another reason too, for the Cenél Eóghan were a wood of refuge and a bush of shelter at all times for every one of the Cenél Conaill itself who opposed and resisted their own true prince, and not only for them but for every one in other territories who was in opposition to or in enmity with the Cenél Conaill by reason of their hatred of them.

[ar ba holc a fhola friu an tan soin uair batarsaidhe occ forran fora thír-siumh ó ro lá laige 7 eneirte fora athair 7 o ro herghababh é badhdéin la Gallaibh. Fáth oile ann dana ar robtar iad Cenél nEoghain ba coill fosccaidh 7 ba dos didin dogres da gach aon do Chenel cConaill fad-hein nó friothardadh 7 no imresnaigedh i nagaidh a fflatha fírdhilis 7 nirbho dóibhsidhe namá acht da gach neach i nechtairchrich no bhiodh i frithbhert nó ind eccraittes fri Cenel Conaill ara mioscais ind.][17]

It was therefore necessary to demonstrate one's power by imposing tribute on subordinate lords as soon as possible after succeeding to the lordship if they did not render their dues voluntarily. It was this which gave rise to the attacks on the Uí Ceallaigh, Clann Pilib and MacCostello in the annalist's story of 1549. In 1601, for instance, after Richard Burke had newly succeeded his father to become fourth earl of Clanricard, Lughaidh Ó Cléirigh, the biographer of Aodh Ruadh Ó Domhnaill observed in a passage of somewhat mixed sentiments

a desire and longing seized him in the pride of his strength, through vanity and vain glory, after his inauguration to go and avenge his wrongs and enmity on all the people who were under the authority and sway of O Domhnaill, and not to stop until he would come to the bank of the Sligeach if he could. This was proper, for he with all his territory had claims on O Domhnaill and his people, if they were able to levy them on them, for many were their plunderings and visi-tations of them in their countries.

[Ro ghabh ierttain ailghes 7 iomtholta eisidhe la borrfadh brighe la huaill 7 ionnoccbhail iarna oirdnedh dul daithe a anfaladh 7 a eccraitis for nach ndruing fors mbaoi smacht 7 cumhachta Uí Dhomhnaill 7 gan oirisiomh co rochtain do co hur Sligicche dia ccaemsadh. Deithbhir ón ar ro dlighsidhe cona chrich uile i ccoitchinne feich dUa

---

17 Paul Walsh (ed.), *Beatha Aodha Ruaidh Uí Dhomhnaill* (2 vols, Dublin, 1948–57), i, pp 42–3.

Dhomhnaill cona mhuintir diemtais tualaing a ttobach foraibh ar robtar iolardha a ccreacha 7 a ccuarta chuca ina ttíribh.][18]

Imposing one's authority by setting up bonds of obligation, especially at the time of a succession, was obviously very important. As the sixteenth-century proverb preserved as the first line of Tadhg Dall Ó hUiginn's poem proclaimed, 'Towards the warlike man peace is observed' [D'fior chogaidh comhailtear síothcháin].[19]

The structured nature of the tribute, as described in the story of Ruaidhrí Mac Diarmada's collection of his dues both by consent and violence, corresponds to what might be described as a 'rental' of dues payable to Mac Diarmada by the lords in the area of Moylurg. Such dues reflected the overlordship claimed by Mac Diarmada over others. As such they were of interest to the annalists as a way of understanding political allegiances. A notebook kept by one of those who compiled the Annals of Loch Cé, Pilib Ballach Ó Duibhgeannáin, for instance, contained a list of Ó Domhnaill's quartering rights over Ulster.[20] Mac Diarmada's rights may have been on a lesser scale, but the status of the lordship which the annalist was so concerned to depict depended on the enforcement of these dues. It is clear that many of these dues were of very recent origin. While Ruaidhrí Mac Diarmada was clearly the largest controller of land in Moylurg he was not the only one. The 1585 Composition of Connacht lists other lords in Roscommon who asserted comparable claims. It is evident that some lords, by virtue of their traditional status, claimed dues from other smaller lordships. MacWilliam, for instance, claimed dues from Ó Conchobhair Ruadh, Mac Diarmada and MacCostello. Mac Diarmada equally claimed obligations from surrounding lordships (fig. 1). The 1499 obituary of Tadhg Mac Diarmada in the Connacht annals noted that he was 'a king who tamed and quieted all his near neighbours so that they submitted respectfully to him' [ri do cennsoigh 7 do chiunaigh gac comorsa na comfhoccus go rabadar umhal orromach dhó].[21] However, at times Mac Diarmada had particular problems in enforcing his rights on those to the north of his lordship. In 1536, for instance, Mac Diarmada with the support of Ó Conchobhair Shligigh and Ó Ruairc raided widely into adjoining lordships and took hostages from a number of lords to ensure their compliance.[22] At an even more remote level Ó

---

18 Ibid., i, pp 294–7. 19 Eleanor Knott (ed.), *The bardic poems of Tadhg Dall Ó hUiginn* (2 vols, London, 1922–6), i, p. 108, ii, p. 72. 20 NLI, MS G1, f. 64. 21 A.M. Freeman (ed.), *The compossicion booke of Conought* (Dublin, 1936), pp 161–5; *AConn*, pp 604–5. 22 *ALC*, ii, pp 300–3.

N

Ó Domhnaill

Mág Uidhir

Ó Conchobhair Shligidh

Ó Dubhda

Ó Ruairc

Mág Shamhradháin

Mac Donnchadha

Ó hEadhra

Ó Gadhra

MOYLURG

Mac Raghnaill

MacWilliam (Burke)

MacJordan

MacCostello

Mac Diarmada

Ó Conchobhair

Ó Fearghail

MacMorris

MacDavid (Burke)

1 The Mac Diarmada lordship and its surroundings in the early sixteenth century

Domhnaill claimed obligations of overlordship from Mac Diarmada and other lordships in east Connacht. To assert these claims was one thing, to enforce them another. This led to raiding and counter raiding. In 1530, for instance, Ó Domhnaill raided into Connacht and imposed a 'defensive tribute' [cíosa cossanta] on Ó Conchobhair Ruadh.[23] As the Ulster annalist expressed it on another occasion in 1499 when Ó Domhnaill raided the Mac Diarmada lord-

23 *ALC*, ii, pp 270–1.

ship 'and Mac Diarmada gave rent of protection to Ua Domnaill for Magh-Luirg from that out.' [7 Mac Diarmada do thabairt chisa cosanta d'hUa Domnaill ar Muigh-Luirg o sin amach.][24] In 1532 and 1538, 1539 and 1540 Ó Domhnaill again ravaged part of the Clann Diarmada lands except for the lands of those who submitted to him.[25] Again in 1542 'O Domhnaill made a hosting into Lower Connacht this autumn and the chieftains thereof came to him in peaceful guise and submissively paid him his rent and lord's dues.' [sluaigedh le h. nDomnaill a níchtar Connocht an foghmursin et maithi íchtair Connacht do thecht 'na cend maille re sithchain et a chís et a tigernus d'ic co humal ris.][26]

Maintaining authority over existing followers and acquiring new ones was an important mark of status and worth the enforcement of tribute, by cattle raiding if necessary. The world of Ruaidhrí Mac Diarmada was not a world of cash transactions or even the extortion of cash from surrounding lords. Rather it was a world of obligations. A lordship was not a great estate in the sense of a discrete block of land, owned and exploited in ordered ways. Rather it was a large and scattered area in which the inhabitants owed something, possibly on a sporadic or temporary basis, to a lord and that would be enforced by raiding if necessary. In this context it is not hard to understand the symbolic importance of the annalist's story.

Another way of thinking about the annalist's story of the aggressive cattle raid on the Uí Ceallaigh, Clann Pilib and MacCostello during which over twelve hundred cows and ten horses were seized, is to recognise the substantial logistical and financial strains which such raiding placed on a lordship. The number of people involved is not known but Mac Diarmada was certainly capable of fielding a significant force. In the 1540s he was said to be able to raise more fighting men than most of the surrounding lordships and in 1557 he was able to raise a large force of cavalry.[27] In 1566, English sources indicate that MacWilliam and Ó Ruairc were the only Connacht lords expected to provide a greater number of horses and men for hostings.[28] Moreover, the geographical spread of the raid was considerable and clearly required sophisticated logistical organisation. The Mac Diarmada lordship had a structure in place to help with such undertakings. The Annals of Connacht refer, in the 1520s, to the Mac Dubhgaill family as 'constapla' of Moylurg.[29] Such constables were usually military commanders in the service of a lord. The Mac Dubhgaill family were Scots gallowglasses who had moved to Connacht in the middle ages and become

24 AU, iii, pp 444–5. 25 AConn, pp 678–9, 708–9, 710–11, 714–15. 26 AConn, pp 726–7. 27 Liam Price, 'Armed forces of the Irish chiefs' in Journal of the Royal Society of Antiquaries of Ireland, lxii (1932), p. 204; ALC, ii, pp 372–3. 28 PRO, SP 63/19, no. 85. 29 AConn, pp 638–9, 640–1.

captains of gallowglass for native lords and in return were supported by lands. In the 1540s, for instance, Mac Diarmada certainly used Clann Dubhgaill gallowglasses.[30] Over time Clann Diarmada would make increasing use of gallowglasses but their use was restricted by the cost involved in hiring them.[31] Thus the rights of 'bonnought' which Mac Diarmada claimed from Ó Conchobhair in the annalist's story were an important resource in maintaining a force. Raiding, such as the annalist described, was neither cheap nor easy. Moreover it was only one of several demands that would be made on the lordship. Some poets, such as Eochaidh O hEódhusa, demanded land under the lord's protection in return for their professional services.[32] Some of the learned class can be identified as living on the property of Mac Diarmada as specified in a 1617 grant discussed below. The Annals of Loch Cé noted under 1581 that 'Fer-caogad O Duibhgennain i.e the son of Ferghal, son of Philip died in Cluain Ui Brian [Cloonybrien]' [Fer caogad O Duibhgennáin .i. mac Fergail mic Pilip dfagail bháis a gcluain I Bhráoin].[33] The precise identity of this Ó Duibhgeannáin is unclear, but Paul Walsh has suggested that he may have been the father of Pilib Ballach who was then at Cloonybrien assisting in the compilation of the Annals of Loch Cé and Pilib Ballach was presumably being supported from this land.[34] There were others also who needed to be supported from the land. For instance, the annals refer to the death in 1566 of Eoghan Mac an Bhaird, 'maor' or steward of Mac Diarmada.[35] Again Cormac Ó Laimhín, who was killed in 1567 had described himself as Mac Diarmada's servant and his father had also served the family in the 1550s.[36] Other officials may have served and been provided for within the Mac Diarmada lordship in the mid-sixteenth century but they have left no trace.[37] There were, for example, medical families in the area but whether they were employed by Mac Diarmada is not known.[38]

Mac Diarmada was reliant on what he could extract from his own lordship to raise money to maintain this retinue and also to fund cattle raiding on the scale necessary to enforce the obligations of lordship. Mac Diarmada did not depend on rents from land for the main source of his income as an English-

30 *ALC*, ii, pp 372–3. 31 *ALC*, ii, pp 364–5, 372–3, 380–1, 382–3, 406–9. 32 Osborn Bergin (ed.), *Irish bardic poetry* (Dublin, 1970), pp 136–7, 274–5; S.H. O'Grady and Robin Flower (eds), *Catalogue of Irish manuscripts in the British Museum* (3 vols, London, 1926–53), i, pp 475–6; Pádraig A. Breatnach, 'The chief's poet' in *Proceedings of the Royal Irish Academy*, lxxxiii, sect. C (1983), pp 60–6. 33 *ALC*, ii, pp 436–7. 34 Paul Walsh, *Irish men of learning* (Dublin, 1947), pp 18–19. 35 *ALC*, ii, pp 392–3. 36 *ALC*, ii, pp 396–7, 358–9. 37 For the possibilities see Katharine Simms, *From kings to warlords: the changing political structure of Gaelic Ireland in the later middle ages* (Woodbridge, 1987), chs 5–6. 38 John Bannerman, *The Beatons: a medical kindred in the classical Gaelic tradition* (Edinburgh, 1986), pp 10, 45, 54, 109, 117. For a 1563 medical MS from north Connacht see TCD, MS 1357.

style landlord might. While the lordship was criss-crossed with a complex hierarchy of property units such as townlands, cartons, treens and quarters, doc-
umented in the seventeenth-century Books of Survey and Distribution, these
were not primarily units of landownership. Rather they were properties held
through a system of obligations owed to a lord. These arrangements were not
the subject of written records and thus proxies must be used to try to recreate
something of the polity they represented. These territorial units were docu-
mented in early seventeenth-century English administrative records when they
were used as the main elements in land grants and surveys under common law.
Thus some clues as to how landed property was understood in the older Gaelic
world of Mac Diarmada is provided by a royal grant of 1617 of land to Brian
Óg Mac Diarmada, a grandson of Ruaidhrí.[39] This grant recorded two cate-
gories of land within the lordship. First there were eighty-seven quarters granted
directly to Brian Óg which seems to coincide with what was described as
'Cowrin Bryen Mc Dermott' in the indenture of Maghery Connaught, which
was part of the 1585 composition settlement of Connacht.[40] 'Cowrin' is evidently an anglicisation of *comhroinn*,[41] meaning share or division, and thus denotes
in this instance the share of the land allocated to be under the control of Brian
Mac Diarmada. The term was repeatedly used to describe land units that were
subdivisions of baronies in the Composition Book of Connacht. The concept
it denoted would appear to derive from the particular form of gavelkind inheritance that had been practised in Connacht where the division of land was made
by the youngest coheir who stood to benefit from an egalitarian apportioning
of land.[42] However, in the case of the 'cowrin' associated with the heads of
lordships in the 1580s, this seems to represent the mensal lands of the chief and
the demesne lands of the lordship.[43] Similar lands were also set aside for the
tánaiste [heir apparent].[44] At the heart of these lands was Carraig Mhic Diarmada
at Lough Key. A poem, probably of *c*.1600, by Eochaidh Ó hEódhusa, '*An tú ar
gcéadaithne, a charrag*', celebrated the Mac Diarmada castle at the core of the lordship (fig. 2). The poet stressed that although it was now in ruins it had been a
centre of feasting and hunting. It was where poets performed their praise poems
for Mac Diarmada in return for gifts, where genealogies were recited 'telling

39 *Cal. pat. rolls Ire., Jas I*, pp 332–3.   40 Freeman (ed.), *Compossicion booke of Conought*, p. 158.   41 *DIL*, s.v.   42
Freeman (ed.), *Compossicion booke of Conought*, passim; K.W. Nicholls, *Land, law and society in sixteenth-century
Ireland* (Dublin, 1976), p. 18.   43 For discussion of the *fearann ríg*, and *fearann tánisteachta* see Katharine Simms,
From kings to warlords (Woodbridge, 1987), pp 129–30, and in an earlier context Fergus Kelly, *Early Irish farm-
ing* (Dublin, 1997), pp 403–4.   44 *ALC*, ii, pp 270–1; Hiram Morgan (ed.), '"Lawes of Irelande": a tract
by Sir John Davies' in *Irish Jurist*, n.s. xxviii–xxx (1993–5), p. 311; Simms, *From kings to warlords*, pp 129–30.

2 The Mac Diarmada castle, Lough Key, County Roscommon. Reproduced
from Francis Grose, *The antiquities of Ireland* (1791)

each hero's nobility' [ag maoidhimh uaisle gach fhir], and it was where the business of the lordship was conducted. Most importantly it was a place for prac-
tising 'hospitality and generosity' [iocht is oineach], values reflected in Mac
Diarmada's dealings with the poets in the annalist's story and clearly essential
to the workings of lordship.[45]

Some of the property mentioned in the 1617 patent clustered around Lough
Key itself. The composition agreement of 1585 had stipulated that Mac Diarmada
might set aside four quarters near Carraig Mhic Diarmada as demesne, which
may represent a continuation of an older pattern of land use.[46] While the castle
on the Rock may have been the focal point of major events within the lordship,
there were a number of high status sites on the land around the lough which

45 Lambert McKenna (ed.), *Dioghluim dána* (Dublin, 1938), pp 207–11, translated in *Irish Monthly* xlviii (1920),
pp 539–44, esp. stanzas 21–3, 37.   46 Freeman (ed.), *Compossicion booke of Conought*, p. 162.

also seem to have been associated with the core functions of the lordship. Ó hEódhusa's poem on Carraig Mhic Diarmada records that wine was drunk at banquets. Such wine would have been purchased from abroad. Again the British Library copy of the Annals of Loch Cé contains ten folios of paper and four of parchment. Such paper was not manufactured in Ireland and needed to be imported.[47] Thus its availability implies some form of trading site in the area. In 1231 the Annals of Connacht noted that 'Cormac son of Tomaltach [Mac Diarmada] began to make a market town at Rockingham [Port na gCarraig]' [Tinscna baili marcaid do denam la Cormac mac Tomaltaig hi Purt na Carce].[48] How long this trading town lasted is not known but the site was certainly well known in the sixteenth century and the Annals of Loch Cé record the death of the son of Mac Diarmada there in 1590.[49] The 1618 grant also contained provisions for a grant of both a fair and a market to Brian Óg Mac Diarmada in this locality.[50] There were other potential trading sites in the region. The substantial settlement around Boyle when surveyed in 1569 was said 'to have been a bigge towne but now there are no more but 3 waste cottages' and hence presumably had attracted traders in the past when it was a major monastic centre.[51] In addition to possible trading centres there are a number of medieval references to another Mac Diarmada fortress, 'longport Meic Diarmada', which seems to have been located on Longford Hill, Rockingham Demesne, but whether this continued to be used into the sixteenth century is not known.[52]

The core lands of the lordship lay around Lough Key with the remainder scattered throughout the northern part of Boyle barony and a further concentration in a block south of Lough Key (fig. 3). While not all of this land can be correlated to the land units described in the Books of Survey and Distribution from the 1660s, the areas that can be identified indicate that the core lands of the lordship were among the best in the barony of Boyle.[53] According to the surveyors of the 1660s the property comprised well over 7,000 acres of which just over two-thirds was reckoned to be profitable land. On this land Ruaidhrí Mac Diarmada settled his followers. Some of these were probably allocated land in return for their services to the lord. Leaving aside the lands necessary for the support of the learned class the remainder could be used by Mac Diarmada to generate wealth for himself. What form that wealth would take is unclear. Some native Irish lords did cultivate this land directly as

---

47 The paper folios are BL, Add MS 4792, ff 27–8, 33–40.   48 AConn, pp 40–1.   49 ALC, ii, pp 508–9.
50 Cal. pat rolls Ire., Jas I, p. 333.   51 Surveys of dissolved monastic property in Connacht, c.1570, BL, Add.
MS 48015, f. 231v.   52 Kieran O'Conor, The archaeology of medieval rural settlement in Ireland (Dublin, 1998), p.
85.   53 R.C. Simington (ed.), Books of survey and distribution: i, county of Roscommon (Dublin, 1949).

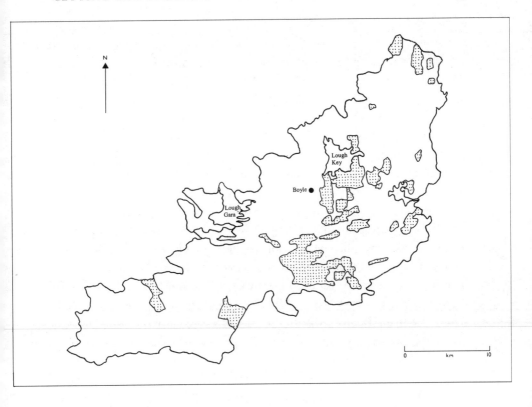

N

Lough
Key

Boyle ●

Lough
Gara

0   km   10

3 The lord's lands in the Mac Diarmada lordship in the mid sixteenth century

demesne.[54] However, there are two indications that this may not have been the case in the Mac Diarmada lordship. The first is the scattered nature of the property which would have made it difficult to manage directly. Secondly a feature of the area seems to have been its low population in relation to the available land. For this reason it would be difficult for Mac Diarmada to muster enough followers to cultivate the lands properly. It is only possible to guess at how Mac Diarmada exploited the lands available to him. It does seem clear that the relationship between Mac Diarmada and the inhabitants of the demesne lands was not that of landlord and tenant as understood in common law. The property was certainly held by the Mac Diarmada family and those who worked it rendered dues to them. The nature of these dues is difficult to ascertain but they were almost certainly paid in kind. Some may have been in the form of labour services which could be used on the lands nearest the core

54 Nicholls, *Land, law and society*, p. 14.

of the lordship. In other cases agricultural produce may have been rendered. Ó Duibhdábhoirenn's sixteenth-century glossary explained the word 'faer' as 'the name of the food that is given to the lord in the autumn' [ainm bid doberar do tiagherna isin fogmar] and 'fuirec' was the 'food given to the lord before Christmas' [bid fertar riadh notlaicc].[55]

The agricultural system of the demesne lands is not clear, and may have varied depending on the availability of human resources to work the land. Livestock, which could be moved easily when people moved, certainly formed a significant element and common pasture features as part of the agricultural organisation of most townlands within the region in the Books of Survey and Distribution compiled in the 1660s. However, substantial quantities of arable land are also recorded in the seventeenth-century sources and ploughmen were mentioned as being killed on the property in 1569.[56] There were also two mills, indicating that grain production was an established feature.[57] Renders may then have consisted of both grain and livestock. It is unclear how and when these renders were taken. In the 1560s at least, as noted earlier, Mac Diarmada had a steward or 'maor' Eoghan Mac an Bhaird.[58] His name may suggest a Donegal origin, but his precise family connections are unknown. Evidence from elsewhere suggests that these men were of fairly low status within the lordship.[59] While it is possible that the renders paid to Mac Diarmada were brought to Carraig Mhic Diarmada there is a second possibility. Throughout the Mac Diarmada lordship there were a number of castles held by the family. Baile na hUama (Cavetown), for instance, was rebuilt by Brian Mac Diarmada in 1554 and rebuilt again on a number of subsequent occasions.[60] Other sites, such as Port Inis Doighre, a crannóg on Drumharlow Lough, also seems to have been used and one of the Clann Diarmada was killed there in 1561.[61] It is possible that rather than renders being brought to the lord at his principal residence the lord went on circuit to collect his renders in the form of entertainment. Certainly stewards travelled this sort of circuit. A 1539 agreement between Ó Domhnaill and Ó Conchobhair Shligigh concerning Sligo castle stipulated that 'Tadhg [Ó Conchobhair Shligigh] shall be obliged to go with the stewards and marshals of O Domhnaill into every place in Lower Connacht to impose the

55 Whitley Stokes (ed.), *Three Irish glossaries* (London, 1862), p. 91. 56 *ALC*, ii, pp 406–7. 57 Simington (ed.), *Books of survey and distribution: i, Roscommon*, pp 145, 146. 58 *ALC*, ii, pp 392–3. 59 Simms, *From kings to warlords*, pp 83–4, 92. 60 *ALC*, ii, pp 367, 383, 419. Three Mheic Diarmata strongholds were mentions by Fitzwilliam in 1571, PRO, SP63/34, no. 29. 61 *ALC*, ii, pp 378–9; Kieran O'Conor, 'The moated site on Inishatirra Island, Drumharlow Lough, Co. Roscommon' in *County Roscommon Historical and Archaeological Society Journal*, vii (1998), pp 1–3.

lordship of O Domhnaill' or to collect his tribute, [a beith d'fhiachaib ar Tadhg imtheacht le maoraibh agus le marusccalaibh I Dhomhnaill in gac uile ait a nIchtar Condacht do thabach tigearnaiss I Domnaill].[62]

This had two important advantages. First, it gave lordship a visible profile outside the centre and cemented social bonds, possibly by retelling the story of Mac Diarmada's successful collection of dues and his raiding. Secondly it differentiated the sort of tribute payable by a lord's own followers from that payable by subject lords and hence defined different hierarchies of relationships. Tributes in cattle were to be taken away, as in the annalist's story, suggesting a stronger power relationship than the less political connotations of a lord feasting on locally produced food.

The second type of land which features in the crown grant of 1617 was land granted to others from which a rent charge was payable to Brian Óg Mac Diarmada. Such arrangements recognise that he had some rights over the property but that those rights did not relate to land title.[63] Rather, they echo the rent charges agreed in the 1585 Composition negotiated with the English administration and payable to local lords in lieu of traditional exactions. A closer look at the levels of rent charges paid to Mac Diarmada according to the 1617 grant suggests that these dues were closely structured. The amounts payable varied a great deal, from under a shilling to almost £2. There is no simple correlation between the size of property and the amount payable. The most frequent sums payable, however, which together account for about half of all payments, are 10½d. or multiples of that sum, such as 1s. 9d., 3s. 6d. or 7s.[64] This does suggest some common assessment unit was being employed by Mac Diarmada over the lands of his followers in the same way as the annalist's story records a structured taking of prey from adjoining lordships.

The arrangements concerning dues in the Mac Diarmada lordship may have a parallel in the money rents levied by Ó Néill in his lordship at the time of the flight of the earls. According to an account of the dues collected by Ó Néill, money rents of 12d. each quarter were chargeable on cattle grazing on the lands of the Ó Néill lordship. However, it was clarified that 'no certain portion of lands' was let to tenants in return for the rent paid. It was also noted in the case of Uí Néill rents that 'the said rent is uncertain, because by the custom of the country the tenants may remove from one lord to another every half year, as they usually do ...'[65] An alternative possibility is presented by the

62 Maura Carney, 'An agreement between Ó Domhnaill and Tadhg Ó Conchobhair concerning Sligo Castle (23 June 1539)' in *Irish Historical Studies*, iii (1942–3), pp 288, 290.   63 *Cal. pat. rolls, Ire., Jas I*, pp 330, 331, 332–3, 349.   64 All these money amounts are also even fractions of a guinea.   65 *Cal. S.P. Ire., 1608–10*, p. 533.

dues levied on the MacWilliam Burke followers in Mayo about 1570 which
recorded that in the barony of Tirawley money rents were collected 'and fur-
thermore it is on the soil MacWilliam's rent is derived' [agus ní eile fós gurab
ar an bhfearainn atá cíos Mhic Uilliam].[66] The MacWilliam text raises yet
another possibility since it stipulates that dues other than cash might be levied
on the lands of followers. These dues included ale, flour, oats, billeting of mercenaries and military service to MacWilliam. The 1585 composition agreement
for Roscommon certainly referred to Mac Diarmada's 'customary duties, exac-
cions and cuttings' levied on followers which seems to imply services other than
cash payments.[67] The cash values mentioned in the 1617 grant most probably
represent a commutation of such services into cash for the purposes of the
patent. It is not possible to be certain that this was the case but it is clear that
these payments were not regarded as rent for the land. They were rather obligations due from a follower to a lord who had traditionally asserted overlordship over the territory but whose claim on the land itself was negligible. It may
well be, again on the evidence of the MacWilliam lordship, that lords had some
claim to the waste lands of their followers but in the main the property was
vested in the families of the followers.[68] The income, however, was vital in maintaining the infrastructure of the lordship, such as providing the funds for raiding, which generated the resources for both getting and spending.

For these followers the sort of story told by the Loch Cé annalist in 1549
was important. It emphasised Mac Diarmada's lordly prowess as a man who
could maintain his status and defend the periphery of the lordship against
attack by adjoining lords. The relationship between a lord and his followers
was a reciprocal one. To his followers Mac Diarmada offered protection. Such
protection was not likely to be consistently available and the borders of lordships were often contested spaces. Thus Eochaidh Ó hEódhusa described the
lordly centre at Lough Key as

> From border-land asking terms
> often would come messengers of peace
> to thy high-walled warm bright court,
> and battle challenges would go forth from thee.
>
> [Meinic thigdís teachta síth
> d'fhoráil chomhadh ó choigcrích

66 Ó Raghallaigh (ed.), 'Seanchus Búrcach' in *Journal of the Galway Archaeological and Historical Society*, xiii (1927),
pp 116–17.   67 Freeman (ed.), *The compossicion booke of Conought*, p. 162.   68 Nicholls, *Land, law and society*, passim.

> dod chúirt ghairthe thaobhaird the
> 's raibhthe i ngach aonaird uaibh-se].[69]

The sources of threat were usually well established. Neighbouring lords might attempt to enlarge their influence by enticing families on the border of one lordship to shift their allegiance. The tale *Leighes coise Chéin* describes how one family shifted allegiances, placing itself under the protection of a different lord.[70] However local families themselves might try to test the strength of their overlord. According to the *Seanchus Búrcach* the inhabitants of the barony of Gallen were unwilling to grant MacWilliam his dues. A late seventeenth-century tale, possibly based on earlier materials, *MeGuidhir Fhearmanach*, also depicts one group refusing to pay their tribute unless the lord, who was ill, appeared in person rather than sending one of his stewards.[71]

II

In the aftermath of the establishment of the parameters of the lordship, either through the peaceful collection of tribute or through raiding those who would not pay, described in the annalist's story, Ruaidhrí Mac Diarmada had now to face the problem of converting his newly acquired wealth into status. How he would go about this was an important test of whether or not he could act correctly in the circumstances. Appropriate actions conveyed status in a way that cash or cattle alone did not. Given that land was abundant, the geographical size of a lordship might count for little. This helps explain why so few lords were concerned about territorial expansion through castle building. Followers might be a better measure of political strength, though not invariably so. Indeed the Connacht annals noted of Cú Maige Ballach son of Donall Ó Catháin in 1524

> Cu Maighe Ballach son of Domnaill O Cathain, who was, consider-

---

69 McKenna (ed.), *Dioghluim dána*, p. 209, trans. *Irish Monthly* xlviii (1920), p. 542.   70 S.H. O'Grady (ed.), *Silva Gadelica* (2 vols, London, 1892), i, 296–305; ii, pp 332–42.   71 Ó Raghallaigh (ed.), 'Seanchus Búrcach', pp 116–17; P. Ua Duinnín (ed.), *MeGuidhir Fhearmanach: the Maguires of Fermanagh* (Dublin, 1917), pp 30, 43; the extant manuscript of this text is dated 1716 and the editor notes on the basis of the style and language that 'it cannot have attained its present form very long before the date 1716' (p. 7). On the background to the manuscript see Bernadette Cunningham and Raymond Gillespie, 'The purposes of patronage: Brian Maguire of Knockninny and his manuscripts', *Clogher Record*, xiii, no. 1 (1988), pp 41–2.

ing [the fewness of] his followers, the best gentleman of his race, was
killed this year by some men from the Route.

[Cú Maighe Ballach mac Domnaill I Chathain, fer a fhédhno fein dob
ferr do duine uasal dá chinedh, do marbad le cuid don Rúta in hóc
andó.][72]

Despite the successful raiding of adjoining lordships and taking of tribute it
might still be possible that Ruaidhrí's actions would not be approved of. For
that reason the annalist's story concentrated as much on spending as getting.

Ruaidhrí Mac Diarmada's response to his new-found wealth was to give
gifts which created bonds of obligation between the lord and his followers and
he paid particular attention to the poets who would increase his status through
their compositions in his praise. Such patronage was a common practice
designed to create symbolic capital within this society.[73] Through his carefully
targeted generosity the status of the giver of gifts would be enhanced. As late
as the 1630s when Bishop William Bedell arrived in his diocese for the first time
he was greeted with gifts of horses, fat oxen and brawns. Convinced that the
local inhabitants were trying to bribe him he offered to pay money for the gifts,
an action which was received 'with indignation as a kind of affront'.[74] Bedell
coming from a more commercialised world clearly misunderstood the importance of gift giving in regulating social relationships.

The first type of gift which Ruaidhrí Mac Diarmada gave to his invited
guests in 1549 was probably a feast. Although the annalist does not specifically
mention feasting in the story other parallels suggest that a feast was common
on these sorts of occasion. Hospitality was an essential social attribute in this
world.[75] In the late life of St Lasair, which was certainly in circulation in the
Roscommon area in the early seventeenth century, there is an episode in which
a band of roving poets arrived at St Lasair's house. The appropriate response
was to provide hospitality but no food was available and as a result Lasair's
modesty was said to be compromised. Her response was to pray and food was
miraculously provided to the honour of God and Lasair.[76]

It is possible to obtain some insight into the sort of bonds which hospitality was meant to create or reinforce from the entry in the Annals of Loch

72 AConn, pp 652–3.   73 The term 'symbolic capital' is from Pierre Bourdieu, Outline of a theory of practice
(Cambridge, 1977), pp 171–83.   74 E.S. Shuckburgh (ed.), Two biographies of William Bedell (Cambridge, 1902),
p. 29.   75 Katharine Simms, 'Guesting and feasting in Gaelic Ireland' in Journal of the Royal Society of Antiquaries
of Ireland, cviii (1978), pp 67–100.   76 Lucius Gwynn (ed.), 'The life of St Lasair' in Ériu v (1911), pp 84–5.

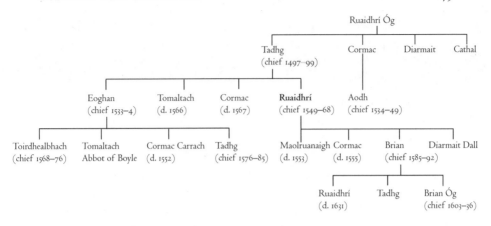

4 Genealogy of the main branches of Clann Diarmada

Cé for 1540 which describes an earlier poetic assembly at the castle on Lough Key. This earlier gathering was hosted by Ruaidhrí Mac Diarmada and his wife, nine years before he attained the title of Mac Diarmada.[77] Many of those present were the local lords within the Mac Diarmada lordship and they had presumably been invited there to bind the lordship more closely together.[78] It was necessary to encourage such cohesion since in 1538, as a result of an internal feud, the lordship had been partitioned between Aodh and Ruaidhrí Mac Diarmada, who hosted the school (fig. 4).[79] Potential rivalries clearly existed which needed to be controlled and it is probably significant that Aodh's name heads the list of those attending, perhaps in a conciliatory gesture. This was not, however, bonding on a principle of equality. The acceptance of a gift from Mac Diarmada placed those attending the feast under an obligation to him and thus they implicitly accepted his lordship over them. Moreover the order in which those present are recorded in the list of those attending the feast is not random but seems to reflect their own relative status within the wider lordship. Thus the attendance of those outside the immediate Mac Diarmada family demonstrates something of the wider Mac Diarmada strategy in consolidating the lordship. The presence of the two sons of Ó Conchobhair Shligigh reflected well-established contacts with Clann Diarmada since they had assisted Mac Diarmada in his expedition against Ó Conchobhair Ruadh in 1536.[80] Another person in attendance, Tadhg son of Cairbre Ó Beirn from near Elphin, also had close contacts with Ruaidhrí Mac Diarmada. The Uí Bheirn were one

77 *ALC*, ii, pp 326–9.   78 The families are detailed in Dermot Mac Dermot, *Mac Dermot of Moylurg* (Manorhamilton, 2000), p. 135.   79 *ALC*, ii, pp 312–13.   80 *ALC*, ii, pp 696–7.

of those families who had arbitrated in the dispute within the Mac Diarmada lordship in 1538, a role which indicates that they were well known to and respected by both parties.[81] Tadhg's brother, Maelsechlainn, had been foster brother to Ruaidhrí but had been murdered in 1536 by two of the Clann Diarmada who were promptly banished by Ruaidhrí.[82] That both of those who had been banished were present at the 1540 gathering strongly suggests a deliberate attempt to reassemble bonds broken by the murder. The fostering of political alliances is also suggested by the presence of Conn son of Brian son of Eoghan Ó Ruairc. Brian was then lord of the Ó Ruairc lordship and had devastated the Mac Diarmada lordship in 1540. Conn, however, was in open rebellion against his father and was murdered by him later in 1540.[83] While he was alive, therefore he was a potentially important ally for Mac Diarmada.

In at least one instance the bonding process failed to work. Although Ó Flannagáin had enjoyed Ruaidhrí Mac Diarmada's hospitality in 1540, two years later Mac Diarmada, together with the Ulick Burke, first earl of Clanricard, attacked the Ó Flannagáin castle of Béal Átha Uachtair. In the 1549 story Ó Flannagáin territory was raided by Mac Diarmada and twenty-four cows were taken. By the 1550s, the Ó Flannagáin and Ó Maelenaigh families (also represented in 1540), were at war with the main Mac Diarmada line.[84] Inevitably perhaps, the impact of generous hospitality could be shortlived, but it is clear that one important function of the poetic school and associated hospitality was to bind together diverse elements within the Mac Diarmada lordship. Hospitality, in the form of a feast, was the gift of the host to those whom he invited to his presence.

The second type of gift to be understood from the Mac Diarmada story of 1549 is the gift given to the poets in return for their poetry. Apart from poets attached to the lord's household visiting poets were more likely to arrive singly. Such mobile figures unattached to a normal social order could be seen as having special qualities and knowledge which may have underpinned some of the near magical powers poets were held to possess in, for instance, the realm of satire. In the tale *Eachtra an mhadra mhaoil*, which was known in early sixteenth-century Connacht, the hero uses the disguise of a poet bringing a poem for the king to gain entrance to a castle, suggesting that this was not an unusual event.[85] The same motif can also found in other prose tales, including *Oidheadh Chloinne*

81 *ALC*, ii, pp 312–13. 82 *ALC*, ii, pp 262–3, 288–9, 292–3. 83 *ALC*, ii, pp 320–1, 328–9. 84 *ALC*, ii, pp 332–5, 366–9. 85 R.A.S. Macalister (ed.), *Two Irish Arthurian romances* (London, 1908), pp 32–3; for discussion of Roscommon provenance and early sixteenth-century dating of BL, Egerton MS 1782 see O'Grady, Flower, *Catalogue of Irish manuscripts in the British Library*, ii, pp 259–61.

Tuireann, reinforcing its typicality.[86] The unfortunate poet and historian Diarmait Ó Cléirigh who was caught up in an affray in 1522, while waiting to go to see Ó Néill, may have intended to present him with a poem, or otherwise seek his patronage.[87] Less commonly groups of poets might go on circuit together looking for hospitality in exchange for praise. Such a group is depicted in the tale *Bás Cearbhaill agus Farbhlaidhe* when their arrival at the king of Scotland's castle generated considerable excitement. On the seventh day a poem was performed and the poet was rewarded with cattle, precious metals, clothing and a sword.[88] The summoning of a poetic band by a lord was a significant event suggesting that a major celebration in praise poetry was planned in tandem with the success of Ruaidhrí's raiding. This also seems clear from the high level of expenditure on the occasion. The text of the annals is unspecific but at minimum the poets received 1,200 cows for their services, a large amount considering that the ransom paid for Mac Diarmada in 1567 was 300 cows.[89] The importance of such payments is clear from the early sixteenth-century history of the Mac Suibhne family which depicts such a poetic gathering at Eastertime, after which the king died, his dying instruction being that the poets were to be generously rewarded.[90] It is apparent that although they were being rewarded they were not being paid for their poetry. The distinction was not an academic one. Poetry was not regarded as a commodity to be bought and sold in a market transaction. The point seems clear from a story involving Ó Conchobhair Shligigh and a merchant which appears in a *crosántacht* written by Domhnall Carrach Mac Eochaidh for Felim Ó Beirn of Wicklow probably at the end of the 1590s or at the very beginning of the seventeenth century. According to the story

> And the evening that he [the merchant] was leaving the town a company of worthy poets came to O'Connor with a praise-poem, artistically designed, poetic and word-clever. The poem was listened to and the band paid liberally with silver and with noble and honourable raiment. And when the merchant saw how liberally the poem was paid for he said: O'Connor, you pay dearly for a poem'. 'I do not', said

86 S. Ua Ceallaigh (ed.), *Trí truagha na scealuidheachta: Oidhe Chlainne Tuireann, Oidhe Chlainne Lir, Oidhe Chlainne Uisnigh* (Baile Atha Cliath, 1927) pp 24–5, we owe this reference to Caoimhín Breatnach.   87 *AU,* iii, pp 540–1; he might also have been a messenger.   88 Paul Walsh (ed.) 'Bás Cearbhaill agus Farbhlaidhe', in *Irisleabhar Muighe Nuadhat* (1928), pp 37–8, Siobhán Ní Laoire (ed.), *Bás Cearbhaill agus Farbhlaidhe* (Dublin, 1986), pp 45–6, translated in James Doan (ed.), *The romance of Cearbhall and Fearbhlaidh* (Dublin, 1985), pp 61–3. Though the tale contains many elements of farce, the underlying representation of generosity towards poets is nonetheless relevant.   89 *ALC,* ii, pp 396–7.   90 Paul Walsh (ed.), *Leabhar Chlainne Suibhne* (Dublin, 1920), pp 36–9.

O'Connor, 'for I have not yet half paid for it'. Having heard that the merchant came back to Dublin. And shortly afterwards a company of poets came to the merchant to buy arms and clothes from him. The merchant asked if they had a poem they would sell him, and they said that they had. 'Well, then, I will pay a good price for it'. He gave them ten pounds for a poem that had been made upwards of a hundred years before and then he went with the poem to O Connor Sligo in the hope that he would give him twice what he had paid for it, although the poem that the merchant had brought with him was not to his father, his grandfather, or to anybody of the race or tribe of O'Connor. However, when O'Connor heard of the merchant's bargain, and [that he had come to him] that he might buy it from him, he gave him twice what he had paid, although he had no use for it.

[Agus an oidhche do-chuaidh don bhaile, tángadar buidhion do dheaghaos dána a gceann I Chonchubhair lé dán ar n-a ghréschuma go fáthamhuil focailghlic. Do héisdeadh an dán agus do díoladh an bhuidhion go daor d'airgead agus d'earraidhibh uaisle onóracha. Agus is eadh adubhairt an ceannuighe an uair do-chonnairc sé a dhaoire do díoladh an dán, 'A I Chonchubhair, is daor chennchus tusa dán', ar sé. 'Ní daor' ar O Conchubhair, 'óir ní thugus a leathluach air fós.' Mar do-chualaidh an ceannuighe sin, táinig to hAth Cliath tar ais. Agus is gearr 'na dhiaidh sin go ndeachadar buidhion ré dán d'ionnsuighe an cheannuighe do cheannach airm agus éadaigh uaidh. Do fhiafruigh in ceannuighe dhíobh an raibhe dán aca do dhíolfaidís ris féin. Adubhradur-san go raibhe. 'Más eadh, ceinneóchad-sa go maith é.' Tug sé deich bpúint dóibh ar an dán do bhí dénta lé forgla chéd bliadhan roimhe sin; agus 'na dhiaidh sin do ghluais sé leis an dán a gceann I Chonchubhair Sligigh a ndóigh go ttiubhrach dá uiread a ttug féin air dhó, agus nách dá athair ná dá sheanathair ná do neach do chineadh ná do chlannmhaicne I Chonchubhair do-rinneadh an dán do rug an ceannuighe leis. Agus giodh eadh mar do-chualaidh O Conchubhair connradh an cheannuighe, agus a raibhe ris in dán fá n-a chomhair féin dá cheannach uaidhe, tug O Conchubhair dá uiread a ttug an ceannuighe ar an dán dó dá chionn, bíodh nách raibhe feidhm aige ris.][91]

91 Seán Mac Airt (ed.), *Leabhar Branach* (Dublin, 1944), pp 215–16, translated in James Carney, *Studies in Irish literature and history* (Dublin, 1955), pp 265–6.

The story has a number of messages but the most important one was that poetry was not a commodity, such as the commodities traded by merchants, but something much more subtle. The value of poetry was not to be defined in simple monetary terms. However, at the beginning of the seventeenth century, as the demand for traditional bardic poetry waned and patronage of the poets dried up, a poem did become much more like any other commodity. Mathghamhain Ó hIfearnáin in the early seventeenth century asked 'Question! who will buy a poem?' [*Ceist! cia do cheinneóchadh dán?*] and he compared himself to a merchant ship with an unwanted cargo.[92] While the sort of patronage and hospitality that Mac Diarmada offered existed, poets could resist the process by which their compositions were turned into a commodity. The liminal nature of the poet's art, neither purely aesthetic nor commercial, in this world ensured its special status. At one level poetry was fleeting and ephemeral in so far as it was composed to suit a specific patron on a specific occasion. Yet Ó Conchobhair Shligigh still valued a hundred-year-old poem even though his perception of it differed from the merchant's commercial interest therein. As poets assured their patrons, the poetry which they commissioned was timeless. Tadhg Dall Ó hUiginn reminded one of his patrons, Cormac Ó hEadhra, of this in the poem '*Maith an ceannaighe Cormac*', composed in the late sixteenth century

> Behold is there any better exchange than the lasting, enduring honour that goest to the pleasant, kindly chieftain in return for vain, transitory wealth?

> Not for long would the riches given by Fermoyle's lord remain, but the praises of his noble, ruddy countenance shall endure eternally.

> A good merchant is he who got in return for a worthless, transitory figment the sincerest of fragrant, lasting panegyric at a time when art was being rejected.

> [Féach an fearr iomlaoid oile
> ná an mhoirn shuthain shíorroidhe
> téid don fhlaith ionfhuair fhaoilidh,
> ar mhaith ndiombuain ndíomhaoinigh.

> Gearr do mhairfeadh na maoine
> bronntar le flaith Formaoile,

92 Bergin (ed.), *Irish bardic poetry*, pp 145–6.

's budh buain na molta ar marthain
dá ghruaidh chorcra chomharthaigh.

. . .

Maith an ceannaighe an fear fuair
air bhréig ndiomolaidh ndiombuain
díoghrais molta bhuain bhaluidh
i n-uair obtha dh'ealadhuin.][93]

This motif of the lasting value of poetry was an extremely common one among the bardic poets of the sixteenth century.[94] Poetry was not entirely intangible. At least some families in the north Connacht area compiled collections of poetry relating to their families by having them transcribed into a family poem book or *duanaire*.[95] This sort of activity generated additional prestige since scribal patronage also accumulated cultural capital. Books, like poets, took on a special quality and were much sought after for the status they brought. Thus in 1470 the Four Masters noted that Ó Domhnaill's tribute from Connacht had been two books, *Leabhar Gearr* and *Leabhar na hUidhre* and in 1522 the Book of Ballymote followed them.[96] In 1497 the traffic was reversed when the *Cathach*, a copy of the psalms, was seized from Ó Domhnaill by Mac Diarmada but was returned as part of a peace agreement in 1499.[97]

The poem or manuscript was, in essence, a gift to the patron which increased his status, for which a counter gift was expected. The gifts bestowed in return varied. Poets mentioned land and cattle but one late sixteenth-century poem listed cattle, clothing, hats, shoes, gloves or the price of a sword or a horse as well as 'from him I got the honour due to an ollav' [furaras uadh onóir ollaimh].[98] What was important, however, was that the gift to the poet should be a generous one, since the display of generosity would enhance the patron's status yet further. Failure to be generous was a legitimate cause for

---

93 Knott (ed.), *The bardic poems of Tadhg Dall Ó hUiginn*, i, pp 220–1, ii, pp 146–7. 94 For examples from north Connacht, Knott (ed.), *The bardic poems of Tadhg Dall Ó hUiginn*, i, pp 246–7, ii, pp 162–3; Lambert McKenna (ed.), *The book of O'Hara* (Dublin, 1951), p. 59. 95 Brian Ó Cuív, *The Irish bardic duanaire or 'poem-book'* (Dublin, 1974). The most significant example from this area is McKenna (ed.), *Book of O'Hara* but other families had smaller collections, for example Tomás Ó Raghallaigh (ed.), 'Seanchus Búrcach' in *Journal of the Galway Archaeological and Historical Society*, xiv (1928–9), pp 30–51, 142–57 and that commissioned in the seventeenth century by the Dillon family, RIA, MS A v 2. 96 *AFM*, iv, pp 1068–9; Robert Atkinson (ed.), *Book of Ballymote [facsimile] … from the original manuscript in the library of the Royal Irish Academy* (Dublin, 1887), p. 2. 97 *AFM*, iv, pp 1232–3, 1252–3. One manuscript was also given in ransom for a prisoner in the 1460s, Myles Dillon, 'Laud 610' in *Celtica*, vi (1963), pp 150–1. 98 Breatnach, 'The chief's poet', passim; Colm Ó Lochlainn (ed.), 'Prince and poet' in *Éigse*, ii (1940), pp 160–1.

complaint and the author of the sixteenth-century life of St Máedóc of Ferns emphasised that the saint gave away his gold and tribute to the poor, musicians and players and poets 'to protect his honour, nobility and worth' [ar sgath a einigh 7 a uaisle 7 a ionnrácais].[99] Where no gold was available God would miraculously provide as in the early sixteenth-century life of St Colum Cille in which a poetic satire against the saint was averted by a gift of gold which was miraculously generated from the saint's sweat.[100] Thus generosity and poetry were often tightly connected and one early sixteenth-century poet connected what he saw as a decline in poetry with a decline in the traditional value of generosity.[101]

Such generosity could come in many forms. The early sixteenth-century history of the Mac Suibhne family of Fanad recorded a story in which a ransom to be paid for Mac Suibhne prisoners held by Enrí Ó Néill was used instead to make gifts to poets who visited Mac Suibhne. Ó Néill, not wishing to seem less generous than Mac Suibhne in his patronage of the poets, released the prisoners because of the way in which the ransom was paid. The poets in return offered the composition 'Fanad, sanctuary of generosity', 'Fanad nurse of generosity' and 'Fanad well of generosity and many others which we shall not mention here.' [Roim na feile Fanuid 7 Buime na féile Fánaid 7 Tobar na féile Fanaid 7 moran eile nach áireomamaid annso.][102] From the perspective of the annalists of Loch Cé generosity was one of the most important social attributes of either a lord or his wife. When obituaries were inserted in the annals generosity to poets and others was a common motif of praise.

Generous sponsorship of praise poetry was therefore an important mechanism through which lords could increase their status and thereby accumulate cultural capital. It was not the only way to attract cultural capital but it was a very significant one. Other dimensions of lordship were often measured against the relationship of poet and lord. Poets, for instance, described themselves as the lord's spouse.[103] The analogy was a good one since marriage was another means of attracting cultural capital by strategic marriage connections with high status or highly influential families. Thus in return for increasing status by the acquisition of a wife the reciprocal process of gift giving was also associated with a wedding. When Brian Mac Diarmada married the daughter of Ó

99 Charles Plummer (ed.), *Bethada náem nErenn* (2 vols, Oxford, 1922), i, p. 264, ii, p. 256. 100 A. O'Kelleher and G. Schoepperle (eds), *Betha Colaim Chille* (Illinois 1918) pp 70–1. 101 Brian Ó Cuív, 'The decline of poesy' in *Celtica*, xix (1987), pp 126–7. For a later poem on the same theme see P.A. Breatnach (ed.), 'A poem on the end of patronage' in *Éigse*, xxxi (1999), pp 85–8. 102 Walsh (ed.), *Leabhar Chlainne Suibhne*, pp 56–7. 103 Breathach 'The chief's poet', pp 42–3.

Conchobhair Shligigh in 1582, therefore, the annalist described the event in much the same way as he had written about the poetic school.

> The great, regal, wedding feast of the lord of the Rock, and of his wife, i.e. Medhbh, the daughter of Domhnall O Conchobhair, i.e. daughter of O Conchobhair Sligigh, was celebrated together by Brian, son of Ruaidhri Mac Diarmada, at which large quantities of all kinds of stock, and of all descriptions of treasure and valuables, were presented and dispensed, according to their wish, to every one of the men of Erinn and Alba that came to solicit them during that year.

> [Bainfheis righdha romhór thigherna na cairrge ocus a mhna, .i. Meadhbh inghen Domhnaill hI Conchobhair .i. inghen hI Conchobair Sligigh, do dhenum a coimhnénecht do Bhrian mac Ruaidhri Mic Dhiarmada, dú inar bronnadh ocus inar bithsgaoiledh ilimad da gach cenél cruidh ocus dá gach arnáil innmhuis ocus édala, do réir a náil-ghis, dá gach aon dfheruibh Erenn ocus Alban dá tánic da hiarrad ar fedh na blíadna sin.][104]

The similar strategies of marriage and poetic patronage were not, however, always foolproof ways of increasing status. Cultural capital, for example, could be decreased through satire which might emphasise meanness towards poets or others, traits well exemplified in Aenghus Ó Dálaigh's satire on many of the families of Gaelic Ireland composed in the early seventeenth century.[105] Such satire, in turn, could raise the wrath of the patron against the poet. One poem of the early 1590s by Eochaidh Ó hEódhusa suggests that this happened in at least one case with Conchobhar Mac Diarmada, the poet having to apologise to his patron for some unspecified offence.[106] The consequences of offending a patron could be even more severe. Tadhg Dall Ó hUiginn's tongue was reputedly cut out by members of the Ó hEadhra family in revenge for a satire written by him against them.[107] More subtly revenge could be exacted in literary contexts where it would be difficult to refute. The motif of the rapacious poet is used in a number of sixteenth-century saints' lives where to take offence would be to question the

---

104 *ALC*, ii, pp 446–9. 105 Aenghus O'Daly, *The tribes of Ireland*, ed. John O'Donovan (Dublin, 1852). For further discussion and examples see Gearóid Mac Eoin, 'Poet and prince in medieval Ireland' in Evelyn Mullally and John Thompson (eds), *The court and cultural diversity: selected papers from the eighth triennial congress of the International Courtly Literature Society* (Woodbridge, 1997), pp 13–15. 106 Lambert McKenna (ed.), *Aithdioghluim dána* (2 vols, London, 1939–40), i, pp 135–7; ii, pp 81–3. 107 Knott (ed.), *The bardic poems of Tadhg Dall Ó hUiginn*, i, p. 278, ii, p. 185.

veracity of the saint and hence risk incurring his or her wrath.[108] In a world where honour and reputation were highly valued and conscientiously defended, the role of poet as propagandist could be risky as well as rewarding as the story of Maghnus Ó Duibhgeannáin, related below, demonstrates.

III

The story of Ruaidhrí Mac Diarmada's imposition of lordship by exacting tribute voluntarily or through raiding and his subsequent bestowal of gifts to the poets is not a lesson in archaic economics. It was about getting and spending but should not be interpreted as an illustration of the lack of commercialism in the lordship of Moylurg. The Clann Diarmada knew a great deal about the cash economy and used it. They consumed luxury goods, such as wine or paper, which could only be purchased in the market. They also used money as ransom. Mac Diarmada hostages, possibly taken during the Clanricard raid into Roscommon in 1542, were ransomed for 160 marks in 1546 and 100 marks was paid for the return of a Mac Donnchadha castle from Mac Diarmada in 1551.[109] In other sixteenth-century lordships, such as that of Ó Néill, lords were well aware of the values and precious metal content of coins in circulation.[110] Again while land was theoretically held by entire families rather than individuals property could be sold in commercial transactions.[111]

The collection of tribute and the giving of gifts in the annalist's story was about something a great deal more important than money. It was about power. If the territories of Mac Diarmada produced, as we have seen, food, rents, and labour services, then the essentials for power had to be sought elsewhere, that is by taking them from those who already had them and thereby asserting authority over them. In this way the spoils of raiding could be distributed through gifts and feasting to create a network of obligations which could be drawn on when required. That nexus of lordship was underpinned by the formation of symbolic capital, dominated by the concerns of honour and the avoidance of shame through satire, according as wealth was generously shared with poets in return for praise. In other instances, the patronage of scribes gave rise to major manuscript compilations such as the Book of Lecan, the *Liber Flavus Fergusiorum*, or *Leabhar Uí Mhaine* (all of which have a fifteenth-century

---

108 For example, Gwynn (ed.), 'Life of Saint Lasair', pp 84–5.   109 *ALC*, ii pp 348–9, 358–9.   110 Michael Dolley and Gearóid Mac Niocaill, 'Some coin names in Ceart Uí Néill' in *Studia Celtica*, ii (1967), pp 119–24.   111 *ALC*, ii, pp 338–9, 422–3.

Connacht provenance) and such works bestowed on their owners tangible signs of prestige. The prestige attaching to the local lord's name, according as symbolic capital accumulated, could attract more followers and hence symbolic capital could be turned into economic capital. From the perspective of the annalist, the 1549 story of Mac Diarmada getting and spending was a single entity. It began with giving gifts to the poets and concluded with the same action. Extracting money and spending it correctly were part of an integrated process and that was part of a wider process of sustaining social relationships within a lordship structure. The story of Ruaidhrí's exactions and raids was a tale about the correct behaviour of a lord as he succeeded to the lordship and its recording in his son's historical annals suggests he passed with flying colours.

2

The dispossession of MacCostello:
land and lineage in Mayo, 1586

A cryptic story involving the MacCostellos in Mayo recorded under the year 1586 in the Annals of Loch Cé provides a good example of a curious event which conceals a complex set of political interactions. In a brief entry the annalist noted

> The great castle of MacGoisdelb, and half the lordship of the country, were given to Tibbot Dillon by MacGoisdelb, i.e. John, son of the Gilla-dubh, son of Hubert. O Gadhra gave five towns in his division, and the castle of Daire-mór, to the same man. (Oilillin O Gadhra that gave those away).

> [Caislen mor Meic gCoisdealb, ocus leath thigernuis in tíre, do thabhairt do Thaboid Diluin do Mac Goisdealbh .i. Sean mac in gilla dhuibh meic Hoiberd. O Gadhra do thabhairt cuig mbaile na rand, ocus caislen Doire mhoir, don fír cedna. Oillilin O Gadhra tug sin uadha].[1]

On a first reading the story would seem to be improbable. It does not seem to be associated with any sort of routine raiding or coercion. Moreover, even if there were evidence of military activity, the taking of a castle would have been unusual in a sixteenth-century context. Local warring activity usually concentrated on plundering and harrying raids rather than on capturing territory or castles.[2] Indeed in this case a particular distinction is drawn between the handing over of the castle of Castlemore itself and the lordship or governance of the country [tigernas in tíre]. There are other reasons why we might be doubtful about the exact meaning of the story as it is related by the annals. The annal

1 *ALC*, ii, pp 476–7. 2 Katharine Simms, 'Warfare in the medieval Gaelic lordships' in *Irish Sword*, xii (1975–6), pp 98–108.

5 MacCostello gives Castlemore to Theobald Dillon from BL, Add. MS 4792

entry itself is added in a different ink in a blank space at the end of the entry
for 1586 although it is written in the same hand as that which wrote part of the
entry for that year, that of Brian Mac Diarmada (fig. 5).[3] There are few other
blank spaces in the manuscript for the 1580s and it is certainly possible that the
entry may not belong to the year 1586 at all and that it was added later as some
sort of justification for later developments. Indeed the closest match for the
ink in which the story of Castlemore is recorded is the entry for 1589, also written by Brian Mac Diarmada. One further piece of evidence which might raise

3 BL, Add. MS 4792, f. 27v.

suspicions about the veracity of the story of the handing over of Castlemore is that in June 1586 Seán MacCostello 'principal and chieftain of his nation' entered into a surrender and regrant arrangement with the crown, the regrant being made in July of that year. The regrant was unambiguous that the lands of Castlemore were still in the hands of MacCostello, with a strengthened land title, in the middle of 1586, the same year as the entry in the annals.[4] A further piece of evidence that must be balanced against this in relation to Castlemore is found in a letter from Sir Nicholas Malby, president of Connacht, to Sir Francis Walsingham, one of the queen's principal secretaries of state, written in June 1580

And amonge the rest one Macostilo dwellinge in eughter Counaught beinge in deede by surname Nangle and possessinge greate territories (albeyt very poore) pretendinge to be alied to the Dyllons (as in p[ro]ffe he ys) hathe called unto him out of thinglishe pale this gentleman bearar herof Mr Tibault Dyllon. And wowinge him to Joyne wth him in frind-ship in the name of his kinsman) hath (wth the consent of all the rest of his surname) gyven him as of free gyfte a greate porcion of his Land wth a fayre auncient castell called castell more, standinge upon a straight of the countrie by wch comonly the scottes must of necessytie (or at leaste) have usually passed when they com from the northe into eughter Conaught alz Mc Will[ia]ms countrie. Mr Dyllon havinge a great devo-cion and good disposycion to advaunce cyvill government as his sur-name ever hathe don, and willinge rather to employ his time in doinge good to his comon seale (where nede ys) then to lye ydell at home where he can not do the like good) hath accepted of the said Macostiloes gyfte (sumwhat to his charges) and hath put on a mynd to sett up his rest to do his cuntrie good. And yet wth that good consideracion as he hathe devysed wth him sellf som meanes to establyshe his enterprise so als bothe he and his posterytie after him shall stick there as a stake for ever, yf yt may be his good happe to obtain the same at her Ma[jes]t[ie]s hands wch he hathe acquainted me wthall and hath prayed my recomendacion unto your honor for the better furtherance therof. For that I am governor in the said province and findeth yt not fyt to deale in any thinge there wthout my knowlege. Wch honest care of his dothe move me to answer his request wch ys this.[5]

4 James Morrin (ed.), *Calendar of the patent and close rolls of chancery in Ireland, Elizabeth, 19th year to end of the reign* (Dublin 1862), p. 113. *Fiants Ire., Eliz.,* nos 4898, 4902. 5 PRO, SP63/73, no. 51.

Malby's evidence deserves to be taken seriously because he was a knowledge-able if not objective commentator. He was clearly a supporter of Dillon and proposed to establish him as sheriff of Mayo and therefore knew something of Dillon's side of the story. He probably also knew at least some version of events from the MacCostello perspective since his technique for governing Connacht was to balance the differing power groups within the province. This he did through assembling local knowledge of power relationships and seek-ing to implement his policies accordingly. There is one further piece of evi-dence that something unusual was in train in the barony of Costello in the mid–1580s. The entire barony was omitted from the inquisition taken in September 1585 which was to form the basis of the scheme known as the Composition of Connacht. No indentures were issued for composition in the barony in that year despite the fact that Seán MacCostello was on the jury for the County Mayo inquisition.[6] Somehow the MacCostellos had remained out-side the government reorganisation of power structures which the composi-tion aimed at.[7] As will be seen, the barony was treated separately at a later date. All this suggests that there is rather more to the story of the handover of Castlemore to Theobald Dillon than an act of philanthropy by Seán MacCostello or an episode of landgrabbing in the career of Theobald Dillon.

To attempt to answer some of the questions raised by this evidence we need to establish what sort of transaction took place between Dillon and MacCostello. There is no doubt that property passed between them. In the better-documented world of the 1630s a survey of the ownership of land in Mayo recorded that Thomas, Lord Dillon, grandson and heir to Theobald Dillon, held 175 quarters of land out of over 270 in the barony of Costello, in which Castlemore was located, as well as seven quarters of land in two bar-onies in County Roscommon.[8] A good deal more precision about the nature of the Dillon landholding in the barony of Costello is possible for a slightly later date since it is recorded in some detail in the 1635 survey of Mayo made in preparation for the plantation of Connacht then proposed by Lord Deputy Wentworth.[9] The property in the barony of Costello then in the hands of the Dillons fell into three large sections. On the east of the barony lay the com-pact property of Castlemore, the acquisition of which seems to be described

6 A.M. Freeman (ed.), *The compossicion booke of Conought* (Dublin 1936), pp 93–4.   7 Bernadette Cunningham, 'The composition of Connacht in the lordships of Clanricard and Thomond, 1577–1641' in *Irish Historical Studies*, xxiv (1984–5), pp 1–14, explains this process.   8 BL, Harley MS 2048, ff 205, 218, 220–1. A quarter of land in Connacht comprised approximately 120 acres of profitable land.   9 William O'Sullivan (ed.), *The Strafford inquisition of County Mayo* (Dublin, 1958), pp 1–6.

by Malby in 1580 and by the 1586 entry in the Annals of Loch Cé. The second part of the Dillon property lay in the middle of the barony, around and to the north of what would become the town of Ballyhaunis, part of which may have been church land. The largest part of the estate lay in the west of the barony in the parishes around Knock and Beckan, and comprised some of the best land in the barony. This property had been in the hands of the Dillons since at least 1610 when Theobald Dillon received a regrant of all his lands from the crown.[10] The ownership of the property can be traced back further to 1587 when a queen's letter for the composition of the barony of Costello recorded that Dillon held land in the barony but was not specific as to its extent.[11] To appreciate something of the complexity of the process by which Dillon acquired this property from MacCostello we need to understand the backgrounds of the two parties to the transaction. The exploration of that context will touch on the nature of political interaction over land, lineage and honour, and on conflict and peacemaking in late sixteenth-century Ireland.

I

The MacCostello family, the first party to the transaction described in the annalist's story, had their origins in the Anglo-Norman settlement of Connacht. The de Angulo family had come to Ireland in the twelfth century and by the early thirteenth century they had moved to Connacht. By the middle of that century they had established themselves at Castlemore and their surname was subsequently hibernicised as MacCostello (Mac Goisdealbh).[12] However they remained conscious of their Norman origins and were prepared to reinvent these when it became necessary. Malby, for example, in 1580 noted that MacCostello claimed to be allied to the Anglo-Irish family of Dillon.[13] By the middle of the sixteenth century they had fallen under the overlordship of MacWilliam Burke. The tract of c.1570 recording MacWilliam Burke's rights in Connacht, the *Seanchus Búrcach* included specific mention of the MacCostellos

> This is MacWilliam's 'rising out' on the Clann Costello and their country, viz. three score mail and three score mercenaries and the cavalry standard of MacCostello and sixteen marks of rent.

10 *Cal. pat. rolls Ire., Jas I*, p. 125; NA, RC4/14, Mayo no. 4 is an inquisition of 1607 which also places the property in Dillon's hands. 11 Morrin (ed.), *Cal. pat rolls Ire., Eliz.*, p. 143. 12 For the background see H.T. Knox, *The history of the county of Mayo* (Dublin, 1908), pp 313–16, 317. 13 PRO, SP63/73, no. 51.

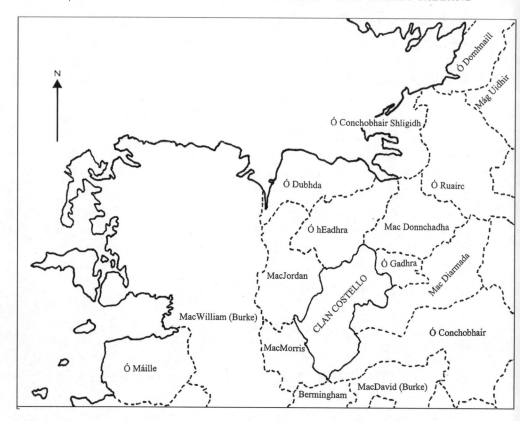

6 The MacCostello lordship and its surroundings in the early sixteenth century

[Sé so eirghe amach Mhic Uilliam Búrc air Cloinn Choisdealaigh trí fichid díolmhanach ar a lón féin agus bratach mharcshluagh Mhic Coisdealaigh agus sé mharg dhéag cíosa.][14]

Exactly what this meant was not spelt out. In theory, MacWilliam would have undertaken to provide some form of protection to the MacCostellos in return for such payments and services but whether the payments were actually made paid or that protection provided is a moot point. The MacCostello lordship lay

14 Tomás Ó Raghallaigh (ed.), 'Seanchus Búrcach' in *Journal of the Galway Archaeological and Historical Society*, xiii (1927), pp 116–17. For the date of the text see Art Cosgrove (ed.), *New history of Ireland: ii, medieval Ireland, 1169–1534* (Oxford, 1987), pp 814–15; The significance of the *Seanchus Búrcach* is discussed in Nollaig Ó Muraíle, 'Settlement and place-names', in P.J. Duffy, D. Edwards and E. FitzPatrick (eds), *Gaelic Ireland: land, lordship and settlement, c.1250–c.1650* (Dublin, 2001), pp 237–40.

at the easternmost point of the MacWilliam Burke influence in Connacht and might not easily have received any significant military protection against incursions into the MacCostello territory from the north, east, or south (Fig. 6). There does seem, however, to have been some role for the MacCostello family in the politics of the MacWilliam Burke lordship in the specific context of the election of the chief of the MacWilliam lordship. In 1595 when Ó Domhnaill became involved in the disputes over the election of the MacWilliam his biographer noted that Ó Domhnaill summoned the contenders to a meeting and

> There came to that same meeting, like the rest, to O Domhnaill, the chiefs and barons of the country, MacCostello (Seaán Dubh), MacJordan, i.e. Edmund of the Plain, and Mac Domhnaill the Galloglass, i.e. Marcus son of the Abbot, and MacMorris, i.e. Edmund, and O Máille, i.e. Eóghan. It was by consultation among these and by election that a chieftain used to be inaugurated over the country, and he was called by the title of MacWilliam on the rath of Eas Caoide and it was MacTibbot used to proclaim him.

> [Dosfangatar isin chomhdail cetna hi cuma chaigh do shaigidh Uí Domhnaill toisigh ⁊ baruin an tíre Mac Goisdelbaig Seaan Dubh, Mac Siurtain .i. Emann an Machaire ⁊ Mac Domhnaill Galloglach .i. Marcus mac an Abbadh ⁊ Mac Muiris .i. Emann ⁊ O Maille .i. Eoghan. Ba hiarna ccomairlisidhe ⁊ iarna ttoghae no hoirdnighthi tigerna foran tír ⁊ i Raith Eassa Caoide do gairthi an tanmaim as Mac Uilliam de ⁊ ba he Mac Teapoitt no goiredh.][15]

On this occasion the candidate supported by MacCostello triumphed.

Amidst the heightened political tension in north Connacht in the 1580s the MacCostellos were not safe from MacWilliam's attempts to assert superiority. From time to time, the MacWilliam Burkes could certainly muster enough strength to raid MacCostello property as a way of ensuring compliance with their wishes, as happened in 1588.[16] However, the payments from MacCostello to MacWilliam cannot necessarily be regarded as some form of 'protection money' to remove the threat of MacWilliam interference, since the main threat to the integrity of the MacCostello lordship came not from the west but from Mac Diarmada and Ó Conchobhair to the east. Threats

15 Paul Walsh (ed.), *Beatha Aodha Ruaidh Uí Dhomhnaill* (2 vols, Dublin, 1948–57), i, pp 114–17.   16 *Cal. S.P. Ire., 1588–92*, p. 245.

from these neighbouring lordships persisted throughout the century. In 1549 the accession of Ruaidhrí Mac Diarmada to the lordship of Mac Diarmada saw him flexing his muscles and raiding MacCostello, taking sixty cows from him in a story discussed in the previous essay.[17] In another instance Aodh Dubh Ó Domhnaill, according to his annalistic obituary, had mustered enough strength to raid MacCostello and forced them to recognise Uí Dhomhnaill overlordship of the area and submissively pay tribute.[18] Even Ó Néill in 1565 was raiding the area around MacCostello's territory asking for the tribute paid 'in old times'.[19]

There were, of course, well-established procedures for the MacCostellos to obtain protection in such situations, and by the late sixteenth century the traditional options were extended by the presence of new power brokers in the province. In 1589, the year after the Burke raid on the MacCostellos, the president of Connacht, Sir Richard Bingham, reported that the MacCostello family wished to shift their allegiance to the Dublin government and hence be protected by them. Accordingly 'divers of the chief of the Barony of Coystellagh are also receaved under protection and have offered to put in assurances for the loyalties when they maie be defended against the supposed Mc William'.[20] In 1592 some chief gentlemen of Costello were said to be attending the common law courts in Connacht.[21] While this may have guaranteed protection it did little to modify traditional habits and in late December William Caech Costello was killed in a raid on the Uí Cheallaigh in County Galway.[22] Within two years, as the influence of Ó Domhnaill spread into Connacht, the MacCostellos had again defected to the MacWilliam camp. A description of Ireland in 1598 noted that most of Mayo was under the control of the MacWilliam Burkes and 'the rest of the countrie is inhabitted by the Mc Jordans, Mc Custulaghes ... who being dependers upon McWilliam, and in a manner his vassals. they are whollie in rebellion'.[23] Allegiance was a matter of military control rather than political ideology.

By the late sixteenth century, however, the sort of payments made by MacCostello to MacWilliam Burke had become important. As factional disputes escalated between the various branches of MacWilliam Burkes, the contenders for power increasingly relied on Scottish mercenaries for the military strength necessary for victory, MacWilliam being described in 1569 as a 'drawer of the Scots to Connacht'.[24] How many Scottish mercenaries were in Connacht

---

17 *ALC*, ii, p. 354. 18 *ALC*, ii, pp 306–8. 19 PRO, SP63/15, no. 15, i. 20 *Cal. S.P. Ire., 1588–92*, p. 317; BL, Cotton MS Titus B XII, f. 653v. 21 *Cal. S.P. Ire., 1588–92*, pp 532–3. 22 *ALC*, ii, pp 504–5. 23 Edmund Hogan (ed.), *The description of Ireland ... in anno 1598* (Dublin, 1878), pp 141–2. 24 PRO, SP63/28,

at any one time is impossible to calculate. The annals mention groups of between 300 and 800 at various points from the 1560s.[25] It is clear that such mercenaries were expensive. In 1544, for instance, a group of English mercenaries were paid 'great wages' [tuarustail mhór] by Ó Domhnaill and by 1561 Scottish mercenaries had become something of a status symbol, the annalist praising Ruaidhrí Mac Diarmada noted that there was not in Ireland a camp containing more learned men or mercenaries.[26] Some idea of the cost of Scottish mercenaries is available from the accounts of the Connacht president in the early 1580s. The cost of 260 Scots hired by the president between May and August 1581 was £508. 8s. 10d. while 100 Irish kerne hired from 1 October 1580 to 30 March 1581 were charged at £440. 16s. 10d.[27] In the early 1580s MacWilliam was said to have incurred debts of £16,800 in the hire of Scottish mercenaries.[28] Such additional sums had to be found by the Connacht lords to fund their factional disputes and hence the exaction of duties on lesser lords became a priority. The attempts of the Dublin government to stop this practice were ongoing. Lord Justice William Fitzwilliam commented in 1571 that his policies would limit the ability of MacWilliam to maintain Scots, and the composition of Connacht implemented in 1585 was designed to put an end to the exactions imposed by Gaelic lords throughout the province.[29]

If the external political demands on the MacCostellos may have been increasing in the late sixteenth century the economic base necessary to fulfil those demands was weak. The MacCostello lordship was centred on a region of poor land. Those sent to assess the area for composition in 1587 described it as 'barren amongst the most barren, which thing beinge so, and yet standing in so discomodious a place, yet can be hardlie brought aboute to be peopled with civill inhabitaunts, excepte a respect of some extraordinarie freedoms or immunitye drawe them thither'.[30] In the middle of the seventeenth century the Books of Survey and Distribution estimated that more than two-thirds of the barony of Costello was 'unprofitable land'.[31] Sixteenth-century descriptions of the MacCostello lordship also stressed its poverty. In 1536 the Annals of Connacht record a raid by a newly created Ó Conchobhair on the MacCostello lordship, the old lord of which had recently died, but 'they did not seize on much prey' [ni rucadar ar morán creichi]. This cannot have been military ineffectiveness since they seized a castle, took MacCostello hostage and forced him

no. 10.   25 *ALC*, ii, pp 383, 392, 406, 410, 442; PRO, SP63/33, no. 15, iv.   26 *ALC*, ii, pp 380–1, 344–5; *AConn*, pp 734–5.   27 PRO, SP63/112, no. 79; SP63/112, no. 80.   28 PRO, SP63/81, no. 42,i.   29 PRO, SP63/34, no. 29; Cunningham, 'The composition of Connacht'.   30 Morrin (ed.), *Cal. pat. rolls, Ire., Eliz.*, p. 142.   31 R.C. Simington (ed.), *Books of survey and distribution: ii, county of Mayo* (Dublin, 1956), pp 79–93.

to hand over armour.[32] In April 1576 Lord Deputy Sidney also commented on the poverty of the MacCostellos when he met them at Galway observing

> at that instant were also with me McPhaten of Englysh surname, Barret, McFaylye of Englysh surname Staunton, McJordan of the lyke Dexter, McCustelo of the lyke Nangle, McMorris of Englysh surname Prendergast and these v shewe matter of some recoorde and creedyt that they have not onely bene Englysh, which every man confesseth but also Lordes and Barons in parliament as they them selves affirme and suerlie they have landes suffitient for Barrons if they might weld their owne quietlie but so bare, barbarous barons are they nowe as they have not three hackneis to carry them and their trayne home.[33]

The economic difficulties of the MacCostellos were not entirely the outcome either of external demands from MacWilliam or a lack of natural resources. Rather it was the way these resources were divided up which created problems. Lordship did not involve the ownership of property within the area of control as the previous essay showed. That lay in the hands of a number of freeholders although the lord had certain rights over their lands.[34] However, the way in which that property was passed from generation to generation was through partible inheritance under which property was divided among all the sons of a family. As one Chancery bill of the early seventeenth century involving land in the neighbouring barony of Clanmorris put it, the

> said barony or territory of Clamorish and all the land therein is and have been beyond the memory of man of the nature of gavelkind by the ancient custom therof and hath always been and is partible betwixt all the sons after the decease of the ancestor and descendable in that sort.[35]

The traces of this system in Costello can be seen as late as 1641 when the holdings of individual MacCostellos were scattered in different parts of a single parish suggesting that what may originally have been a compact holding was fragmented by subdivision as a result of inheritance practices.[36] This may have

---

32 *AConn*, pp 690–2.   33 PRO, SP63/55, no. 34.   34 K.W. Nicholls, *Land, law and society in sixteenth-century Ireland* (Dublin, 1976).   35 NA, Chancery Bills Y 38. For other examples claiming gavelkind in Mayo and all Connacht, NA, Chancery Bills I 206, R 135, R 63, V 63.   36 This is clear from O'Sullivan (ed.), *Strafford inquisition*.

been seen in a positive light in some quarters. Writing in the 1630s Geoffrey Keating, probably thinking of the sixteenth-century experience wrote

> Neither was it possible to dispense with the second custom obtaining in Ireland at that time, that is to say, to have fraternal partnership in the land. For, the rent of the district would not equal the hire which would fall to the number of troops who would defend it: whereas, when the territory became divided among the associated brethren, the kinsman who had the least share of it would be as ready in its defence, to the best of his ability, as the tribal chief who was over them would be.

> [Níor b'fhéidir fós gan an dara nós do bheith ar marthain i n-Éirinn an tan soin, mar atá roinn chomhmbráithreach do bheith ar an bhfearann. Oir, níor bh'fhiu cíos na críche an tuarasdal do rachadh do'n líon buannadh do choiseonadh í: gidheadh, an tan do roinntí an chríoch idir na comhmbráithrigh, do bhiadh an bráthair budh lúgha mír dhi coimhéasgaidh re n-a cosnamh fa n-a dhícheall, agus do bhiadh an ceann-feadhna do bhíodh aca.][37]

While the effect of gavelkind may well have been to create at one level a community within a lordship it also had the effect of weakening the economic viability and political influence of certain families of freeholders and leave the lordship open to internal disputes.

If the economics of lordship were posing problems for the MacCostello family by the 1580s those problems were compounded by internal political difficulties. The expanding MacCostello lineage which may have contributed to their economic difficulties also nurtured political rivalries within the lordship. In 1536 Seán Mac Giolla Dubh MacCostello, who had been lord of Costello since 1487, was killed by his nephew in a family feud. The annalist noted

> MacCostello, i.e. John, son of the Gilladubh, a generous, humane man, and a good captain, was killed by Piers MacCostello, and by some of the people of Airtech, *in hoc anno.*

> [Mac Goisdealbh .i. Seun mac an ghiolla dhuibh, neach deirluictech daonnachtach deigh chennuisfeghna, do marbadh do fPíarrus Ma[c] Goisdealbh agus do chuid do lucht Airtigh in hoc anno].[38]

---

37 Geoffrey Keating, *Foras feasa ar Éirinn* (4 vols, London, 1902–14), i, pp 68–9.   38 *ALC*, ii, pp 304–5.

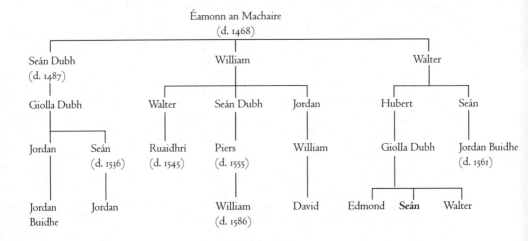

7 Genealogy of the main branches of the MacCostello family

He was succeeded by Walter, uncle of Piers, of the line based at Mannin, and in 1545 by Piers himself. After Piers's death – killed by his own relatives apparently as part of an internal lordship dispute – the succession is uncertain (fig. 7).[39] The next clear MacCostello is Seán of the Castlemore line, the man who subsequently surrendered the castle to Theobald Dillon. Seán was not the most obvious choice; none of his line of the family had previously held the position of MacCostello and he had acquired it only after an acrimonious dispute. The evidence for the succession dispute comes from a number of sources. In September 1586 Sir Richard Bingham, in an account of his actions against the Scots at Ardnaree in County Sligo, mentioned camping at Castlemore where 'our guide was Edmond McCostello (the one that pretended to have been McCostello but that Theobald Dillon maintained another against him)'.[40] This seems to represent Edmond, brother of Seán of Castlemore. The dispute may have been in progress for some time and may have been more extensive that Bingham understood. In January 1585 both Edmond and Seán were pardoned for what seems to have been a row over land since one of the conditions of the pardon concerned land held at the time of the dispute.[41] However, others were also named in the pardon including William, son of Piers of the Mannin line, which suggested that other branches of the family may have been involved. Moreover the dispute seems to have gone on longer

39 ALC, ii, pp 368–9.   40 Cal. S.P. Ire, 1586–8, p. 178.   41 Fiants Ire., Eliz., no. 4599.

than Bingham realised. According to a Chancery suit taken by Theobald Dillon a number of MacCostellos, including Edmond and his son William, attempted to evict Dillon's tenants and occupy the property of Castlemore causing £100 worth of damage in November 1586.[42] Two other pieces of information point to disturbed conditions in the MacCostello lordship. In June 1586 Edmond was pardoned for some criminal offence and, according to the annals, William, son of Piers of the Mannin line, was hanged in that year by the sheriff of Roscommon thus eliminating their challenge for the lordship.[43] The dispute may have rumbled on. In July 1587 the privy council ordered that Edmond was not to be disturbed.[44] Edmond may well have continued to play factional politics in Connacht since his name appears on a 1587 petition to the queen in support of Sir Richard Bingham. Bingham's opponent, Dillon, had backed Edmond's rival for the lordship.[45] This cluster of evidence all points to a complex succession dispute raging in 1585 and 1586, not just between Seán and his brother Edmund of the Castlemore branch, but also involving the Mannin branch of the family. This was a situation in which all parties would look for external allies and Theobald Dillon's role in settling the dispute seems to have been significant.

There was one further political problem which impinged on the integrity of the MacCostello lordship: the growing power of the Connacht presidency and the influence of the English common law. The MacCostellos seem to have remained outside the first composition agreement in Connacht drawn up in 1577 by the president of Connacht, Nicholas Malby. It is unclear why this was so but they do not feature in the presidency accounts among those who paid composition rent in the late 1570s or early 1580s.[46] In 1585 when a new composition scheme was introduced, the MacCostellos were again exempted.

The annalists perceived the new composition as a tribute to be paid to the Dublin government commenting,

> A great tribute was imposed on Connacht by Saxons, i.e. an ounce of gold on every quarter, both ecclesiastical and lay; and the sovereignty of each Gaelic lord was lowered by them.
>
> [Doeirchis mor do cur ar Connachtuib do Saxanchuib .i. uingi dór sa

---

42 NA, Chancery Bills, B 97.   43 *Fiants Ire., Eliz*, no. 4877; *ALC*, ii, pp 468–9. The hanging of Piers may be mis-dated by the annalist since according to Richard Bingham a 'Pers' MacCostello was hung by the sheriff of Roscommon in 1588 who may well be William son of Piers, *Cal. S.P. Ire., 1586–8*, p. 496.   44 PRO, SP63/130, no. 57.   45 BL, Cotton MS Titus B XIII, ff 418–8v.   46 PRO, SP63/106, nos 50–2.

cethramain itir cill ocus thuaith, ocus tigernus gach uile tigerna gaide-
alach dissleghadh doib.][47]

Coming as this did at a time of internal difficulty for the MacCostello lordship it required some expedient action to exempt the lordship from the composition arrangements. It seems certain that the alliance with Theobald Dillon
was pivotal in achieving this. One observer commented that because of Dillon's
involvement in the area 'the whole country [of Costello] at the time of the
composition was omitted out of our survey'.[48] Ultimately however, the exemp-
tion benefited Theobald Dillon rather than the MacCostellos themselves.

II

The second family in the annalist's story, the Dillons, were like the MacCostellos
Anglo-Norman in origin, settling finally in Westmeath and by the early seventeenth century the main branch of the family had become earls of Westmeath.
Theobald Dillon was the third son of Thomas Dillon of Ballynakill. Theobald
and his family, like the MacCostellos, took a creative approach to their ances-
try. By the early seventeenth century the family in Connacht behaved much as
any native Irish family might, commissioning a family *duanaire* or poem book,
one poem in which explained the family's origins in terms of the traditional
Irish origin legend of the Clann Mhíleadh.[49] As a younger son, Theobald
Dillon's opportunities for advancement in Westmeath were limited and this
probably explains why he chose to look elsewhere. It seems that he became
involved in Connacht as a result of prior family connections with the province.
Robert Dillon, who described himself as Theobald's kinsman and wrote in
support of his position in Connacht, was a justice in the Connacht presidency
and Lucas Dillon, who also wrote to London in support of Theobald, was
involved in Connacht provincial affairs.[50] On the evidence of Nicholas Malby,
Dillon had already established his genealogical connection with the MacCostello
family by 1580. Dillon's claims may have been invented and he may have deemed
the move necessary given that genealogy provided the framework for political
activity within Irish society. However, the claim may have had a remote basis

47 *ALC*, ii, pp 466–7.   48 PRO, SP63/139, no. 73.   49 RIA, MS A v 2 (Dillon poembook). For a mid-
seventeenth-century account of the origins of the Dillons by Dubhaltach Mac Fhirbhisigh see Brian Ó
Cuív, 'Bunús Mhuintir Dhíolún' in *Éigse*, xi (1964), pp 65–6.   50 PRO, SP63/87, nos. 35, 36; *Cal. S.P. Ire*,
1574–85, pp 228, 335.

in fact. In the early seventeenth century one Chancery suit involving the Barrett family of Mayo did rest on remembered medieval connections with the Cusack family of Meath and in the sixteenth century the MacWilliam Burkes certainly preserved a medieval origin legend of their family.[51] Whatever the origin of the Dillon-MacCostello connection it provided the basis for Dillon's career in Connacht politics. He seems to have been living in Connacht by 1581 for in that year Lord Deputy Grey reported that he was living 'in that barbarous nook only to do good among the savage people'.[52] Dillon rapidly acquired political office for himself in Connacht. By March 1582 he was sergeant at arms for the Connacht presidency and by May was a cessor and collector of the composition money for the province. His career went from strength to strength and by 1599 he was knighted by the earl of Essex for his part in the Nine Years' War. Finally in 1622 he achieved what may have been a long-held ambition when he purchased the viscountcy of Costello-Gallen.[53] The title confirmed his status within Connacht society on terms that he would have particularly valued.

Within Connacht, Dillon carved out a role for himself as a broker linking local interests with the provincial and central governments and providing protection for local personalities within the province. In 1586, for example, when Thomas Roe Burke was killed by a sub-sheriff in Mayo Dillon, together with the provost marshall of Connacht, Francis Barkley, intervened. According to the evidence of the president of Connacht, Sir Richard Bingham, Barkley and Dillon 'the better to win credit with the ill-qualified and to bring their purposes to pass' promised 'that they would repair to Dublin and procure their pardons, which as they said would be easily obtained'. Dillon was operating as a broker between the local lords and the Dublin administration, acting as protector of local interests from which he might be expected to gain. As it transpired the lord deputy, Sir John Perrot, did not grant pardons to the Burkes on the basis of Barkley's intervention but the fact that all parties believed he might have done so was significant.[54] Again in 1586 it seems to have been Dillon and Barkley who were responsible for drafting a justification of the Burke rebellion in the English language for an illiterate MacWilliam Burke to use in his defence.[55] The result was, from the perspective of at least some in the Dublin administration, that Dillon was operating in collusion with 'many ... ill disposed persons there [in Mayo] to maintain them in all their causes'.[56] The moti-

---

51 NA, Chancery Bills, I 84, I 85, U 31; Ó Raghallaigh (ed.), 'Seanchus Búrcach', pp 119–37.   52 PRO, SP63/87, no. 37.   53 Historical Manuscripts Commission, *Eighth report* (London, 1881), appendix 2, p. 30.   54 PRO, SP63/125, no. 53; SP63/126, no. 53, i.   55 PRO, SP63/126, no. 83.   56 PRO, SP63/126, no. 53, i.

vation in all these acts was complex. Clearly Dillon's undisguised dislike of Sir Richard Bingham was a factor but the gaining of local trust and support from which Dillon might personally benefit was equally significant.[57]

A clearer example of his actions as a local protector and broker is provided by his dealings with the sheriff of Roscommon, Henry Eyland, who in 1586 had been accused of arbitrary conduct towards local people.[58] The people, whose knowledge of the workings of the common law was probably limited, turned to Dillon and it was he who initiated proceedings against the sheriff in the court of Castle Chamber.[59] Certainly by 1589 Dillon had acquired a reputation as an effective protector in this area. In that year Feardorcha Ó Ceallaigh, a tenant on the Clanricard lands of Aughrim was accused of rebellion by Bingham. He responded by using Dillon 'to be a meane to her majesty' to have Bingham removed.[60] Dillon was clearly an influential political intermediary in Connacht because of his contacts with the Dublin and provincial administrations and his knowledge of how they worked. Such local effectiveness quickly translated itself into considerable local power and influence.

III

The sort of asymmetrical power relationship demonstrated by the families of MacCostello and Dillon was a well-known phenomenon in late sixteenth-century Ireland and there were well-established techniques for dealing with it. The first was violence, a feature with which the MacCostellos were familiar. The relationship between Clann Diarmada and Jordan Buidhe MacCostello of the Castlemore branch of the family, although never chief of the family, illustrates how feuds might break out between more powerful and weaker elements. In 1547 Jordan Buidhe went to the house of the Mac Diarmada chief to look for stolen property. A scuffle ensued and significant individuals on both sides were wounded. Over the next twenty-four years Jordan repeatedly raided the Mac Diarmada lordship and, in retaliation, Clann Diarmada raided him.[61] It was hardly surprising that on Jordan's death in county Sligo in 1561 the Loch Cé annalist noted that 'this man was noble [and] destructive' [fa huasal aidhmillte an fer sin].[62] Low grade violence over prolonged periods could dictate local power relationships.

---

57 *Cal. S.P. Ire.*, 1586–8, p. 267; BL, Cotton MS Titus B XII, ff 238v–9.   58 PRO, SP63/126, no. 90.   59 BL, Add. MS 47172, ff 82–82v.   60 PRO, SP63/142, no. 30.   61 *ALC*, ii, pp 350–1, 358–9, 362–3, 364–5, 376–7.   62 *ALC*, ii, pp 378–9.

The second way of dealing with the emergence of a powerful lord in a troubled area was a simple process of intimidation. This is what some at least thought had happened in the relationship between Dillon and MacCostello. Sir Richard Bingham, the Connacht president, was deeply suspicious of the methods by which Dillon had acquired his land in Costello barony. In 1586 Bingham hinted darkly at Dillon's activities in Mayo. He observed that Dillon was one of those 'men [who] had gotten in those parts horses and hackneys and a great store of land of many lewd and ill disposed persons there'.[63] Two years later, writing to Lord Burghley, the queen's principal secretary of state, Bingham was more forthright complaining that

> if Dillon had his right and no more that he ought to have he should not have any one foot of land in all Clancostulo for what he hath there he hath got by practising and by very indirect ways from the inhabitants there in time of his collectorship when he did what he list being well known that he is as dangerous a man and as great a dissembler as any can be, a great extortioner, a favourer of rebels and malefactors and one that hath been driven to his pardon for matters of treason.[64]

Bingham was no friend of Theobald Dillon and hence his comments are hardly impartial but the fact that he made the allegations at all suggests that they fell within the bounds of what was credible.

A third way of dealing with disputes was a more complex one, that of negotiating an agreement. This was a common mechanism for resolving disputes in Gaelic Ireland. Such peacemaking could occur in the aftermath of military campaigns. The annals frequently mention the making of peace at the end of campaigns but usually give little detail on how the negotiation was carried out. There is some evidence that the poets may have acted as intermediaries.[65] Occasionally such peacemaking agreements could prevent violence. The Annals of the Four Masters, for instance, recorded one such agreement in 1560 between the earl of Desmond and the earl of Ormond.

> A declaration of battle, and promise of conflict, between the earl of Desmond (Garrett, the son of James, son of John) and the earl of

63 PRO, SP63/126, no. 53, i. 64 Cal. S.P. Ire., 1586–8, p. 482. 65 Reginald Walsh (ed.), 'Irish manners and customs in the sixteenth century' in Archivium Hibernicum, v (1916), p. 19, par. 23. We owe this reference to Edel Bhreathnach. For additional evidence see Pádraig A. Breatnach, 'The chief's poet' in Proceedings of the Royal Irish Academy, lxxxiii, sect. C (1983), pp 55–6.

Ormond (Thomas, the son of James, son of Pierce Roe, son of James, son of Edmond). The cause of these hostilities was a dispute concerning the lands about the Suire and Eoghanacht Chaisil, the lawful patrimonial inheritances of the descendants of Owen More and Cormac Cas, which those Earls of foreign extraction were parcelling out among themselves; and as the nobles were not able to terminate their dispute, they [themselves] agreed to appoint a certain time for deciding the affair by a battle; and the place of battle which they selected was Bothar Mor, adjacent to Cnamhchoill and Tipperary ... When [however] these great hosts had come front to front, and face to face, the great God sent the angel of peace to them, so that concord was established between the hosts, for, having reflected concerning the battle, they parted without coming to any engagement on that occasion.

[Comhfhuabairt chatha ₇ imghealladh iorghaile etir iarla ndeasmumhan .i. Gearóid mac Semais, mic Seaain, ₇ iarla urmumhan .i. Tomás mac Sémais mic Piarais ruaidh mic Semais, mic Emainn, ₇ do bé adhbhar a nimreasna fearainn chois Siúire, ₇ eóganacht caisil (dúthaigh shleachta Eoghain mhóir, ₇ chloinne Corbmaic cais) gá roinn ré roile ag na hiarladhaibh anduthchasacha sin, ₇ ó nár fédadh síodhucchadh do na saorclandaibh do aontaigheattar dol i naimsir airidhe i naireas catha ré roile ₇ así tulach teagmhala do thoghattar an Bóthar mór a ccomhghar Cnámhchoille, ₇ Tioprat arann ... Ar tteacht do na tromshluacchaibh tul i ttul, ₇ aghaidh i nacchaidh do chuir an taon ndia aingel na siothchana dá saighidh ionnas gur síodhaigheadh etir na sochaidhibh ₇ gur gabhsatt céill imon ccathucchadh gur sccarsat gan deabhaidh don dul sin].[66]

Such negotiated settlements might come in a number of forms. Land did not have to be involved and agreements could involve the respective rights of lordship. The Ulster annalist noted after an outbreak of hostilities between Ó Néill and Ó Domhnaill in 1514

And it came of the grace of the Holy Ghost and of the counsel of worthy persons that cordial peace was made by them and they went to meet each other on the bridge of Ard-stratha and gossipred was

66 *AFM*, v, pp 1578–81.

made by them with each other. And new charters, along with confirmation of the old charters, were granted by Ua Neill to Ua Domnaill for Cenel-Moen and for Inis-Eogain and for Fir-Manach. And O'Domnaill delivered to O'Neill his son, namely, Niall O'Neill, who was for a long time before that in pledge for fidelity.

[Ocus a techt do rath an Spirita Naim ⁊ do comairle na n-deghdaine ríth cairdemail do denam doib ⁊ a n-dol a cend a celi ar droicheat Arda-sratha ⁊ cairdes-Crist do denam dóib ré ceile. Ocus cartacha nuaídhe, maille ré daingniughudh na sencartach, do thabairt la hUa Neill dU[a] Domnaill ar Ceniul-Moain ⁊ ar Innis-Eogain ⁊ ar Feruibh-Manach. Ocus O Domnaill do thindlacudh a mic d'O Neill, idon, Niall O Neill, do bí a fad roime sin a n-gill ré tairisecht].[67]

Such charters clearly did not convey property but rather rights of lordship by which the overlord could collect tribute and count on military support in return for protection within that area. A number of these documents have survived from sixteenth-century Ireland. The earliest of these dates from the 1530s. The first, of 5 November 1532, deals with the overlordship of the earl of Kildare over the Mac Raghnaill lordship. In return for a shilling from every quarter of land controlled by Mac Raghnaill the earl promised to defend the family and its property.[68] A more sophisticated form of the same sort of agreement was concluded in August 1566 between Conor Mac Eochagáin and Bresal Fox in King's county. In this it was agreed that Mac Eochagáin would be overlord to Fox and a tribute of pigs was to be rendered to Mac Eochagáin as 'the sign of lordship' [comartha tighearnuis]. Provision was also made for mortgages, the payment of cess levied on the territory by the crown. In return Mac Eochagáin promised to defend Fox and his followers and resolve their legal disputes.[69] A variant on this sort of lordship agreement was that of 1539 between Ó Domhnaill and Tadhg Ó Conchobhair over Sligo castle. Ó Conchobhair promised to be a loyal follower of Ó Domhnaill and to surrender the keys of Sligo to him when required. He also promised to send the cocket of the port of Sligo to Ó Domhnaill.[70] None of these 'charters' con-

67 *AU*, iii, pp 514–5. A similar entry appears in the Annals of Connacht, *AConn*, pp 626–7. 68 Charles W. Russell, 'On an agreement in Irish between Gerald, ninth earl of Kildare and the Mac Rannalds' in *Proceedings of the Royal Irish Academy*, x (1866–9), pp 480–96. 69 John O'Donovan (ed.), 'Covenant between Mageoghegan and the Fox' in *The miscellany of the Irish Archaeological Society*, i (Dublin, 1846), pp 190–7. We have used a revised translation kindly supplied by Edel Bhreathnach. For discussion of the correct dating of the document see Paul Walsh, *Irish chiefs and leaders* (Dublin, 1960), pp 255–6. 70 Maura Carney (ed.), 'Agreement between

veyed or recorded the conveyance of land. They were all about lordship, in various forms. In most cases the contexts are rather obscure and only that of Sligo can be related to the capture of the castle. How long the agreements lasted was a moot point. Such documents are clearly what the poet Tadhg Dall Ó hUiginn had in mind in a late sixteenth-century poem to Cormac Ó hEadhra of Sligo as

> The old charters of the tributes of the plain of Leyney have fallen out of remembrance, so that it is a bright, clear charter this is renewed for his heirs.
>
> [Seanchairt chíosa chláir Luighne
> ar ndul uatha ar éagcuimhne
> go mbí 'na glanchartaigh gil
> athglantair í dá oighribh.][71]

These charters almost certainly lay behind the composition of prose tracts on the rights of individual lords. Thus the rights of MacWilliam as they were set down in *Seanchus Búrcach* were 'according to the testimony of the stewards and of the charters' [D'fhiaghnuisí na maor agus na cartach].[72]

While such charters were mostly about rights it was possible that some peace agreements could include an element of land transfer. In 1541 the Connacht annalist recorded that Ó Domhnaill had ravaged both the eastern and the western shores of Lough Erne, attacking the Mág Uidhir lordship both by land and water. The following year the same annalist recorded the terms of the peace made between the two parties

> Magnus O Domnaill gave Toorah and Lurg to Sean son of Cu Chonnacht Mag Uidir, against whom he had previously committed great depredations. In consideration of this re-grant, Mag Uidhir acknowledged himself to be O'Domhnaill's vassal, surrendering to him his land and estate and undertaking to lead a levy of his followers on all O Domnaill's hostings, during his own life-time, or to pay a fine in lieu of such service not performed. He also granted to O Domnaill half the *éiric* for manslaying throughout Fermanagh.

Ó Domhnaill and Tadhg Ó Connchobair concerning Sligo Castle (23 June 1539)' in *Irish Historical Studies*, iii (1942–3), pp 288–91. 71 Eleanor Knott (ed.), *The bardic poems of Tadhg Dall Ó hUiginn* (2 vols, London, 1922–6), i, p. 240, ii, p. 158. 72 Ó Raghallaigh (ed.), 'Seanchus Búrcach', p. 111.

[Maghnus O Domnaill do tabairt Tuath Rátha 7 Luirg do hSean mac
Con Connacht Meg Uidir ar milled morain fa Mag Uidir reme sin
d'O Domnaill, 7 Mag Uidir arna thabhairt fein d'O Domnaill, 7 do
thabairt a thíre 7 a thalman do et do tabairt eirghe amac ar fein 7 ara
thalmain co gnathach rena lind ara hson sin, no cáin san ergh[e] amach
nac fuighti; et tuc fos leth er(ca) marbthu duine ar fedh Fer Manach
uile d'O Dhomnaill.][73]

It seems likely that in this case some of Mág Uidhir's mensal land may well
have been surrendered.

The details of how such accords were made are frustratingly vague.[74] As
noted above, poets may have had a role in the negotiations. The wording of
some of the extant charters would suggest that church officials had some role
in their construction. In the case of the Mac Raghnaill agreement the seal of
the chantry college of Maynooth was attached to the document. The document was sworn on 'the faith of God and the oaths of the church' [slana Dé
agus minna na h-eclaise] and suitable ecclesiastical sanctions were also invoked
in the case of Ó Conchobhair and Ó Domhnaill as well as the satire of the
poets.[75] The Mag Eochagáin charter begins by invoking the name of the Trinity.
In some cases an oath taken on relics may have been involved. In 1539 the relics
of the convent at Donegal were certainly used in some form of peacemaking
between Ó Néill and Ó Domhnaill and in 1600 during the Nine Years' War an
alliance was forged between the earl of Desmond and Ó Néill at Holy Cross
where they could 'consecrate themselves with new oaths before that idol [the
relic of the true cross]'.[76] In other cases, however, the making of such charters
about overlordship arrangements seems to have been entirely secular affairs,
agreed without clerical intervention. In the case of a 1580 agreement over lands
set aside to establish a Franciscan house at Lisgoole, county Fermanagh, no
ecclesiastical sanctions were included. However, those who failed to observe
the agreement were to be fined and poets were to 'reprove, infame and repre-
hend the disturbers in their taunting poems'.[77] In some cases the overlord of
feuding lordships brokered the peace and arbitrated between parties. In one
case the lord deputy acted as a broker to bring the two parties together and in

73 AConn, pp 720–1, 726–7. 74 There is an account, probably fictionalised, of one failed negotiation in
James Carney (ed.), A geneaological history of the O'Reillys (Cavan and Dublin, 1959), pp 45–6, 92–3. 75 Russell,
'On an agreement in Irish between Gerald, ninth earl of Kildare and the Mac Rannalds', p. 482. 76 AU,
iii, pp 524–5, 626–7; Cal. S.P. Ire, 1599–1600, p. 456. 77 K.W. Nicholls (ed.), 'The Lisgoole agreement of
1580' in Clogher Record vii (1969–72), p. 32.

another the Connacht annalist recorded that peace was made by friends.[78] Such peacemaking may well have been sealed by feasting or other communal celebrations.[79]

Choosing from among these processes – raiding, forceful seizure of land, or an agreement whose meaning could be negotiated later – was a complex decision. In the case of the MacCostellos there were clearly practical considerations of access to power and wealth which influenced their dealings with Dillon. There was, however, another important if less tangible consideration which makes the suggestion of handing over land seem less strange. MacCostello with his mounting political and economic problems in the 1580s had few options when faced with a more powerful political operator. He could hold on to his land and risk being killed in internecine warfare or lose his land in legal tussles. By handing over land to Dillon he gained security and a protector. In this bargain honour played an important part. In choosing to convey the property to Dillon, MacCostello had seized control, for a brief moment, of the direction of the action and had rejected the pressures to conform being exerted by both MacWilliam and the Dublin administration. His sense of honour made it difficult for MacCostello to ignore the growing pressures. To have done nothing would have reduced his status and honour by allowing the encroachment of outside forces. The importance of honour in determining status and maintaining the integrity of the lordship was again alluded to in 1581 when the Four Masters recorded that Ó Domhnaill, unprepared for war, was forced to fight an Ó Néill army because

> He could not, however, brook that an extern army should come into his territory without opposing them, even though he were certain of meeting immediate death.
>
> [Ar a aoí bá forrán lais sluagh eachtaircheneóil do thocht dia thír gan frithbeart friú dia madh deaimhin lais a oidheadh fo chedóir.][80]

The importance of honour in this sort of situation is difficult to overestimate. Irish lords were very sensitive to suggestions that they did not act in honourable ways. One episode recorded by the Annals of the Four Masters for 1567 might help to explain the role of honour in such situations. With the lordship of Tirconnell under attack from Ó Néill, Aodh Ó Domhnaill had been forced to

78 *AConn*, pp 564–5, 648–9, 650–1, 654–7, 658–9; *AU*, iii, pp 610–11; *ALC*, ii, pp 368–9.   79 *AConn*, pp 710–11; *AU*, iii, pp 518–19.   80 *AFM*, v, pp 1766–7.

retreat after a battle near Letterkenny. He had hoped to receive reinforcements from other families but few of these appeared.

> To these chiefs O'Donnell complained of his distress and injuries; and he protested to them that he would deem it more pleasing and becoming to fall and to die in the field, than to endure the contempt and dishonour with which he himself, his kindred, and his relations had been treated by the Kinel-Owen, such as his ancestors had never suffered or endured before; but more especially the insult and indignity they had offered him on this occasion, by violently expelling and banishing him from his fortress.

> [Ro acaoín ua Domhnaill a imneadh 7 a ettualang fris na maithibh sin, 7 atbeart friú gur bhó lainne 7 gur bhó maisi lais a écc, 7 a oittheadh do maighin, riasiú no fodaimhfeadh an do radsat cenel eoccain do thár 7 do tarcasal fair budheain, for a dhearbhfhine, 7 for a chomhfuilidhibh amhail ná ro fhulaing 7 ná ro fhodhaimh a bhunadh chenél riamh roimhe, 7 go sonnradhach an dímiadh 7 an dimhiccin ro imirseat fair don chur sin .i. a athchur 7 a ionnarbadh co foireicneach as a longport.][81]

In his own way MacCostello had acted honourably in that his actions had maintained his status. He had also sought to ensure that his own status would be maintained into the future through the activities of a patron of his own choosing.

IV

With some knowledge of the background of the MacCostello and Dillon families and a sense of how relationships between two parties could be constructed in Gaelic Ireland, it is possible tentatively to reconstruct the circumstances which led up to the Castlemore incident described by Brian Mac Diarmada under the year 1586. There seems little reason to doubt that in the early 1580s MacCostello did indeed give the castle of Castlemore and some surrounding land to Dillon. In addition to the evidence of Nicholas Malby quoted at the beginning of this essay there is the December 1581 testimony of one of Theobald Dillon's relatives, Robert Dillon, chief justice of the common pleas, which accords almost exactly with that of Malby.[82] Precisely how it came about

81 *AFM*, v, pp 1612–13.   82 PRO, SP63/87, no. 35.

that the MacCostellos fixed on Theobald Dillon as their ally, using a genealog-ical fabrication, may not be fully established. It is clear, however, that they needed an influential broker who would act as their agent and protector in a changing political climate. The events of 1579–80 seem to have convinced the MacCostellos that a realignment of Connacht politics was under way. The MacWilliam Burkes did not join with the earl of Desmond in his rising of 1579, despite appeals to do so. This may have been interpreted by the MacCostellos as an indication that MacWilliam's strategy was to increase his power by aligning it with that of the recently appointed president of Connacht.[83] If there were any doubts of the power of the English provincial government, which the MacCostellos had managed to evade by not being included in the 1577 composition arrangements, those were dispelled by the warfare of 1581.[84] In this context an intermediary with contacts in the provincial government was required, and this was the sort of role as broker that Dillon excelled in. It is uncertain precisely what sort of agreement MacCostello initially struck with Dillon. Castlemore may well have changed hands but given that MacCostello was recorded as still holding Castlemore in 1586 it was probably not an out-right grant.[85] The language of the annal entry for 1586 probably preserves the more important part of an agreement of c.1580. It was not really about land but rather about the specific issue of 'a half-share in the lordship of the coun-try' [leath-thigernuis in tíre]. Such a deal would have been designed to allow Dillon equal status with MacCostello within the context of a Gaelicised lord-ship. Lordship, as opposed to ownership, lay at the heart of this agreement. For Dillon, it was a crucial first step in establishing himself in north Roscommon. This kind of agreement whereby both land and lordship were transferred is not entirely unknown in the annals. The Annals of the Four Masters record an instance where

> The peace of Sil-Murray was again ratified; and the lordship of the descendants of Cormac O'Beirne, the half townland of Baile-an-Chlair, and the five townlands of Ceann-Coradh, being part of the share of Cormac Oge, were given, by consent of the descendants of Turlough Oge, to Felim O'Conor. A portion of the territory of Clann-Chathail-mic-Murray, which had been for some time in the possession of the Clann-Maelruain, was given to Felim Finn O'Conor.

83 Knox, *History of the county of Mayo*, pp 187–8; PRO, SP63/81, no. 15; Sean Murphy, 'The Sligo papers, Westport House, Co. Mayo: a report' in *Analecta Hibernica*, no. 33 (1986), p. 30. **84** *ALC*, ii, pp 432–46. **85** Morrin (ed.), *Cal. pat. rolls Ire., Eliz.*, p. 113.

[Sidh shil Muireadhaigh do naidhm doridhisi, ⁊ tighearnas sleachta Corbmaic ui Birn ⁊ leath Baile an cláir, ⁊ cóicc baile chinn coradh do chuid ronna Toirrdhealbhaigh óicc, do mhaitheamh dá shliocht dFeidhlim ua Conchobhair. Bladh do chloinn Cathail mic Muireadhaigh do baí athaidh daimsir illaimh cloinne Maolruain do tabhairt dFeidhlimidh fhionn ua Cconcobhair.][86]

It is worth noting in passing the parallel arrangement between Dillon and Ó Gadhra which is also mentioned in the 1586 annal entry, and in each case the entry in the annals may have been intended as an official record of what had been agreed. The property reputedly given to Dillon by Oillilin Ó Gadhra in 1586 does not appear in Dillon hands in seventeenth-century surveys. However, Dillon continued to operate as a patron and protector of the Uí Ghadhra and acted as ward of the young Fearghal Ó Gadhra in the early seventeenth century.[87]

None of this necessarily explains why the annalist should have chosen to record his version of events under the year 1586. It seems probable that the impetus to record the agreement between MacCostello and Dillon was prompted by a significant change in the nature of their relationship in the mid-1580s. A succession dispute had weakened the power of the MacCostello family and Dillon found a role for himself as a king maker in determining the succession and, in 1586, Seán Mac Costello became head of the lordship. The combination of needing a protector in the face of external threat and the growing influence of Dillon in the politics of the lordship, made the MacCostellos increasingly dependent on him. The price ultimately exacted by Dillon was land; his ambition went way beyond what he had acquired in 1580. Dillon's ambition to extend his landholding may well be the context of the 1586 surrender and regrant of the MacCostello lands. The arrangement may well have been orchestrated by Dillon to provide good title for the land and thus clearing the way for a subsequent conveyance to himself.

The most significant issue that affected the MacCostello lordship from an external point of view in the mid-1580s was the negotiations surrounding the 1585 composition of Connacht. The payments to local lords agreed under the 1585 composition were negotiated in proportion to their status and influence. Dillon's manipulation of the composition for the barony of Costello resulted

86 *AFM*, iv, pp 1154–5.   87 *Cal. pat. rolls, Ire., Jas I*, p. 311. In later life Fearghal Ó Gadhra acted as patron of the compilers of the Annals of the Four Masters, Alexander Boyle, 'Fearghal Ó Gadhra and the Four Masters' in *Irish Ecclesiastical Record*, 5th ser, c (1963), pp 100–14.

in a deal which excluded the MacCostellos from the main composition and left them without the kind of recognition that Oillilin Ó Gadhra and others who were party to the main agreement of 1585 managed to achieve.[88] Instead it was Dillon whose special status in the barony was recognised through the grant of exemptions from composition rent in a separately negotiated deal.[89] It was in 1587, when Bingham, the English governor of the province, was out of the country, that a very advantageous arrangement for the barony of Costello was made. It was not MacCostello but 'Theobald Dillon, in behalf of himself and his tenants and the rest of the inhabitants of the said barony [of Costello]' who entered into the agreement.[90] The terms, under which composition rent was to be charged on only eighty-three of 275 quarters of land in the barony, was decidedly beneficial to Dillon since the unchargeable quarters were very attractive to potential settlers who did not have to pay composition rent on them. The agreement was strongly opposed by the Connacht president, Sir Richard Bingham, but Dillon personally took the matter to the court in London to ensure that it was accepted.[91] It was later alleged by Bingham that he was supported by Sir Nicholas Walsh, second justice of the queen's bench and speaker of the parliament of 1585, but Dillon was also a regular correspondent of Sir Francis Walsingham, one of the queen's principal secretaries of state, who may have been his patron. The reality was that no one, not even Bingham, really knew the details of how Dillon achieved this feat.[92] Indeed it dawned only slowly on the government how advantageous the deal was, both to Dillon and MacCostello.[93]

The entry in the Loch Cé annals for 1586 reflects not a simple transfer of property but a reorientation of the political and economic relationship between MacCostello and the newcomer Dillon, and was one element of a wider process of accommodation. While Dillon certainly remained as a 'broker' between the MacCostello lordship and the Dublin administration he now also became a significant landowner in the area. The 1586–7 surrender and regrant arrangement had provided MacCostello with good title to the property and armed with this knowledge Dillon began acquiring further property from various

88 Freeman (ed.), *The compossicion booke of Conought*, pp 137–8.   89 *Cal. S.P. Ire., 1586–8*, pp 482, 486–7; Morrin (ed.), *Cal. pat. rolls Ire., Eliz*, pp 141–2.   90 Morrin (ed.), *Cal. pat. rolls Ire., Eliz*, pp 113, 141–3.   91 PRO, SP63/133, no. 79; *Cal. S.P. Ire., 1586–8*, pp 482, 486–7, 500–1.   92 BL, Cotton MS Titus B XII, f. 238v; *Cal. S.P. Ire., 1574–85*, pp 239, 334, 425, 444, 512, 562, 573, 584; PRO, SP63/195, no. 22. There is evidence that Dillon had earlier achieved similar special concessions in relation to other lands he held in Longford and Westmeath, PRO, SP63/74, no. 14; SP63/87, no. 28.   93 *Cal. S.P. Ire., 1586–8*, pp 482, 486–7, 500–1; PRO, SP63/133, no. 99; SP63/136, no. 88.

MacCostellos. Castlemore passed into his hands in this way. A chancery suit in 1586 recorded that he had also acquired the property of Binfadda.[94] He may also have acquired the land from the Mannin branch of the MacCostellos about this time following the execution of William MacCostello in 1586.[95] After the transfer of the property of Castlemore was completed, presumably in 1586, the MacCostello lordship was effectively divided between MacCostello and Dillon although there may well have been some later minor readjustments in occupancy to accommodate both parties.

IV

When the Costello estate was sold under the land purchase scheme in 1885 the conveyance mentioned that the townland of Tullaghanmore, or Edmondstown demesne a few miles to the west of Castlemore where the Costello family had their seat, was subject to a rentcharge of £31. 6s. 10d. 'now payable to Lord Viscount Dillon, created by some ancient deed or other assurance not now forthcoming'.[96] It seems likely that this arrangement may date from the 1580s and allowed the Costello family to establish themselves near their former seat. Similar arrangements may have existed in other parts of the property since the Strafford survey of the 1630s recorded that Theobald Dillon's family held a number of rentcharges on property in Costello barony.[97] After 1587, Theobald Dillon began developing the lands to which he had established title. According to an early seventeenth-century description of Connacht he introduced settlers from the Pale, the population of which was growing rapidly in the late sixteenth century and in the process began an informal settlement of east Mayo which would continue after his death.[98]

The events surrounding Castlemore described in the Annals of Loch Cé for 1586 were therefore not a reckless gesture or the result of panic by MacCostello but were rather the outcome of a calculated survival strategy. Just how successful that strategy was is clear from the fact that in 1873 Arthur Richard Costello, J.P., the descendant of the family who had granted Castlemore

---

94 NA, Chancery Bills, B 97. Dillon's associate Sir Francis Barkley also acquired property from the MacMorris family of Clanmorris in 1585 in similar circumstances, NA, Chancery Bills, I 196, V 63.   95 This was leased to his brother Gerald in 1614 and appears in later surveys under Gerald's name, NLI, D 10389, D 10390.   96 Quoted in Máire McDonnell-Garvey, *Mid-Connacht: the ancient territory of Sliabh Lugha* (Manorhamilton, 1995), p. 176.   97 O'Sullivan (ed.), *Strafford inquisition*, p. 6.   98 BL, Lansdowne MS 255, ff 363v–4.

to Dillon, was the thirty-third largest landowner in Mayo in terms of both the acreage and the value of his estate. In this he was among the top 13 per cent of Connacht landowners (assuming that anyone holding less than 500 acres was not worth calling a landowner) and among the top 11 per cent of Irish landowners. Admittedly his 7,513 acres in Mayo and 1,038 acres in Roscommon were dwarfed by Viscount Dillon's 83,749 acres in Mayo and a further 5,435 acres in Roscommon but Costello was the last of the sixteenth-century landowners to maintain a presence in the county.[99] Clearly such survival cannot be ascribed simply to the surrender of Castlemore to Theobald Dillon. Fortuitous marriages, the production of male heirs, political caution and provident living all played their part but all this would have been futile had they not survived the problems of the sixteenth and seventeenth centuries. In such a turbulent world a patron was essential and patrons had their own price.

99 Based on figures in *Thom's almanac and official directory of the United Kingdom and Ireland, 1881* (Dublin, 1881), pp 737–41, 751.

3

The murder of a historian: lineage, learning and morality in Fermanagh, 1534

In their annalistic record of the year 1534 the Four Masters included the rather blunt entry 'Maghnus buidhe O'Duigenan was strangled in the night by his own wife' [Maghnus buidhe Ó Duibhgheannáin do tachtadh dá mhnaoí fein san oidhche].[1] The annalists added nothing by way of explanation or qualifi-cation to their rather stark assertion leaving the reader to wonder whether this murder was simply a rare annalistic occurrence of the outcome of domestic violence or perhaps the result of a *crime passionnel*. While not all aspects of this case can be recovered it is possible to see beyond the rather terse entry of the Four Masters. According to the preface, in which they set out the sources of their work, the Four Masters consulted two works for the year 1534, 'Book of the O'Duigenans of Kilronan' [*Lebhar Muintere Duibgeandáin chille Rónáin*] which extended to the year 1563, and 'a portion of the Book of Cú Choigcríche son of Diarmait Ó Cléirigh' [bladh do *Leabhar Choncoiccriche meic Diarmatta ... Uí Clerigh*] which extended to the year 1537.[2] The Annals of Connacht do not mention the event.[3] Whether or not the Book of Cú Choigcríche Ó Cléirigh recorded the event is not known since that manuscript cannot now be iden-tified with any certainty. However, the source the Franciscans described as *Leabhar Sheanaidh mec Maghnussa*, now better known as the Annals of Ulster, sur-vives in two manuscripts, one of which contains the following detailed account of the murder of Maghnus Ó Duibhgeannáin as part of the entry for 1534 (fig. 8).

> An untimely, hurtful deed was done in Fir-Manach Martinmas night [11 Nov.] precisely: to wit, Maghnus Ua Duibhgennain the Tawny, an eminent historian, was strangled and smothered and concealed in his

---

1 *AFM*, v, pp 1418–19. 2. *AFM*, i, pp lxiv–vi. 3 See above, p. 16, note 8, for the presumed link between the Annals of Connacht and the Book of the O'Duigenans of Kilronan.

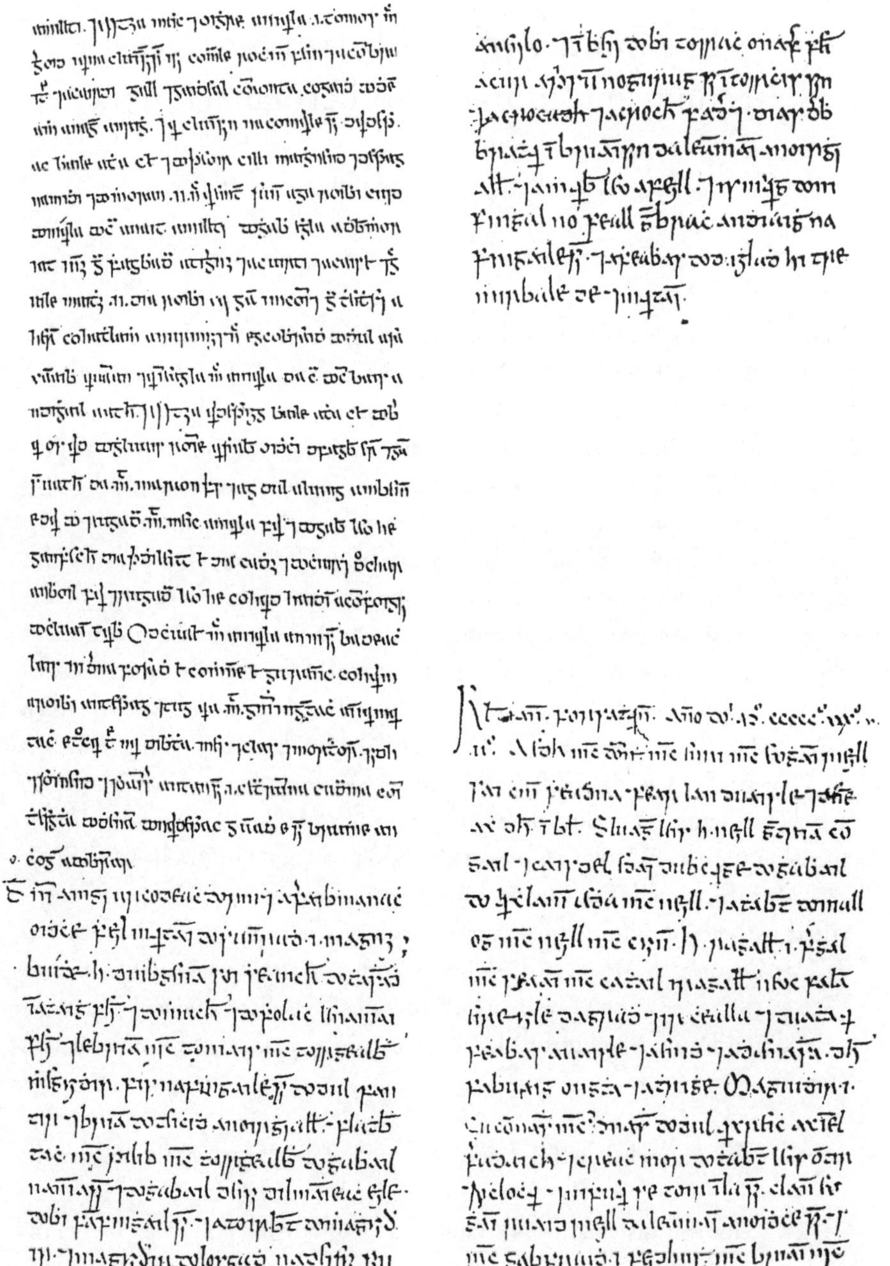

8 The murder of Maghnus Ó Duibhgeannáin from Bodl. Ms Rawlinson B 489

own house by his own wife and by Brian, [son of Thomas], son of Toirdelbach Mag Uidhir. Tidings of that murder went through the territory and Brian fled into Oirghialla. And Flaitheartach, son of Philip, son of Toirdelbach, arrested that woman and arrested two other culprits who were [implicated] in that murder and gave them up to Mag Uidhir and Mag Uidhir burned those two in one day. And the woman, who was pregnant by her own husband, was put in prison until she brought forth that birth and was hung at the end. Two brothers of that Brian pursued him into Oirghialla and he was killed by them in treachery. And woe is the one who does murder, or deceit, to doom, after that murder and the excellence wherewith it was punished through miracles of God and Martin.

[Gnim amgi urcodeach do rinedh a Fearaibh-Manach oidhche fheil Martain do shunnradh; idon, Maghnus buídhe hUa Duibhgena[i]n, soi seanchaidh, do thachtadh i n-a thaigh fein ⁊ do mhuchádh ⁊ do fholach le n-a mnai fhein ⁊ le Brian, mac Tomais, mic Toirrgealbhaigh [sic] Mheg Uidhir. Fir na fínghaile sin do dul fa'n tír ⁊ Brian do teichidh a n-Oirghiallaibh. Ocus Flathbhertach, mac Philib, mic Thorrghealbhaigh [sic], do ghabhail na mna sin ⁊ do ghabhail deisi dilmhaineach eile do bhi fa'n fínghail sin ⁊ a toirbert do Mhag Uidhir ⁊ Mag Uidhir do losgadh na deissi sin a n-en lo. Ocus in bhean do bhi torrach o n-a fer fein, a cur a prisun no gu rug si in toirchis sin ⁊ a crochadh fa deredh. Días derbhbhrathar in Bhriain sin d'a leanmhain a n-Oirghiallaibh ⁊ a mharbadh leo a feill. Ocus is mairg do ni fínghal, no feall, gu brach a n-diaigh na fíngaile sin ⁊ a fheabhas do dighladh hi tri mhírbale De ⁊ Mhartain.]⁴

This longer narrative of the murder of Maghnus Buidhe Ó Duibhgeannáin suggests a more complicated version of events than that of the staccato entry of the Four Masters.⁵ The form of murder, strangling or suffocation, is an

4 *AU*, iii, pp 594–7. The English translation provided by Hennessy and MacCarthy omits 'mac Tomais' and thus wrongly describes the accomplice to the murder as Brian son of Toirdhealbhach Mág Uidhir rather than Brian son of Tomás son of Toirdhealbhach Mág Uidhir. 5 This episode is found only in the version of the Annals of Ulster preserved in Oxford, Bodleian Library, MS Rawl. B. 489, ff 129v–130. The version consulted by the Four Masters is believed to be that preserved in TCD, MS 1282 (formerly H.1.8), and they asserted that the text they saw extended only to 1532. It is now incomplete and ends in 1504. It would appear that the Four Masters either saw or heard about the story recorded in Sir James Ware's manuscript of the Annals of Ulster (now Bodleian MS Rawl. B. 489) or that they consulted another source

unusual one for the annals. Similarly the fact that the person who committed
the act was Maghnus's wife lends an intimacy to the story which suggests that
there was a layer of personal intrigue which is not now recoverable given the
nature of the evidence. This may provide a clue as to why the story made its
way into the Ulster annals. It seems unlikely, however, that this was simply a
matter of domestic violence given the involvement of Brian mac Tomáis Mhéig
Uidhir and at least two other accomplices. Thus a more complex explanation
seems necessary for these events.

There are several features of this incident which seem to mark it out as
unusual. The narrative implies that the local lord, Mág Uidhir, became directly
involved in the case and issued summary justice. Cú Chonnacht Mág Uidhir,
who held the position of Mág Uidhir from 1527 to 1537 was certainly regarded
as a lord who ruled his lordship firmly. As his obituary in the annals expressed
it

> and it was a good rule, for it was a long time since there had appeared
> in his land a lord who gave better law and governance and who more
> firmly put down robbery and violence and all criminals whatsoever,
> who settled the country in greater peace and comfort

> [et dobad maith an smacht-sin, uair ní thanic 'na dhuthaig fein re chian
> d'aimsir tigerna dob ferr recht 7 ríagail et is mo do choisc goid 7 eigen
> 7 aos gaca huilc eli archena et do chuir na tírthi 'na suighe co socoir
> sichánta].[6]

That the lord of Fermanagh should become so directly involved in admin-
istering justice in a case of murder seems remarkable. While lords did involve
themselves directly in legal cases it was more usual for killings to be settled by
the lord's brehon who established a money amount, an *éiric*, or honour price,
which would be shared between the two parties and the lord.[7] As Sir John
Davies, who knew something of the legal practices of south Ulster having travelled extensively there, noted in his 'Lawes of Irelande' tract 'and murder were
but fineable, the fine they called an Ericke which was assessed by the lord and
his Brehons'.[8] That the *éiric* was usually collected in Fermanagh by local lords

---

that is not now known to survive. 6 *AConn*, pp 706–7. 7 Fergus Kelly, *A guide to early Irish law* (Dublin,
1988), pp 126–7; Eleanor Knott (ed.), *The bardic poems of Tadhg Dall Ó hUiginn* (2 vols, London, 1922–6), i, p.
42, ii, p. 28. 8 Hiram Morgan (ed.), '"Lawes of Irelande": a tract by Sir John Davies' in *Irish Jurist*, n.s.
xxviii–xxx (1993–5), p. 312.

is also clear from the entry in the Annals of Connacht for 1542 which records a settlement between Mág Uidhir and Ó Domhnaill under which Mág Uidhir 'granted to Ó Domhnaill half the *éiric* for manslaying throughout Fermanagh.' [tuc fos leth er[ca] marbthu duine ar fedh Fer Manach uile d'O Dhomnaill.][9] However it was true that an *éiric* could be understood, at least in Fermanagh, to be a piece of property (such as a castle) or indeed a life. As the annals record for 1513, two of the sons of Pilib mac Briain Mhéig Uidhir were killed by the family of Ó Flannagáin 'in *éiric* of their brothers whom those slew before that.' [a n-éruic a mbraithrach do mharbadur san roime sin.][10] The aim of such exchange was to prevent a further act of violence which the offender and his kindred would have treated as an insult to their honour, prompting an escalation into a full-scale feud. The effectiveness of the *éiric* depended on whether the revenge killing was regarded as a sufficient price to end the feud. In one case recorded by the Annals of Loch Cé in 1581 the arrangement clearly did not work. The explosion of a feud between Ó Conchobhair Shligigh and the Scots in Sligo meant that 'there was neither peace nor promise between them afterwards' [gan ríth iná gealladh etorra ina dhiaidh]. Sons of the two protagonists were slain 'although they were not an *éiric* for each other' [gidh nár bhéruic i naghaid aroile íad] and the feud continued.[11] Such considerations do not seem to apply in this case. Indeed given that Flaitheartach Mág Uidhir was in open dispute with Cú Chonnacht Mág Uidhir over the murder of his son, and would kill Mág Uidhir during a dispute a few years later, it is remarkable that he assisted the lord of the territory at all.

The punishment of death by burning meted out by Mág Uidhir to the two apprehended accomplices was also unusual. In the previous century the Ulster annals recorded only one other burning enforced as a punishment by a lord and this too occurred in untypical circumstances. In 1490 the Annals of Ulster recorded

> The wife of Ua Ruairc, namely, Mor, daughter of Eogan Ua Neill, was slain in treachery by a kern of her own people, namely, the son of Cathal Ua Ardlamaigh and he himself was burned afterwards.
>
> [Ben hUi Ruairc, idon, Mor, ingen Eogain hUi Neill, do marbadh a fill do cethernach n'a muinntir fesin, idon, mac Cathail [U]i Ardlamaigh 7 se fein do loscadh iarum].[12]

---

9 *AConn*, pp 726–7.   10 *AU*, iii, pp 508–9, 512–13.   11 *ALC*, ii, pp 444–5.   12 *AU*, iii, pp 350–1.

The more usual punishment adopted by lords to maintain order within their own lordship was that of hanging, a punishment sanctioned by legal practice in a way that burning was not.[13] From the 1490s onwards the annals record a handful of hangings by local lords.[14] Mág Uidhir's gallows, for example, were eulogised in 'Urra ac oighreacht Éiremhóin', a late sixteenth-century bardic poem to a later Cú Chonnacht Mág Uidhir by Cú Choigcríche Ó Cléirigh, which declared

> The criminals cannot buy off their headhalters by bribes; women by their side sighing heavily have made everyone sad. Your gallows are bent from all the guilty men you have hanged; nobody dared to knock them down without your permission.

> [A ccendghaid do chrochairibh
> ní cealgthar re comhadhaibh,
> maoith ar cách do chuireadar
> mná re [t]taoibh ac tromossnadh.

> A legadh nír lamhadair
> gan do cheadsa ac comharsain;
> ód chrochadh ar chiontachaibh
> do chrocha do chromadair.][15]

A third unusual feature of the story of the murder of Maghnus Ó Duibhgeannáin was the revenge exacted on the accomplice Brian Mág Uidhir. The annalist clearly approved of the actions of Brian's two older brothers, Donn and Reamonn, who followed the culprit into Monaghan and killed him.[16] This act was portrayed by the narrator as constituting a divinely sanctioned punishment. Yet Brian, despite his having been implicated in the murder, was nonetheless described as having been slain 'in treachery' [a feill]. This phrase occurs frequently in the fifteenth-century entries in the Ulster annals, usually in the context of killings within a closely knit circle, usually a family or the artificial kin group created by fosterage. As if to emphasise the point the annalist describes the killing of Brian as fíngal or kin-slaying which was regarded as

13 Kelly, Guide to early Irish law, pp 217–18.   14 AConn, pp 568–9, 596–7, 682–3, 624–5; AU, iii, pp 370–1, 376–7, 384–5, 450–1, 510–11, 530–1, 570–3, 606–7, 630–1. For reference to hanging as punishment in late fifteenth- and early sixteenth-century Ireland see Siobhán Ní Laoire (ed.), Bás Cearbhaill agus Farbhlaidhe (Dublin, 1996), p. 52. 15 David Greene (ed.), Duanaire Mhéig Uidhir (Dublin, 1972), pp 186–7.   16 Fleeing into an adjoining lordship seems to have normal practice to avoid revenge as Keating noted in the early seventeenth century, Geoffrey Keating, Foras feasa ar Eirinn ed. David Comyn and P.S Dinneen (4 vols, London, 1902–14), i, pp 68–9.

a particularly heinous crime.[17] Clearly the messages being sent about the revenge exacted by Brian's brothers were mixed – a repulsive but necessary act.

Enough has been said to suggest that the murder of Maghnus Ó Duibhgeannáin was not a simple or insignificant domestic event. By the time the Four Masters were writing in the 1630s the incident had lost much of its original context and hence its impact. Since the social context of the murder and its aftermath is central to understanding why the event attracted the attention of the Ulster annalist, it is worth exploring whether key elements of that context can be reconstructed. This investigation of what this murder meant to those who lived in south Ulster in the early sixteenth century and why it provoked such distinctive responses is ultimately an attempt to achieve a clearer understanding of social interaction within Gaelic society.

I

Placing the demise of Maghnus Ó Duibhgeannáin in the context of the complicated dynastic politics of the Mág Uidhir lordship in the early sixteenth century is a difficult task. Even the poets admitted that the Mág Uidhir genealogy was complex.[18] An important starting point is the fact that those who were responsible for the murder were arrested by Flaitheartach, son of Pilib, son of Toirdhealbhach Mág Uidhir. From this it may be assumed that Maghnus was under the protection of Flaitheartach perhaps in a client-patron relationship since, as a recent arrival in the lordship, Maghnus would have no well-established kin group to support him. Flaitheartach's position in the Mág Uidhir genealogies is relatively easily fixed as the eldest grandson of Toirdhealbhach son of Pilib Mág Uidhir (fig. 9). By the early sixteenth century the Meig Uidhir, descendants of Tomás Mór (d. 1430), had resolved themselves into two main families, one descended from the ineffective Tomás Óg (d. 1480) and the other descended from Tomás Óg's ambitious younger brother Pilib (d. 1470), who had established himself as tánaiste by 1447. Pilib's immediate family effectively achieved control of West Fermanagh with the remaining half of the lordship available to the descendants of Tomás Óg. For two hundred years the title 'Mág Uidhir' had regularly alternated between the two related kin groups, the extent of the internal divisions within the lordship being exacerbated by the ease with which Ó Néill and Ó Domhnaill assistance could be invoked by either party.[19]

17 Kelly, *Guide to early Irish law*, pp 127–8.   18 Greene (ed.), *Duanaire Mhéig Uidhir*, pp 200–1, ll 2599–600.
19 Katharine Simms, 'Gaelic lordships in Ulster in the later middle ages', unpublished Ph.D. thesis,

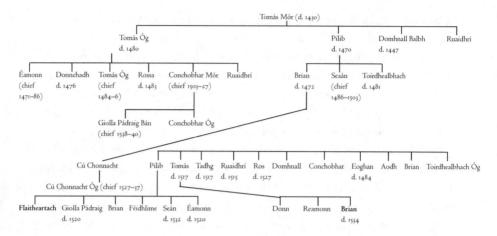

9 Genealogy of the family of Pilib Mág Uidhir

By the early sixteenth century disputes had begun to emerge among the descendants of Pilib. Cú Chonnacht Óg, the then Mág Uidhir and descendant of
Brian mac Philib, had been drawn into disputes with Flaitheartach and his
brothers descendants of Toirdhealbhach mac Philib. This dispute intensified
in 1532 when one of Flaitheartach's brothers was killed by a son of Mág Uidhir.
Then, in 1537 Cú Chonnacht Óg was killed by Flaitheartach, possibly in revenge,
and the following year Flaitheartach continued to raid the new Mág Uidhir's
territory.[20] The descendants of Pilib were also at odds with the descendants of
Aodh an Einigh, whom they appear to have displaced in the territory of Fir
Lurg by the mid-fifteenth century, and Toirdhealbhach mac Philib (Brian Mág
Uidhir's grandfather) died at their hands in 1481.

Toirdhealbhach's older brother, Seaán, held the title Mág Uidhir for an
extended period from 1486 to 1503, having profited from the dissension within
Clann Tomáis Óig. The Ulster annalists indicate that Seaán was an effective
leader, and his obituary expressed this in the accepted form

> … the unique choice of a sub-king of Ireland about that time and
> the one Gaidhel who was of most mercy and humanity that was in
> his own time and best maintained and defended his own territory and
> land against the power of border lands and had best sway and rule in
> church and state.

University of Dublin, 1976, pp 483–93.   20 *AU*, iii, pp 584–5, 614–15, 620–1.

> [... en rogha uirrigh Erenn 'mun am sin 7 an t-aen Ghaeidhel do bo
> mo trocaire 7 daenacht do bi i n-a aimsir 7 is ferr do chothaigh 7 do
> chosain a thir 7 a thalmain fein ar nert coicrich 7 dob' ferr smacht 7
> riaghail a cill 7 a tuaith.][21]

Nevertheless at Seáan's death the title of Mág Uidhir reverted to the rival Clann
Tomáis Óig. Seáan's younger brother, Toirdhealbhach, had eleven sons whose
prospects within Fermanagh did not include attaining significant social or political influence within the lordship. As one early eighteenth-century historian of
Fermanagh observed 'the progeny of Thorlagh son of Philip, who was the son
of Thomas surnamed great was a remarkable branch in this country'.[22] The
fragmentation of the power of Clann Philib Mac Thomáis Mhóir that the existence of such a large family implied was a significant limiting factor on their
political, economic, and social aspirations. Toirdhealbhach's family established
themselves in the barony of Clanawley in west Fermanagh and in 1603 a survey
of the boundaries of the county listed 'Sleught Tirleogh Magwire' as one of
the chief freeholders in the barony (fig. 10).[23] Where the group's mensal land
lay or where Brian Mág Uidhir lived cannot be ascertained precisely but it seems
that it lay in the east of the barony around the River Arney, since it was in that
area that Giolla Pádraig, a cousin of Brian Mág Uidhir, was attacked by Ó
Domhnaill in 1512. Again a description of an attack on the family in 1502
describes their property as 'eachreidh an Tire' meaning the level part of the
country which must be near Lough Erne rather than in the more mountainous
western part of the barony.[24] As the lineage expanded with Toirdhealbhach's
eleven sons, two brothers, and numerous nephews, tensions inevitably developed. The rivalries were probably due in part to land hunger and were expressed
in disagreements over the relative share of wealth within the family.[25] In 1506
the Ulster annalists record a division of the family property among the sons
of Pilib Mág Uidhir but in the course of the division a dispute arose and one
branch of the family sought to enforce its claims with the support of Scottish
mercenaries. The result was that 'destruction of the whole country came of
that, both church and laity, such as came not for a long time before that and
so on;' [milledh an tire uile do thecht de sin, eter cill 7 tuaith, mar nach tainig
re haimsir fhada roime sin 7 araile;], one of Brian's cousins was killed and his

---

21 *AU*, iii, pp 462–3.   22 P. Ó Maolagáin, 'An early history of Fermanagh' in *Clogher Record*, ii, no. 1 (1957),
p. 56.   23 *Inquisitionum in officio rotulorum cancellariae Hiberniae … repertorium* (2 vols, Dublin, 1826–9), ii, p.
xxxiv.   24 *AFM*, v, pp 1318–19, note o; *AU*, iii, pp 458–9.   25 See Simms, 'Gaelic lordships in Ulster', p.
492.

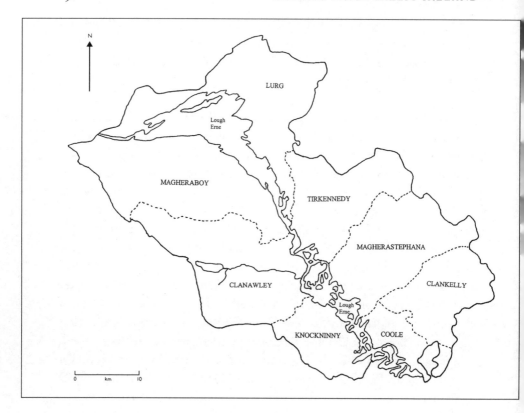

10 Baronies of County Fermanagh

uncle dangerously wounded.[26] Given that a lineage was both expanding and
fragmenting, raiding of adjoining lordships was a predictable and acceptable
activity. In 1498 and again in 1502 Pilib mac Tomáis Mhéig Uidhir, Brian's uncle,
raided Uí Raghallaigh territory in Cavan and in the 1520s one of Pilib's sons
was killed while raiding into Cavan for prey.[27] These activities confirm the internal expansion and fragmentation of one branch of the Mág Uidhir kin group
in the early sixteenth century. Within that lineage the aggressive actions were
those carried out by Pilib mac Toirdhealbhaigh and his sons, the eldest of
whom, Flaitheartach, was responsible for apprehending the accomplices to
murder in 1534.

The world of Brian Mág Uidhir, who was implicated in the 1534 murder of
Maghnus Ó Duibhgeannáin, was one typified by the declining expectations of

26 *AU*, iii, pp 480–3.   27. *AU*, iii, pp 434–6, 458–9, 532–5.

the branch of the family to which he belonged, as a result of the expansion of the power of his cousins. Brian was the youngest of three sons of Tomás, second of the eleven sons of Toirdhealbhach Mág Uidhir. The holder of the title Mág Uidhir at the time of the murder, Cú Chonnacht Óg, the eldest son of an eldest son, was Brian's second cousin. It was Brian's first cousin, Flaitheartach, eldest son of Pilib mac Toirdhealbhaigh, who took immediate action in the aftermath of the murder by apprehending two of the accomplices and referring them to Mág Uidhir for punishment. This world of family politics, connections, and rivalries would play a central part in the murder of the historian.

II

The social and political world of the Mág Uidhir kin group of Fermanagh within which the *seanchaí* Maghnus Buidhe Ó Duibhgeannáin was living prior to his murder was one of complex and contested lineage politics. This was the world in which he sought to make his living as a member of the learned class.[28] Why he was in Fermanagh at all is not entirely clear. As a learned family Muintir Dhuibhgeannáin specialised in history and genealogy and provided scholarly services to the families of Mac Diarmada, Mac Donnchadha and Ó Fearghail in north Connacht and north Leinster, but not usually to Mág Uidhir. There is not enough genealogical detail in the entry in the Annals of Ulster to be certain of his identity but one Maghnus does feature in genealogies of the Ó Duibhgeannáin kin group at the correct time as part of the junior branch of the family based at Castlefore in county Leitrim.[29] It was not unknown for members of the Ó Duibhgeannáin family to drift east into Fermanagh but it was unusual. The Elizabethan fiants provide evidence for one Ferfeassa O Dwgenan at Enniskillen in 1586.[30] It is much more common to find mention in the Elizabethan fiants of various members of the Ó Duibhgeannáin family in Sligo, which suggests that a move westward was more usual for them. However, by the late sixteenth century one member of the main line of the family was employed in Ulster by both Ó Néill and Ó Domhnaill.[31] By the early seventeenth century two members of the Ó Duibhgeannáin family were based in north Antrim under the patronage of Raghnall Mac Domhnaill, earl of Antrim, suggesting a wider dispersion of the family by this stage.[32]

28 No examples of the work of this Maghnus Ó Duibhgeannáin have been identified in extant manuscripts. 29 Paul Walsh, *Irish men of learning* (Dublin, 1947), pp 1–12, genealogy on p. 4. 30 *Fiants Ire. Eliz.*, no. 4810. 31 P.A. Breatnach, 'The methodology of *seanchas*' in *Éigse*, xxix (1996), pp 1–3. 32 Brian Ó Cuív, 'Some Irish

It is clear that Maghnus Buidhe had come from outside the Mág Uidhir
lordship to exercise his craft as a *seanchaí* there. Such movement, though unusual,
need not be regarded as exceptional. It is certainly true that specific learned families tended to be associated with particular lords over a number of generations.[33]
Fermanagh did not lack such families. Sir John Davies in 1606 commented of
the county that 'generally the natives of this county are reputed the worst swords-
men of the north, being rather inclined to be scholars or husbandmen than to
be kern or men of action, as they term rebels in this kingdom'.[34] Part of the
explanation for this apparent surfeit of learned men in Fermanagh may be the
extensive coarb and erenagh lands which were used to support such families.[35]
By the early sixteenth century, families such as Ó Caiside, Ó Luinín and Ó
Breisléin were all associated with different branches of the Mág Uidhir family
of Fermanagh in various branches of learning. There were also members of the
Irish learned class who were not tied into such a network of patronage. They
moved freely from one part of the country to another, offering their services to
a wider range of patrons. The careers of some of these, which must be rather
like that of Maghnus Ó Duibhgeannáin, can only be sketched out. In 1540, for
instance, the Annals of Ulster noted the death of one Mac Caba from
Monaghan as constable of the family of Pilib Mág Uidhir.[36] Again, in 1579,
Seán mac Ruaidhrí Uí Uiginn, was touting his poetry around Leinster deni-
grating various Irish families in the hope of attracting the patronage of others
but he also probably composed poetry for Cú Chonnacht Mág Uidhir in 1589.[37]
Certainly the late sixteenth-century poems directed to Cú Chonnacht Mág
Uidhir contain terms which can best be translated as 'visiting poets' as opposed
to the poets attached to the lords household on a permanent basis.[38] In the 1530s
there was enough surplus people among the Irish learned families to ensure that
some were willing to move into the Pale in search of patronage. The 1534 ordi-
nances for the government of Ireland provided that no

Yryshe mynstrals, rhymours ne bardes, unchaghes, shannaghes nor
messangers should come to desire any goodes of any man dwellinge

---

items relating to the MacDonnells of Antrim' in *Celtica*, xvi (1984), pp 139–40. 33 See, for example, the comments of Dubhaltach Mac Fhirbhisigh *c.*1650 on the process in Toirdhealbhach Ó Raithbheartaigh (ed.),
Genealogical tracts, I (Dublin, 1932), p. 8. 34 Henry Morley (ed.), *Ireland under Elizabeth and James the first* (London,
1890), p. 370. 35 Proinsias Mac Cana, 'The rise of the later schools of *filidheacht*' in *Ériu*, xxv (1974), pp 130–6.
36 *AU*, iii, pp 632–3. 37 Paul Walsh, *Gleanings from Irish manuscripts* (2nd ed., Dublin, 1933), pp 182–93. 38
Greene (ed.), *Duanaire Mhéig Uidhir*, pp 41, 49, 73, 79, 83, 87, 103, 179, 181. For the importance of official as
compared with visiting poets see P.A. Breatnach, 'The chief's poet' in *Proceedings of the Royal Irish Academy*, lxxxiii,
sect. C (1983), pp 37–40.

within the Inglyshrie, uppon peyne of forfayture of all theyr goodes, and theyr bodyes to prison.[39]

This ruling clearly had little immediate effect since Robert Cowley reported to Thomas Cromwell in 1537 that

> harpers, rymours, Irish chronyclers, bardes and isshallyn, comonly goo with praisses to gentilmen in the English pale, praising in rymes, otherwise callid danes, their extorcioners, roboties and abuses, as valiauntnes, which rejoysith theim in that their evell doinges.[40]

It seems clear that the presence of an outside historian or genealogist in west Fermanagh in the early 1530s can best be explained as being the result of political initiative. Historians or genealogists were, almost by definition, political actors. Their task was described by the Dublin apothecary Thomas Smith in the 1560s as

> the seconde sourte is the Shankee, which is to say in English, the petigrer. They have also great plaintye of cattell, wherewithall they do sucker the rebells. They make ignoraunt men of the country to belyve that they be discended of Alexander the Great, or of Darius, or of Caesar, or of some other noteable prince; which makes the ignorant people to run madde, and cerieth not what they do; the which is very hurtfull to the realme.[41]

The function of the *seanchaí* was the recording of genealogies and the composition of chronicle poems.[42] These were not always subject to the stringent metrical demands of bardic poetry. Such learned men not only prepared these compositions but regularly updated them to take account of both the availability of new evidence and new political realities.[43] Thus when a new lord came to power in a lordship two things needed to be done. The levies on the freeholders had to be affirmed, as the first essay in this book has shown, and genealo-

---

39 *State papers, Henry VIII* ([London], 1834), iii, p. 215. 40 *State papers, Henry VIII*, ii, p. 450. 41 H.F. Hore (ed.), 'Irish bardism in 1561' in *Ulster Journal of Archaeology*, 1st ser., vi (1858), p. 166. 42 The division of intellectual labour was, in practice, not as clear cut as it was in theory, see Seán Mac Airt, '*Filidecht* and *coimgne*' in *Ériu*, xviii (1958), p. 139. 43 Breatnach, 'The methodology of *seanchas*'. For the learned class as 'concealers' of change see Marc Caball, *Poets and politics: reaction and continuity in Irish poetry, 1558–1625* (Cork, 1998), pp 24–5.

gies had to be consulted and modified, if necessary. In another example, Tadhg Dall Ó hUiginn described the process at the succession of Cormac Ó hEadhra in the 1580s in the following terms.

> He gathers their books to discover their genealogical branches; every recondite matter concerning his stock he seeks in the regnal list.
>
> [Tionóiltear leis a leauoir
> do thúr a ghég ngeinelaigh;
> gach diamhair dá fhréimh roimhi
> iarroigh san réim ríoghroidhi.][44]

Such genealogists, and indeed other members of the learned class, were therefore intensely political figures working under the protection of one lord and acting as his legitimiser. Because of their considerable importance members of the learned class were not usually the subjects of violence. Most died in their beds but there were a few exceptions. Toirdhealbhach Mág Uidhir, who was also a participant in this story, was involved in a raid in 1502 in which a physician was killed and in 1522 one of Ó Domhnaill's historians was killed in battle.[45] Rather closer to the case of Maghnus was the murder of the poet Tadhg Mac Conmidhe near Enniskillen in 1493 'by a churl of his own people' [le bodach d'a muinntir fein].[46] These cases were exceptional and the more usual security enjoyed by the learned families came from the patronage of a lord. Yet this was not absolute and in a notorious incident in 1572 Conchobhar Ó Briain, third earl of Thomond, was responsible for the execution of a number of poets.[47] Less severe was the cutting out of Tadhg Dall Ó hUiginn's tongue by members of the Ó hEadhra family reputedly in revenge for a satire written by him against them.[48] Being political drew opposition and thus carried problems as well as advantages and this reality may help to explain the murder of Maghnus Buidhe Ó Duibhgeannáin.

The outcome of the historian's task was not the preparation of a manuscript designed for private consumption by an individual but rather for communication to the wider world through public oral performance. It is perhaps significant that when in 1569 Domhnall Ó Duibhdábhoirenn defined the word 'coimgni' in his glossary as meaning 'seanchas' he illustrated this with a quotation from

---

44 Lambert McKenna (ed.), *The book of O'Hara* (Dublin, 1951), pp 42–3. 45 *AU*, iii, pp 458–9, 540–1. 46 *AU*, iii, pp 368–71. 47 Brian Ó Cuív, 'The earl of Thomond and the poets, A.D. 1572' in *Celtica*, xii (1977), pp 125–45. 48 Knott (ed.), *The bardic poems of Tadhg Dall Ó hUiginn*, i, p. 278, ii, p. 185.

the *Leabhar Breac*: 'chants synchronisms, the dignities of everyone' [drechta comgni cataig caich].[49] Again elucidating the word 'duil' or 'book' Ó Duibhdábhoirenn glossed his example with the phrase 'i.e. you should recite the books of family names i.e. genealogies' [.i. aircella na duili sloinnti .i. genelacha].[50] Tadhg Dall Ó hUiginn's poetic description of Enniskillen castle in '*Mairg féagas ar Inis Ceithleann*' in the late sixteenth century, for instance, speaks of those in the court of the castle at Enniskillen 'those who exposed the recondites of the genealogy of the Grecian Gaels.' [lucht foilgheasa sgéal do sgaoileadh fréamh gcoibhneasa Ghaoidheal nGréag.][51] In another instance, after the flight of the earls in 1607, Eoghan Ruadh Mac an Bhaird described in '*Anocht as uaigneach Éire*' the desolation resulting from the flight in terms of loss of performances by the *seanchaí*,

> No reciting of panegyrics,
> no telling of sleep inducing story,
> no wish to examine a volume,
> nor hear a roll of genealogy.
>
> [Gan rádha rithlearg molta
> gan sgaoileadh sgeóil chodalta
> gan úidh ar fhaicsin leabhair
> gan chlaistin ghlúin ghenealaigh.][52]

The contrast between reading as a private matter and the public oral performance of genealogy is particularly striking in this context and points to the importance of public recitation of genealogies, thus making them available to wide audiences.[53] The objective of this task was the assertion of individual rights and due entitlements within the community. Occasionally this could take on a very real meaning as one poem addressed to Mág Uidhir in the late sixteenth century described how 'hostages recite genealogies to your warriors to get quarter.' [géill ag gabháil ghenealaigh / dot fhéin d'fhagháil anadhail.][54]

The political importance of such public literature was clearly appreciated by Brian Mág Uidhir's grandfather, Toirdhealbhach, since in his obituary in the

49 Whitley Stokes (ed.), *Three Irish glossaries* (London, 1862), p. 62. 50 Stokes (ed.), *Three Irish glossaries*, p. 73. 51 Knott (ed.), *Bardic poems of Tadhg Dall Ó hUiginn*, i, p. 75, ii p. 50. 52 Paul Walsh (ed.), *Beatha Aodha Ruaidh Uí Dhomhnaill* (2 vols, London, 1948–57), ii, pp 140–1. The stanza also occurs in a poem attributed to Ainnrias Mac Marcuis on the same subject which has nine stanzas in common with this one, Eleanor Knott (ed.), 'The flight of the earls' in *Ériu*, viii (1915–16), pp 192–4. 53 For a late example of this see Henry Piers, *A chorographical description of the county of Westmeath* (repr. Tara, 1981), pp 109–10. 54 Greene (ed.), *Duanaire Mhéig Uidhir*, pp 104–5.

annals for 1481 it noted '[he] most bought of bardic composition that was in Ireland in his own time that Toirdelbach.' [is mo ro chennaig do dhan do bi i nErinn i n-a aimsir fein in Toirrdelbach sin.][55] The move was clearly an astute one for someone wishing to establish his own junior branch of the family as a significant force in local politics. The same motivation may have been behind the presence of the *seanchaí* Maghnus Buidhe Ó Duibhgeannáin in Fermanagh. He was most probably living under the patronage of the family of Flaitheartach Mág Uidhir, the man who took it upon himself to revenge the historian's death. As we have seen above the upwardly mobile family of Flaitheartach had been involved in on-going disputes with the family of Cú Chonnacht Óg Mág Uidhir as he tried to consolidate his hold on part of his fragmented lineage. The presence of the historian may well have been part of a propaganda campaign associated with such competitive raiding within the Mág Uidhir lordship and intended to underpin the position of Flaitheartach's branch of the family.

That Ó Duibhgeannáin's presence was probably an innovation is also suggested by the fact that in the late fifteenth century the recruitment of learned men for the family had usually been done on the basis of the extended lineage of Pilib Mág Uidhir. In 1495, for instance, the Annals of Ulster noted the death of Uilliam Glas son of Pól Ó Caiside who was physician to Pilib Mág Uidhir and his sons, and in 1520 the death of Feidhlimidhe Ó Caiside chief physician to the descendants of Pilib Mág Uidhir was recorded. In 1540 likewise Giolla na Naomh Ó Caiside, 'ollam' to the descendants of Pilib Mág Uidhir, was noted.[56] As the family fragmented in the 1530s some of the branches seem to have required their own propagandists but needed to recruit them from further afield, hiring them to extoll the virtues of the branch of the family that patronised them. When the family of Flaitheartach son of Pilib son of Toirdhealbhach established themselves as patrons, the learned men they employed to praise their branch of the family would inevitably have implied a reduction in status of the brothers of Pilib mac Toirdhealbhaigh and their descendants. This was the group of people to which Brian Mág Uidhir belonged. In exalting one branch of the family – that of his patron – Maghnus, the historian, may have implicitly cast a slight on other branches, or indeed members of other learned families. It is relevant in this context that the early seventeenth-century biography of Aodh Ruadh Ó Domhnaill contains a clear disclaimer by the author, Lughaidh Ó Cléirigh, that he had no wish to trespass on the areas reserved to the learned men of other families lest he be accused

55 *AU*, iii, pp 274–5.   56 *AU*, iii pp 386–7, 534–5, 632–3.

of pride, presumption and vanity and be criticised for it.[57] The dangers of using inappropriate genealogical material in the wrong contexts was clear from the actions of a number of poets at a Christmas feast given by Toirdhealbhach Luineach Ó Néill in 1577. The poets had offered him genealogies but Toirdhealbhach's claim to the lordship was extremely weak in genealogical terms and he wanted instead stories of his victories in battle. The poets were summarily dismissed for their misjudgment of the situation.[58] It can thus be suggested that the murder of Maghnus might be interpreted as an episode in genealogical politics in which he did not quite realise what was admissible and what not in the political world of the Meig Uidhir in Fermanagh.

III

Although the political murder of the *seanchaí* Maghnus Buidhe Ó Duibhgeannáin can perhaps be located within the murky world of dynastic disputes in which a member of the learned class had become involved it cannot be fully explained by that context alone. In its content the account of the murder is certainly unlike most other entries in the sixteenth-century annals. Moreover it is very accurately dated in a way that many annal entries are not. The dating may be, in part, a rhetorical device. By providing the date as the feast of St Martin the annalist allows himself to draw a moral from the events so that justice was portrayed as being achieved not by human intervention alone but through the miracles of God and St Martin. The use of St Martin in this context is unusual. If any saint was to be invoked it should perhaps have been St Lasair since the Ó Duibhgeannáin family were under her patronage.[59] There is scant evidence, though, of a significant local cult of St Martin in the Fermanagh area and no churches there were dedicated to him.[60] Just four indications of a local connection with St Martin have been traced. The first is the inclusion of Martin in a litany of saints, including Ciarán, Colum Cille, Patrick and Mongan, contained in an anonymous poem, copied into the early sixteenth-century *Leabhar Chlainne Suibhne* written in Donegal. Whether this indicates a local cult of Martin is

---

57 Walsh (ed.), *Beatha Aodha Ruaidh Uí Dhomhnaill*, i, pp 170–3.   58 Knott (ed.), *Bardic poems of Tadhg Dall Ó hUiginn*, i, pp 50–6', ii, pp 34–7. For a possible reply by a poet see in Dáibhí Ó Cróinín, 'A poem to Toirdhealbhach Luinneach O Néill' in *Éigse*, xvi (1975–6), pp 50–66.   59 Lucius Gwynn, 'The life of St Lasair' in *Ériu* v (1911), p. 73.   60 Dorothy Lowry-Corry, 'Ancient church sites and graveyards in Co. Fermanagh' in *Journal of the Royal Society of Antiquaries of Ireland*, xlix (1920), table 1. An early seventeenth-century list of church dedications in the diocese contains no dedication to St Martin: TCD, MS 6404, ff 99–99v.

uncertain since a slightly longer version of the poem, 'Réalta [an] chruinne Caitir Fhíona', also occurs in the early sixteenth-century Scottish text The book of the dean of Lismore and given the Mac Suibhne links with Scotland it may have moved from Scotland to Donegal.[61] The second piece of evidence is a reference in a vernacular life of St Molaise of Devenish, a late life (probably fifteenth century) copied in Fermanagh in the early sixteenth century, which contains a passage in which Molaise on his way to Rome meets St Martin at Tours and returns to Devenish with Roman relics including, somewhat problematically, an ankle bone from the still-alive Martin.[62] Whether these relics ever generated a local cult or even survived into the sixteenth century is uncertain. In the second vernacular life of Máedóc of Ferns, which seems to post-date the vernacular life of Molaise since it refers to it, the relics brought to Ireland by Molaise were said to be in the church of Drumlane in County Leitrim, which Máedóc founded. Whether they were in Fermanagh by 1500 is unknown.[63] Another fragment of evidence comes from the early sixteenth-century text known as the Book of Fenagh, compiled in 1516 from older materials at Fenagh, County Leitrim. At one point in the narrative St Caillin was said to have brought from Rome relics of the eleven Apostles and relics of SS Martin, Laurence and Stephen the Martyr together with a cloth made by Mary and used to feed Christ. The three saints were depicted on the 1536 shrine of St Caillin and if there was a local relic of St Martin it might have been enshrined there. There may have been no relic.[64] Other relic lists in the Book of Fenagh omit St Martin. The original motive for his inclusion may have been to increase the status of the church given Martin's supposed family connection with St Patrick and his appropriation by monastic communities in twelfth-century Ulster.[65]

Part of the explanation for the invocation of St Martin in the context of the murder may come from a wider popular tradition. In folklore the dominant theme of the feast of St Martin is sacrifice which is usually associated with the killing of an animal in honour of the saint.[66] The story certainly occurs

61 McKenna (ed.), Aithdioghluim dána, i, p. 358, ii, p. 223.   62 BL, Add. MS 18205 edited in S.H. O'Grady (ed.), Silva Gadelica (2 vols, London, 1892), i, pp 30, 31–3; ii, pp 27, 29–31. We are grateful to Pádraig Ó Riain for his advice on this text.   63 Charles Plummer (ed.), Bethada náem nErenn (2 vols, Oxford, 1922), i, p. 266, ii, p. 258.   64 W.M. Hennessy and D.H. Kelly (eds), Book of Fenagh (Dublin, 1875, rept Dublin, 1939), pp 12–13, 108–11, 192–3; Colum Hourihane, Gothic art in Ireland, 1169–1550 (New Haven, 2003), pp 126–9.   65 Máire Herbert, 'The life of Martin of Tours: a view from twelfth-century Ireland' in Michael Richter and Jean-Michel Picard (eds), Ogma: essays in Celtic studies (Dublin, 2002) pp 76–84.   66 The folklore evidence is reviewed in Seán Ó Súilleabháin, 'The feast of Saint Martin in Ireland' in W.E. Richmond (ed.), Studies in folklore in honour of distinguished service, Professor Stith Thompson (Indiana, 1957), pp 252–61. The more formal evidence of the cult is dealt with in Aubrey Gwynn, 'The cult of St Martin in Ireland' in Irish Ecclesiastical

in the fifteenth-century manuscript *Liber Flavus Fergusiorum*, which may have been written in Roscommon, and Ó Duibhdábhoirenn's glossary of the 1560s contains the entry 'Lupait is the name of the young pig which is killed at the festival of Martin, and my opinion is that it is given to the Lord' [Lupait .i. ainm in bainb marbthar imféil Márta[i]n, ocus dom doich is don tiagharna doberar.][67] The annalist may have had this tradition in mind when recording the story so that the sacrifice became a metaphor for the murder which was in turn redeemed by the revenge of the saint.

Whether or not such a complex reading of the events was intended by the annalist is not certain but what does seem clear is that he turned the report of a murder into a moral tale. Such a transformation is not unknown in the annals. Under 1535 the Connacht annalists recorded the death of Silken Thomas with the obituary

> Now there never lived, of all the Galls of Ireland, a man of his years whose death was a greater loss, both as regards humanity and military leadership, than this Thomas, the earl's son; nor do recent times afford a better sermon than the swiftness with which the line of the earldom, which had held the ascendency in all Ireland for a long time before this, was blotted out of Ireland.

> [7 ni thanic do Ghallaib Erenn fer a aosa fein dobad mó do sgel do thaob daonachta et cendois fédhna ina in Tomas-sin mac ann Iarla, 7 ni mo senmoir da tanic a ndeired na haimsire ina a girre do bi slicht na hiarlachta do sgris a hErinn 7 tren Erenn uile aca re fado d'aimsir roime sin.][68]

The performance analogy of the oral form of a sermon for this sort of moral tale may indeed be a rather good one for the Annals of Ulster in the 1530s. While the obit on the death of Cathal Mac Maghnusa in 1498 had asked 'And let every one that shall *read* this book and avail of it bestow his benison upon that soul of Mac Maghnusa' [Ocus tabrad gach nech dia *leghfa* ind lebur sa 7 dia foighena, a bennacht for an anmain sin Mic Mhaghnusa],[69] the obit for Seán Ó Craidhéin and his wife in 1528 asked 'And every one who shall *read or listen* to this year, let him bestow benison on the souls of that couple aforesaid

Record, 5th ser., cv (Jan.-June 1966), pp 353–64. **67** *Catalogue of Irish manuscripts in the Royal Irish Academy*, fasc. x, p. 1260; Stokes, *Three Irish glossaries*, p. 103. For another reference from 1561 see, BL, Add. MS 30512, f. 17v. **68** *AConn*, pp 688–9. The Annals of Loch Cé have a similar entry, *ALC*, ii, pp 286–7. **69** *AU*, iii, pp 430–1.

we mentioned above' [Ocus gach neach *légfus* 7 *éisdfius* an challuinn siu, tabraid bennachtain ar anmandoibh na lanamna remráite sin adubhromur romainn] (our emphasis).[70] It may well be that the entries for a year were read publicly or were quarried for public reading in, for example, the form of a sermon. If this were the case the story of the murder of Maghnus Ó Duibhgeannáin, by his wife and her accomplices would serve a very similar purpose to the traditional *exempla*, or moral tales, much favoured by medieval preachers as a means of enlivening their sermons.[71] This homiletic style, in a more developed form, appears in an entry in the Annals of Ulster for 1492. The entry tells the story of the murder of two innocent farmers and embellishes it into a moral story replete with six scriptural quotations, provided in Latin in the text, as would be appropriate for a sermon form.[72]

The importance of the story of Maghnus Ó Duibhgeannáin as a moral one is emphasised by the punishments meted out to the conspirators. It was, after all, a double case of *fingal* or kin slaying. On the one hand a wife had murdered her husband and then two men had been forced to kill their brother. Given the attitudes towards women, the murder of a husband was the equivalent of a moral inversion. Sixteenth-century proverbial wisdom, as captured in texts such as *Bídh crínna*, held that women should be kept under control. Thus a man was advised to 'rule your wife' [Smachtaigh do ben]. A more elaborate version advised 'Do not give your wife authority over you, for if you let her stamp on your foot to-night, she will stamp on your head tomorrow' [Na tabhuir cumachta dot mhnaoi os do chionn oir da leige tu dhi saltradh ar do chois anocht sailteoraid si ar do chionn amaireach].[73]

The punishment meted out to the central figure in the case, the unnamed woman who, together with accomplices, murdered her husband, is revealing both of attitudes to women and lineage within Fermanagh society. That an otherwise detailed narrative should omit the woman's name is suggestive of her insignificance in the eyes of the narrator. Nevertheless, she may well have been closely related to the other parties to the crime. The possibility that she was a Mág Uidhir and perhaps a relative of Flaithteartach, who was at hand to appre-

---

70 *AU*, iii, pp 574–5. 71 In this context it may be relevant that in medieval *exempla* it was frequently women who were depicted as the sinners who failed to confess particularly serious sins including infanticide and some sexual sins. See Máirín Nic Eoin, *B'ait leo bean: gnéithe den idé-eolaíocht inscne i dtraidisiún liteartha na Gaeilge* (Dublin, 1998), pp 128–31. For *exempla* in the Irish preaching tradition, Alan Fletcher, 'Preaching in latemedieval Ireland: the English and the Latin tradition' in Alan Fletcher and Raymond Gillespie (eds), *Irish preaching, 700–1700* (Dublin, 2001), pp 56–80. 72 *AU*, iii, pp 366–7. 73 Carl Marstrander, 'Bídh crínna' in *Ériu*, v (1911), pp 126–41.

hend her, cannot be discounted. It does seem unlikely, however, given that Flaitheartach would probably have been inclined to protect his closest relatives in such a situation. The feud with the family of Cú Chonnacht Mág Uidhir would have strengthened such an urge for protection. The deferral of her hanging until after the birth of her husband's child may best be interpreted in lineage terms as being out of respect for the child's father rather than its mother. The fate of the woman who murdered her husband was not the point of the annalist's narrative.

The sentence of burning passed on the male conspirators is certainly best explained in terms of the moral interpretation of the crime. Certainly in 1493, when a poet had been murdered near Enniskillen, hanging was the punishment meted out to the perpetrator.[74] Burning was usually reserved for something particularly heinous. A 1575 list of aphorisms from county Clare, for instance, contains the advice (presumably to a ruler)

> Punish evildoers, that everyone may avoid wrongdoing. Cut off the hands of thieves. Hang robbers. Burn them who do witchcraft. Put to the sword them who commit adultery.
>
> [Tabhair pian do lucht na ndrochghniom ionnus gu sechnoait cach na cionta. Gerr lamha na ngatuighthi. Croch na bithbhinaigh. Loisc lucht na bpiseocc. Claoidhme lucht an adhaltrannuis.][75]

One example of these injunctions being put into action is provided by the Arthurian tale *Eachtra an mhadra mhaoil* which was circulating in Connacht in the early sixteenth century. In this, one of the daughters of the king of Scythia, Beibheann, murders her sister, Beadhchrotha, using magical means

> so that the daughter who was oldest of them (Beibheann) put a sleep-spell of druidry on Beadhchrotha, so that she fell in a stupor of sleep and long slumber; and she took out the blade of a sharp-pointed knife that she had, and struck her in the lower part of her breast, so that she split her fair body to the apple of her throat. The story reached the king, and he takes Beibheann and ordered her to be bound hard and grievously; and fires and brands were lit around her, and she was burnt in the presence of the host, as her evil deeds earned it for her, so that fine ashes were made of her.

74 *AU*, iii, pp 370–1.   75 Marstrander, 'Bídh crínna', pp 134–5.

[ionnus gur chuir an inghean fá sine díobh (eadhón Beibheann) suain-
bhreacht draoidheachta or Beadhchrotha, gur thuit sí n'a toirchim suain
agus síor-chodalta; agus thug altán scéine scoithghéire do bhí aici
amach, agus do bhuail i n-íochtar a broinn í, gur scoilt a sciamh-chorp
go hubhall a brághad. Ráinig an scéal chum an ríogh, agus gabhas
Beibheann, agus thug fá ndeara a ceangal go daor dochrach; agus do
faduigheadh teinnte agus teandála 'n-a timcheall, agus do loisceadh i
bhfiadnuise na sluaigh í, mar do thuill a míghníomhartha féin di é, go
ndearnadh mion-luaith di.][76]

In the case of the execution of the male conspirators in the murder of the historian, it is not necessary to assume from the punishment that witchcraft was
involved, although that was certainly a possibility. The advice to burn witches
may not even reflect the reality of late sixteenth-century Ireland but rather may
be modelled on the biblical injunctions contained in Exodus 22 (including that
on witches in verse eighteen). Other explanations need also to be explored. One
county Meath case of 1647 resulted in the burning of a woman not for witchcraft but for infanticide. The rationale for the burning was that she had committed a religious offence by killing her child before it could be baptised and
therefore assigned it to limbo.[77] In this case the moral offence requiring punishment of burning may well be the inversion of the social order in which a
high-status figure, the historian, was killed by people of a much lower status.
Certainly the few annalistic references which exist to punishment by burning
conform to this type of crime.[78] Such inversion of the normal social order
could well be seen as a moral offence and the punishment of burning emphasised this. For this reason the *éiric* or honour price would have been seen as
inappropriate. The essence of such an honour price was that the requirement
to pay was not, of itself, dishonourable and if a family group could afford the
payment they could be quickly reintegrated into the community. In this case
the inversion of the normal social order was regarded as being too serious a
matter to leave honour intact.

Such moral tales are not common in the Ulster annals. In the fifty years
before 1530 there were only four occasions on which the annalists had felt it

76 R.A.S. Macalister (ed.), *Two Irish Arthurian romances* (London, 1908), p. 54. The earliest manuscript copy
of this tale is dated 1517, BL, Egerton MS 1782, ff 26–30. For other copies see Alan Bruford, *Gaelic folktales
and medieval romances* (Dublin, 1969), p. 260.   77 Raymond Gillespie, 'The burning of Ellen Ní Gilwey, 1647:
a sidelight on popular belief in Meath' in *Ríocht na Midhe*, x (1999), pp 71–7.   78 *AConn*, pp 580–1; *AU*, iii,
pp 350–1.

necessary to make a pointed moral comment on events.[79] In the 1530s alone there are four further episodes, including that of the punishment meted out to the killers of Maghnus Ó Duibhgeannáin, on which the annalist makes moral observations after particular events.[80] In part this may be related to the particular inclinations of the annalists. The annals themselves record the death of Ruaidhrí Ó Luinín, who wrote most of the book, in 1528 while in 1541 they record the death of Ruaidhrí Ó Caiside, archdeacon of Clogher, who wrote the greater part of the book.[81] Exactly what these entries mean is unclear. In the first case writing may simply refer to the transcription by Ó Luinín of the earlier part of the annals. At a conservative interpretation the second reference may mean that at least some of the entries between 1528 and 1541 were compiled by Ruaidhrí Ó Caiside.[82] Ó Caiside as archdeacon of Clogher was closely associated with the reforming bishop of Clogher in the 1520s, an Augustinian friar named Patrick O Cuilinn.[83] The annalist, for example, compiled a register of the diocese for the bishop.[84] It may be that the archdeacon, like Bishop Patrick, was of a reforming cast of mind and wished to use the annalistic compilation as a repository of moral stories or *exempla*.

Another interpretation is also possible. Half the moral tales found in the Ulster annals involve saints, usually operating at a local level to exact revenge for some offence given to them. In the case of the killers of Maghnus Ó Duibhgeannáin it is St Martin; in the case of the desecration of a statue at Downpatrick the saint mentioned is St Catherine. In the other two cases direct divine intervention is suggested. The common theme is the restoration of the normal order of the world after a disturbance. Thus authority in the community was restored by divine means and the divinely appointed order re-established.

IV

The story of the murder of Maghnus was contained within a number of narrative and interpretative frames. The story was certainly a moral tale but it also contained a message about the importance of order in a local community and the centrality of the supernatural forces of religion in maintaining that order. In the disturbed years of the 1530s, with the advent of religious change in a

79 *AU*, iii, pp 288–9, 366–7, 486–7, 512–13. 80 *AU*, iii, pp 596–7, 608–9, 616–17, 624–5. 81 *AU*, iii, pp 572–3, 632–3. 82 The scripts of the Bodleian copy of the annals have been discussed by Brian Ó Cuív, *Catalogue of the Irish manuscripts in the Bodleian Library at Oxford and Oxford College libraries: part 1* (Dublin, 2001), pp 156–61. 83 Aubrey Gwynn, *The medieval province of Armagh* (Dundalk, 1946), pp 180–3. 84 K.W. Nicholls, 'The register of Clogher' in *Clogher Record*, vii, no. 3 (1971–2), pp 361–431.

politically divisive context, such tales of moral order may have had added significance. For the tight-knit community that experienced at first hand the murder of a historian, the necessity of enforcing a punishment appropriate to the seriousness of the crime, thereby restoring order in their world, would have been understood by all concerned.

4

The burning of Domnach Magh Da Claine: church and sanctity in the diocese of Clogher, 1508

When the compiler of the Annals of Ulster came to assemble his entry for the year 1508 he included a long, and somewhat unusual, story:

> The son of Mag Mathgamna, namely, Redmond junior, son of another Redmond Mag Mathgamna, was slain this year in the church of Magh-da-claine, the feast day of Patrick, by the son of Mag Uidhir, namely by Philip, son of Edmond Mag Uidhir. And in this way that befell, to wit: Philip went in honour of Patrick to hear Service to the town and, whilst they were hearing Mass in the church, Redmond junior came [with] a large force around the church and fires were lighted by them at the four angles of the church. And the son of Mag Uidhir said felicitously, auspiciously that he would not allow the church of Patrick to be burned and incited his people to act well. And Philip and his kinsmen went forth in the name of God and Patrick and Redmond junior was thrown from his horse and slain and his foster-brother, namely, the son of Brian Mac Gilla-Brighde the Red, was slain along with him and prisoners were taken there also. And the name[s] of God and Patrick was [were] magnified through that.

> [Mac Még Mhathgamna, idon, Remann óg, mac Rémainn aile Mheg Mhathgamna, do mharbadh a n-Domnach Muighi-dá-claine, lá fheili Padraig, lé mac Mhég Uidhir, idon, lé Pilib, mac Emhainn Mhég Uidhir, an bliadhain so. Ocus mar so tharrla sin, idon: Pilib do dhul a n-onóir Padraig d'eistecht serbhise do'n bhaile 7, mar do bhádur ag estecht an Aithfrinn 'sa tempoll, Rémunn óg do thecht, fedhan mór, fa'n tempoll 7 téinnti do adhuint doibh a ceithri ardigh an tempuill. Ocus mac Még Uidhir gu sona, senamail d'á rádh nach léigfedh sé tempoll Padraig do loscadh 7 a muinntir do brosdughudh docum maithe do dhenum. Ocus Pilib 7 a braithri do dhol amach a n-ainm

Dé 7 Padraig 7 Remonn óg do trascart d'á eoch 7 a mharbadh 7 a com-
dalta do marbadh fáraon ris, idon, mac Briain ruaidh Mic Ghilla
Bhrighdi 7 braighdi do gabail ann fós. Ocus do moradh ainm Dé 7
Padraig trit sin].[1]

The annalist was clearly impressed by the events which he related. The length
of the story – 156 words in the original Irish text – ranks it among the longest
entries in the late fifteenth- and early sixteenth-century part of the Annals of
Ulster. Few others, however, seem to have regarded the story with the same fascination as the Ulster annalist. While the compilers of the Annals of Connacht
were certainly aware of some of the developments in Fermanagh in 1508 which
the Ulster annalist recorded, such as the taking of Mág Uidhir's castle at
Enniskillen by Ó Domhnaill, the story of the burning of Domnach Magh da
Claine was not noted by the Connacht annalists. It was only in the 1630s that
the Annals of the Four Masters retold the story from the Ulster annalist's
record. The interest shown by the Four Masters in the story was almost certainly because of its religious content. They amended the language of the entry
to ensure that there could be no ambiguity over that message. The Ulster annalist had declared that Pilib Mág Uidhir had gone to the place for a 'Service'
[serbhis]. However, that word in the context of the Reformation of the sixteenth century had come to take on a rather Protestant meaning and so the
Four Masters recorded instead that Mág Uidhir and his followers had gone 'to
the town to hear Mass, in honour of St Patrick' [i nónóir Patraic déisteacht
oiffrinn don bhaile].[2]

It is not immediately clear why this event held such interest for the Ulster
annalist. One explanation might be a purely personal one. The Ulster annals
for 1498 record the death of Aibhilin daughter of Cathal Mac Maghnusa, the
compiler of the Ulster annals, who also died in 1498. Aibhilin was the wife of
Pilib son of Edmond, the central character in the story of Domnach Magh da
Claine.[3] It is certainly true that, during the period when Cathal compiled the
annals, events relating to his immediate family were prominently featured in
them. After his death, when others took up the task, references to Cathal's
family occur less frequently so this family association, of itself, is an insuffi-
cient explanation for the account of an event that took place in 1508. Moreover,
church burnings, whether accidental or not, were incidental to the purpose of
the annals. The entries in the annals focus on people rather than buildings and

1 *AU*, iii, pp 482–5; For the revised translation of *brosdughudh* as 'incited' see *DIL*, s.v.   2 *AFM*, v, pp 1294–5.
3 *AU*, iii, pp 426–7.

descriptions of the destruction of physical structures were usually despatched fairly briskly by the annalists.[4] There was, however, a general assumption, drawn from the decrees of the church, that local lords should protect church property. The register of the diocese of Clogher, compiled in the early sixteenth-century by Ruaidhrí Ó Caiside, who also contributed to the annalistic account of the burning of Domnach Magh da Claine, included the 1296 constitutions of Pope Boniface which excommunicated those who overtaxed the church. The response of the lords in the diocese of Clogher to those constitutions was to declare that they would protect the churches in their lordships from 'thefts, spoils, burning and all violence and injuries'.[5] The idea that the lord should protect church property in his lordship is also expressed in sixteenth-century bardic poetry. One poem, 'Leis féin moltar Mág Uidhir', addressed to Cú Chonnacht Mág Uidhir in the later sixteenth century by Maoilín Ó an Cháinte declared that

> He has achieved much of the royal instruction – protecting the right, preventing crimes, restraining strife, guarding churches, getting hostages in his fetters.

> [Mór Tárraidh don teguscc ríogh
> Díden córa, cosg feilghníomh,
> bac gliadh, gabháil ac ceallaibh,
> fagháil giall 'na ghéibheandaibh].[6]

Another poem, 'An áil libh seanchus síl gCéin', addressed to Cormac Ó hEadhra at the end of the sixteenth century also listed his protection of the church among his virtues

> he settles the land of Leyney, both as regards laity and church;

> [áitighthear críoch Luighni lais
> idir thuaith uile is eaglois.][7]

4 For a survey of this theme see A.T. Lucas, 'The plundering and burning of churches in Ireland, 7th to 16th century' in Etienne Rynne (ed.), *North Munster studies* (Limerick, 1967), pp 172–229. 5 K.W. Nicholls, 'The register of Clogher' in *Clogher Record*, vii, no. 3 (1971–2), pp 409–23. 6 David Greene (ed.), *Duanaire Mhéig Uidhir* (Dublin, 1972), pp 208–9. The poet's allusion to the 'royal instruction' recalled the old Irish text on the advice of king Cormac to his son, Kuno Meyer, (ed.), *The instructions of King Cormac Mac Airt* (Todd Lecture Series, xv), (Dublin, 1909). Contrary to the poet's assertion the guarding of churches was not a priority in that text. 7 Lambert McKenna (ed.), *The book of O'Hara* (Dublin, 1951), pp 42–3.

However, in practice lords proved rather ineffective protectors. Indeed during one affair in the 1460s the Mac Mathghamhna family protected two men who had killed another in the parish church of Derrybrusk and incurred a threat of excommunication as a result.[8] In particular the family of Pilib Mág Uidhir had little respect for churches. According to the annals for 1484 Giolla-Padraig Mág Uidhir, one of Pilib's brothers, was killed 'in treachery' [a feall] at the foot of the altar of the church of Ardnalurchur by five of his brothers.[9] Two years later one of those brothers, Donn, was himself killed in treachery by some of his uncles in a graveyard beside a church.[10] The family of Reamonn Mac Mathghamhna can claim no better record of respect for churches. In 1469 letters of excommunication had been issued against three men, Hugh Óg, Magonius, and Glashyne Mac Mathghamhna for plundering and burning the church and lands of Julianstown in county Meath.[11] Exactly who these individuals are is not clear but Glaisne may have been Reamonn's brother and Maghnus and Aodh Óg his cousins. In the 1530s the family of Reamonn Mac Mathghamhna of the Lucht Tí branch of the family, were in further difficulties with the ecclesiastical authorities for burning the churches and lands of three Monaghan parishes. Again they were excommunicated but evaded ecclesiastical censure by attending Mass at the Franciscan church of Monaghan. Whether they were admitted to Mass by the friars there out of Christian charity or from a sense of self preservation is unclear.[12]

In the fifty years before the incident of 1508 the annals record nine individual churches being burnt, one of them on two separate occasions. There are also a number of more general entries noting the burning of property including churches. Some of these church burnings had involved buildings that were occupied at the time of the incidents. In 1492 the Annals of Ulster record the burning of a church of Cell Srianain and the death of sixteen people 'both men and women' [itir fhiru 7 mhna] as a result.[13] As the Annals of Connacht recorded on another occasion, a man was killed in the church at Tully, near Strokestown,

> Ruaidri son of Conn Mac Branain was killed by the sons of Echmarcah son of Conchobar Buide and Toirrdelbach Ruad son of Tadc Buide in the church of Tulach, the church being burned over his head.

8 Anthony Lynch, 'Calendar of the reassembled register of John Bole, archbishop of Armagh, 1457–71' in *Seanchas Ard Mhacha*, xv (1992–3), p. 131.   9 *AU*, iii, pp 285–6.   10 *AU*, iii, pp 307–8.   11 M.A. Sughi (ed.), *Registrum Octaviani alias Liber Niger* (2 vols, Dublin, 1999), ii, no. 435.   12 Aubrey Gwynn, 'Archbishop Cromer's register' in *Journal of the County Louth Archaeological Society*, x (1941–4), p. 169.   13 *AU*, iii, pp 360–1.

[Ruaidri mac Coinn Meic Branain do marbad le clainn Echmharcaig meic Conchobair Buide ⁊ le Toirrdelbach Ruadh mac Taidc Buide a tempoll Tulcho ⁊ an tempall do loscad fair.][14]

The year before the events at Domnach Magh da Claine the Annals of Ulster had summarily despatched one such burning as 'The church of Achadh-beithi was burned this year and very much of the chattel of all the country was burned in it.' [Tempoll Achaidh-beithi do loscadh an bliadhain so ⁊ urmhór maithisa is tíri uile do loscadh ann.][15] Such entries, it should be remembered, record events at those churches whose status or connections were such as to allow an annalistic entry. There may well have been others that did not merit such a mention. Indeed, concern about church burning seems to have ranked relatively low in the priorities of the ecclesiastical authorities. In 1528 one man responsible for the burning of a church of Tullycorbett in County Monaghan was fined fourteen marks by the church court. At first he offered to pay in wool and iron but eventually he paid only a horse, valued at three marks, to the dean of Clogher.[16]

One possible explanation for the annalists' interest is the seemingly ritualistic form of the attack on the church with the lighting of fires at each of the four corners of the church. However even this may not have been as strange to contemporaries as it seems to us. There are earlier Irish parallels to this sort of attack but they are not confined to Ireland. In the late 1570s a similar method was used by the Mac Domhnaill in an attack on the church occupied by Mac Leod at Trumpan on the Isle of Skye.[17] To recover some of the local fascination which seems to have existed for the story of events at Domnach Magh da Claine we need to reconstruct more closely the contexts in which that event was set. In that way we can hope to understand its real significance.

I

The attack at Domnach Magh da Claine was clearly a premeditated act. It was not the result of a chance encounter or the by-product of a raiding party. Reamonn Mac Mathghamhna clearly knew that Pilib Mág Uidhir would be at Mass at a particular place and at a particular time, a point to which we shall

14 *AConn*, pp 660–1. 15. *AU*, iii, pp 484–5. 16 L.P. Murray, 'Archbishop Cromer's register' in *Journal of the County Louth Archaeological Society*, viii (1933–6), p. 349. 17 S.H. O'Grady (ed.), *Silva Gadelica* (2 vols, London, 1892), i, p. 372; ii, p. 410. Alexander Mackenzie, *History of the Macleods with genealogies of the principal families of the name* (Inverness, 1889), pp 47–8, 51.

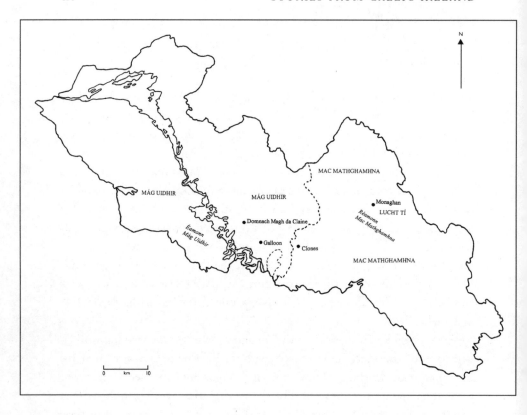

11 The Mág Uidhir and Mac Mathghamhna lordships in the early sixteenth century

return, and organised a raid specifically to attack Pilib. This is the clear message of the annalist's account, which is written from the perspective of Pilib,
the victor in the encounter. Attacking a congregation at Mass was not unknown
in the annals but it was rare. In the previous fifty years just one other instance
is recorded. In 1465 the Annals of Ulster noted

> treachery was done by Domnall, son of Tadhg Ua Ruairc, on Mac
> Con Shnama this year; to wit, himself and his son and many of his
> people were killed at Mass on Sunday.

> [Feall do dhenum do Domnall, mac Taidhg hUi Ruairc, ar Mac Con
> [Sh]nama in bliadhain si, idon. é fein, ⁊ a mac do marbadh oc aiffrenn
> Dia-Domnaigh ⁊ moran dia muinntir.][18]

18 *AU*, iii, pp 212–15.

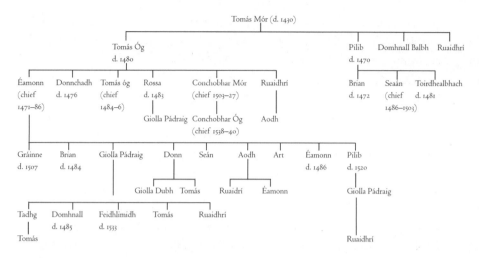

12 Genealogy of the family of Éamonn Mág Uidhir

That this was a heinous act the annalists had no doubt. The Connacht annalists also noted that Mac Con Snama and his son 'were treacherously killed' [do marbad per dolum].[19] While the burning of a church building might be condoned, doing so while it was being used for Mass was clearly an offence of a different degree. To understand why Réamonn Mac Mathghamhna was prepared to breach such social rules and why he might plan such an attack it is necessary to understand the relations between the families involved. Thus, the first context of the burning of Domnach Magh da Claine is clearly that of the relationship between one branch of the Mág Uidhir family and one branch of the Mac Mathghamhna family.

Before the beginning of the sixteenth century the family of Éamonn Mág Uidhir, including Pilib, had little to do with the family of Réamonn Mac Mathghamhna, father to the Réamonn killed in the raid. Geography was one factor contributing to this since Réamonn's family were located at the northern part of the Mac Mathghamhna lordship, the Lucht Tí group in the barony of Monaghan (fig. 11). Raiding into south-west Fermanagh would have required considerable logistical preparations which were not worthwhile. Only once, in 1486, did Brian Mac Mathghamhna, brother to Réamonn junior (d.1508), raid the territory of Éamonn Mág Uidhir. On that occasion he killed one of Pilib's brothers.[20] However, there do not seem to have been any reprisals for that killing and during most of the late fifteenth century the annalistic entries give the impression that the family of Éamonn Mág Uidhir were involved predominantly in internal feuds (fig. 12).

In 1501 that changed. The immediate context is uncertain but a dispute broke out within the Mac Mathghamhna lordship between the family of Réamonn and the family of Aodh Ruadh from Farney. The dissension, which had been simmering since the 1470s, escalated into full-scale war. Factions in support of the Uí Néill were drawn into the dispute on both sides and with them some of the Mág Uidhir kin group. This was a bloody conflict. In one episode, according to the Ulster annalist, forty-seven were killed somewhere on the Slieve Beagh mountains. The Connacht annalist was more vague, simply referring to 'countless' deaths [co n'ár diáirmhe uime].[21] According to the list of names recorded in the annals three brothers and two nephews of Pilib Mág Uidhir were killed on that occasion. From this point in time relations between the two groups deteriorated rapidly. In 1504 Pilib attacked the Lucht Tí branch of the Mac Mathghamhna family at night, killing two. Nine of the raiding party were captured, but Pilib escaped 'triumphantly' [co haithuseach] according to the Ulster annals. That none of the other annals mention the event suggests that it was seen as relatively unimportant out of its immediate context of the heroic exploits of Pilib Mág Uidhir.[22] The attack on Pilib four years later in the church at Domnach Magh da Claine seems to have been one of the last throws in the internecine warfare begun in 1501 and the murder of Réamonn, son of Mac Mathghamhna, may have been regarded as a sufficient éiric [compensation or honour price] for the earlier deaths.

The immediate circumstances of the raid on the church of Domnach Magh da Claine may even have been provoked by a rather murky episode in the politics of dynastic possession, manifested in the rights of the church. If, as is argued below, the church of Domnach Magh da Claine is to be associated with the early modern parish of Drumully in Fermanagh, now contained within the larger parish of Galloon, then it represented one of the elements of the coarbania of Clones. An agreement of 1503 confirmed this relationship between Drumully and Clones and a supplication to Rome of 1537 also named the parish of Drumully as one of the parishes that was to pay an annual rent to the coarb of St Tigernach at Clones.[23] In 1587 after the dissolution of the religious houses the property of Clones was granted to Henry Duke. Among the properties

---

21 *AU*, iii, pp 453–4; *AConn*, pp 606–7. 22 *AU*, iii, pp 473–4. 23 BL, Egerton MS 189, ff 120–20v; Michael Haren, 'Vatican archives *Minutae Brevium in forma gratiosa* relating to Clogher diocese' in *Clogher Record*, xii (1985–7), pp 57–8.

included in the grant was the rectory of 'Dromullye'.[24] While the position of coarb may have been a religious one in the early medieval period, by the late fifteenth century it was given to laymen who enjoyed the revenues. The holders of the title in the late fifteenth century were from the Mac Mathghamhna kin group: Séamus who died in 1502 and his son Pilib who had predeceased him in 1486. Séamus was the uncle of the Reamonn killed on the raid at Domnach Magh da Claine. Indeed so closely were the revenues of the parish of Drumully linked to the Mac Mathghamhna family that the grant to Henry Duke in 1587 specified that the parish was 'in the [barony of] Dartrye in Mac Mahon's country'.[25] However in the early sixteenth century the rights of Mac Mathghamhna had not been so clear cut. From the late fifteenth century the Mág Uidhir kin group were pressing their claim to the *coarbania* of Clones and by 1513 the chief of the Mág Uidhir lordship was described as 'the coarb Mág Uidhir' [comarba Mhág Uidhir] in the Annals of Ulster.[26] The request to Rome in 1537 was for the grant of the office to a Mac Mathghamhna which may suggest that the matter continued to be a source of contention.[27]

This problem may well have been personified in the priest saying Mass on St Patrick's day at Domnach Magh da Claine. While the annalist does not record his name it was probably the parish priest of Drumully, Muiris Mac Domhnaill, who had been appointed to the parish in 1504 after a long vacancy.[28] It seems likely that Muiris was of the Clankelly family of Mac Domhnaill and he had petitioned for the benefice of Drumully as early as 1494.[29] The territory of Mac Domhnaill was disputed, being part of the mensal lands of the bishop of Clogher but in 1493 leased to Ruaidhrí Mac Mathghamhna, the vicar of Clones.[30] However, relations between the Mac Domhnaill family and the clergy of Clones were poor and in 1486 the Ulster annals noted the murder of Art, son of Mac Domhnaill of Clankelly at Clones 'in a quarrel he made with clerics' [a trodan do righne se re cleircib] all of whom were members of the Mac Mathghamhna family.[31] Muiris himself was not unused to violence since before he could be granted the benefice of Drumully in 1504 he had required an apostolic declaration that he was not rendered ineligible on account of a homicide which he had committed.[32] In the context of the burning, the presence of Pilib Mág Uidhir at this church which was claimed as part of the sphere

24 *Fiants Ire., Eliz.,* no. 5042. 25 *Fiants Ire., Eliz.,* no. 5042. 26 Aubrey Gwynn, *The medieval province of Armagh* (Dundalk, 1946), pp 177–80. 27 Haren, 'Vatican archives', pp 57–9. 28 *Calendar of papal letters, xviii: Pius III and Julius II (1503–13),* p. 236. 29 *Calendar of papal letters, xvi (1492–8),* p. 636. 30 *Calendar of papal letters, xvii, part 2 (1492–1503) Alexander VI,* pp 5–6. 31 *AU,* iii, pp 300–1. 32 *Calendar of papal letters, xviii (1503–13),* p. 236.

of influence of the family of his rival Réamonn Mac Mathghamhna can only have added salt to the wounds of a dynastic dispute which was still fresh in the minds of the participants and provided yet a further motive for violence. The presence of a Mac Domhnaill priest of the Clankelly branch of the family would have added yet further fuel to the fire.

II

If one context for the burning at Domnach Magh da Claine was feuding between lordships, then the second context within which the burning needs to be understood is provided by the precise circumstances of the attempted raid. That Pilib Mág Uidhir should have been attending Mass was not improbable. Given that the events reputedly took place on the feast of St Patrick (17 March), it was likely that he would be present at Mass on that day. The decrees of the provincial synod of Armagh in 1556, presumably reflecting existing practice, declared that the feast of St Patrick was a day on which no servile work could be done and Mass attendance was expected.[33]

What Pilib's expectations were as he attended Mass can only be guessed at. One Roscommon text that was circulating in south-west Ulster in the sixteenth and seventeenth centuries may provide some insight into Pilib's perception of his religious obligations. The text on the fourteen virtues of the Mass appears in the *Liber Flavus Fergusiorum*, probably compiled in fifteenth-century Roscommon, and the text is also found in a Donegal manuscript of *c.*1513–14. Later copies in a Cavan manuscript of 1630 and a late seventeenth-century Fermanagh manuscript suggest that it was well known in south-west Ulster.[34] The text may derive originally from a Latin source and was well known in fifteenth-century England as well as in Ireland. In return for hearing Mass from beginning to end the text promised fourteen rewards. Some of these promised spiritual benefits including forgiveness of sins, protection from evil spirits, a holy death and remission of time spent in purgatory. Others promised physical gain such as guarding against loss of sight, temporary protection from aging, and protection from sudden death that day. One benefit linked Mass attendance directly with worldly prosperity. Pilib's motives in attending Mass may not have been entirely spiritual and he may well have expected some material reward for his devotion.

33 L.F. Renehan, *Collections on Irish church history* (2 vols, Dublin, 1861–74), i, p. 134.   34 Gearóid Mac Niocaill (ed.), 'Disiecta membra' in *Éigse*, viii (1955–7), pp 74–6; BL, Add. MS 40766, f. 90v; BL, Egerton MS 136, f. 46.

Despite the spiritual, and indeed temporal, motives for attending Mass at Domnach Magh da Claine there still remains a puzzle as to why Pilib should be at that particular church. This issue arises from the identification of Domnach Magh da Claine. In the nineteenth century the editor of the Annals of the Four Masters and onomastic guru, John O'Donovan, was inclined to equate the place-name with the parish of Donagh in the barony of Trough in north Monaghan but this seems incorrect.[35] Under the year 1507 the Four Masters included the entry 'O'Dunan of Domhnach-maighe-da-Chlaoine was killed with a stab of a knife by his own brother, Gilla-Patrick, son of Philip.' [Ua Dúnáin Dhomhnaigh maighe da claoíne do mharbhadh do shadhadh do scín la a bhrathair feain Giolla Padraicc mac Pilip.][36] Assuming that this is the same Domnach Magh da Claine then the location is not the parish church of Donogh in north Monaghan but rather the chapel of Donagh in the parish of Drumully, barony of Clankelly in county Fermanagh. According to a docu-ment of 1503, surviving in a transcript of 1658, there were two chapels apart from the parish church in the parish of Drumully: Domnach Magh da Claine and Machaire Miolioc.[37] By the time of the early seventeenth-century surveys these seem to have been reduced to one, that of Donagh. The 1609 survey of church lands in Fermanagh records that 'in the said parish of Drumulchy is a chapple of ease called Donoghmoyline, with half a tate of land belonginge to the same, whereof O'Downan is the duoghasa'.[38] The 1605 survey of Fermanagh likewise refers to the 'chappell of Doawny [which] hath one tate of land; it is possessed by O'Doonan as corbe'.[39]

Identifying Domnach Magh da Claine not with a parish church but with a relatively small chapel presents a number of problems. The first is a simple geographical one. It is not possible to be precise about where Pilib Mág Uidhir lived but a good approximation can be reached. In the 1603 survey of the boundaries of county Fermanagh the property of Sliocht Éamonn Mhéig Uidhir was fixed in the barony of Knockninny in the southern part of the county.[40] References in the annals to the kin group confirm this general posi-tion. In 1486, for instance, the Ulster annals record the raid on the family of

35 AFM, v, pp 1294–5, note q. Edmund Hogan, Onomasticon Goedelicum locorum et tribuum Hiberniae et Scotiae (Dublin, 1910) followed O'Donovan's incorrect identification. 36 AFM, v, pp 1290–1. 37 BL, Egerton MS 189, f. 120. 38 Inquisitionum in officio rotulorum cancellariae Hiberniae ... repertorium (2 vols, Dublin, 1826–9), ii, appendix vi; Charles Mac Neill (ed.), 'MS Rawlinson A.237' in Analecta Hibernica, no. 3 (1931), p. 201. 39 Inquisitionum in officio rotulorum cancellariae Hiberniae, ii, p. xxxix. O'Dunan's church at Donagh also features in an early seventeenth-century satire by Aonghus Ó Dálaigh but with the site mis-identified in the editor-ial notes, Aenghus O'Daly, The tribes of Ireland, ed. John O'Donovan (Dublin, 1852), pp 50–1. 40 Inquisitionum in officio rotulorum cancellariae Hiberniae, ii, p. xxxiii.

Éamonn Mág Uidhir by the sons of Réamonn Mac Mathghamhna discussed above. They note that the raid was made at Cuil-na-n-Oirear, which O'Donovan identified with a point of land jutting into Upper Lough Erne, which seems to have been the core of the sept lands. The same place is again mentioned in 1506 as the place a prey was taken from by Ó Néill. One of the sons of Éamonn Mág Uidhir was killed in the ensuing dispute.[41] The Annals of the Four Masters add Doire Cenainn to the list of the places associated with Éamonn Mág Uidhir's sons.[42] This may be identified as Derrycannon in the parish of Kinawley and barony of Knockninny in south-west Fermanagh near the western shore of Upper Lough Erne. Cuil-na-n-Oirear was probably close by. If these identifications are correct it suggests that Pilib had travelled some way to the other side of Lough Erne to a relatively minor church, which was not his parish church, and not even in his own diocese of Kilmore, to hear Mass. The church itself was shown in the 1609 barony maps of Fermanagh to be in the property of 'Sleught Donogh I Callogh Magwire' on the edge of the barony of Clankelly, which adjoined Knockninny barony (fig. 13).[43] Moreover, as noted above, Réamonn clearly knew, when he was planning the raid, that he would find Pilib at this specific church on St Patrick's day. Understanding why Pilib had undertaken this journey may help us to understand the motives for his other actions as recorded in the annalist's story.

Part of the reason for Pilib's journey may be explained by the date of the events, 17 March, the feast of St Patrick. In the form in which it is recounted in the annals, St Patrick plays an important role in the story. Pilib's attendance at the church was to the honour of Patrick and it was the saint's name that was honoured by Pilib's victory over the enemies who had attacked the church. One possible explanation of these references is that the church at Donagh was dedicated to St Patrick and Pilib's presence there could have been connected with a local pilgrimage to a holy place associated with Patrick for his feast day. The early history of the church is obscure but, given its name, it may well be a pre-Norman foundation and may have had Patrician associations.[44] If the church at Domnach Magh da Claine were dedicated to the saint, it would have been the closest Patrician church to Pilib's residence. According to an early seven-

---

41 *AU*, iii, pp 300–1, 478–9.   42 *AFM*, iv, pp 1144–5.   43 *Maps of the escheated counties in Ireland, 1609, copied at the Ordnance Survey Office, Southampton. Col. Sir Henry James*, (Southampton, 1861), map 2.6. This is confirmed by the 1603 survey, *Inquisitionum in officio rotulorum cancellariae Hiberniae*, ii, p. xxxix.   44 Ann Hamlin, 'The archaeology of early Christianity in the north of Ireland' unpublished Ph.D thesis, Queen's University Belfast, 1976, pp 718–19. Many church sites named 'Donagh' are early establishments and have Patrician associations.

13 Church of Domnach Magh da Claine, and adjacent townlands in County Fermanagh, 1609. From *Maps of the escheated counties in Ireland, 1609, copied at the Ordnance Survey Office, Southampton. Col Sir Henry James* (Southampton, 1861), map 2.6

teenth-century list of church dedications in the diocese of Clogher copied by Sir James Ware, presumably from a now-lost visitation return, only six parish churches in the diocese were dedicated to St Patrick.[45] These were the parishes of Donaghmoyne, Aghnamullen, Kilmore, Tullycorbet, Donagh and Tehallan,

45 TCD, MS 6404, ff 99–99v.

all of which lay in the south and east of the diocese where the influence of
Armagh was strongest. None of the parish churches in the western part of the
diocese had such Patrician dedications.

If the hypothesis of a local pilgrimage to a chapel dedicated to Saint Patrick
were correct then two things would follow from this. The first is that the church
at Domnach Magh da Claine was capable of having a dedication different from
that of the parish church. According to a 1504 entry in the papal registers, the
parish church of Drumully was dedicated to St Coman whose feast is mentioned by the early seventeenth-century Martyrology of Donegal as being on
4 January.[46] It is entirely possible that within that parish a chapel with a different dedication could be established. According to the early seventeenth-century attorney general, Sir John Davies, who spent some time in Fermanagh, the
procedure for establishing a church was

> When any lord or gentleman had a direction to build a church, he did
> first dedicate some good portion of land to some saint or other whom
> he chose to be his patron; then he founded the church, and called it
> by the name of that saint and then gave the land to some clerk not
> being in orders, and to his heirs for ever with this intent that he should
> keep the church clean and well repaired, keep hospitality and give alms
> to the poor for the soul's health of the founder.[47]

A similar version of the process of the establishment of churches was recounted
by the jurors summoned in the 1609 inquisition concerning the church lands
of Fermanagh. According to this version the lands for the support of the church
were originally given to saints, 'some were confessors, some deacons and some
virgins', and that the saints chose septs to guard the lands and to provide for
the church.[48] Such local initiatives are certainly suggested by the presence of
large numbers of highly localised cults of saints who usually have no more than
one church dedicated to them.[49] In fact in one case it is possible to see the workings of the process of foundation and dedication by a lay founder. The Ulster
annals record under the year 1498 that

---

46 *Calendar of papal letters xviii (1503–13)*, p. 236; J.E. McKenna, *Parishes of Clogher* (2 vols, Enniskillen, 1920–30),
ii, p. 115.   47 Henry Morley (ed.), *Ireland under Elizabeth and James the first* (London, 1890), p. 367.   48
Inquisitionum in officio rotulorum cancellariae Hiberniae, ii, appendix vi, Fermanagh.   49 *Inquisitionum in officio rotulorum cancellariae Hiberniae*, ii, appendix vi, Fermanagh. The same is true of the adjoining diocese of Kilmore.
For dedications there, Canice Mooney, 'Topographical fragments from the Franciscan library' in *Celtica*, i
(1946–50), pp 65–7.

Margaret, daughter of Domnall Mag Uidhir the Freckled, namely,
wife of Ua Flannagain of Tuath-ratha, namely Gilbert Ua Flannagain,
died this year. And by that couple was built a chapel in honour of
God and Mary on Achadh-mor, the town[land?] of Ua Flannagain.

[Mairgreg, ingen Domnaill Ballaigh Meg Uidhir idon, ben hUi
Fhlannagain Tuaithi Ratha, idon, Gillibert hUa Fhlannagain d'heg in
bliadhain si. Ocus leisin lanamhain sin ro cumdaighedh seipel a n-
onoir Dia 7 Muire ar in Achaidh mhór, bhaile h[U]i Fhlannagain.][50]

It seems clear from this entry that the initiative for the building and naming
of the church came from Margaret and her husband. It is therefore highly probable that a similar non-parochial chapel existed at Donagh, endowed by a
layman, and that it had a separate dedication from the parish church.

The second piece of evidence which strengthens the supposition that the
church may have been dedicated to St Patrick is that there was a strong cult of
the saint in the south Fermanagh area. While local interests may have pre-
dominated in the dedications of parish churches the wider cult of St Patrick
made itself felt in many ways. Patrick, for instance, featured in the lives of
Fermanagh saints which were known to be circulating in the diocese in the sixteenth century. In the version of the life of St Molaise copied at Devenish in
the early sixteenth century, Patrick predicts Molaise's birth. An early sixteenth-
century poem, quoted in a document contained in the early sixteenth-century
register of Clogher, seems also to make a claim for a connection between Patrick
and Devenish.[51] In the life of the patron of the diocese, St Macartan, revised
in 1528 by the bishop of Clogher, Patrick is portrayed as Macartan's contemporary and patron.[52] This may have an even older tradition in the diocese if the
text known as the *Codex Salmanticensis*, which contains the life of St Macartan,
was indeed in the monastic house at Clogher in the later middle ages.[53] The
importance of the Patrician cult is also demonstrated by the use of St Patrick's
day by the compilers of the Annals of Ulster as an important feast day for

50 *AU*, iii, pp 430–1.   51 O'Grady (ed.), *Silva Gadelica*, i, p. 18; ii, p. 19; Pádraig Ó Riain, 'Saints in the catalogue of bishops of the lost register of Clogher' in *Clogher Record*, xiv, no. 2 (1992), pp 72–4.   52 Nicholls,
'Register of Clogher', pp 424–7.   53 Pádraig Ó Riain, 'Codex Salmanticensis: a provenance *inter Anglos*
or *inter Hibernos?*' in Toby Barnard, Dáibhí Ó Cróinín and Katharine Simms (eds), *A miracle of learning: studies in manuscripts and Irish learning* (Aldershot, 1998), pp 91–100. For a counter view see William O'Sullivan,
'A Waterford origin for the Codex Salmanticensis' in *Decies*, no. 54 (1998), pp 19–21. The volume also contains a life of Patrick drawn from the Anglo-Norman life by Jocelin of Furness.

dating events. Between 1450 and 1530 the Ulster annalist used a range of saints'
days to fix the dates of events being recorded. The feast of St Patrick features
twelve times for dating purposes, the most frequently used saint's day for dating
purposes, followed by the feast of the Holy Cross in May and All Saints in
November, each with seven citations. Hardly surprisingly Easter, Christmas
and the feast of St Brigit are the next most significant feasts for dating purposes. For the local annalists, at least, the feast of St Patrick was an important
marker in the ritual year in the diocese of Clogher.

The cult of St Patrick was strongest at the pilgrimage site of Lough Derg
at the north-western end of the diocese and here it is possible to identify some
of the elements of the local cult. First, place-lore was seen as important. The
McGuidhir Fhearmanach text, associated with the Mág Uidhir family in county
Fermanagh, and probably dating from the late seventeenth-century in its current form, begins with a story of the origins of the name Lough Derg describing the encounter of St Patrick with a monster which was slain 'to magnify the
name of God and Patrick for that wonder' [do mhóradh ainm Dé agus Pádraig
tréas na míorbhuile sin.][54] The same story is repeated in an early eighteenth-
century history of Fermanagh and also in John Richardson's 1727 account of
the pilgrimage.[55] Such place-lore gave a tangible reality to the power of the saint
at that place. These stories informed the popular imagination which shaped
traditional religion. Place-lore emphasised real features that could be seen in
the landscape. In the same way, poets made the cult of the saint real by identifying special features in the landscape associated with them. The early seventeenth-century poet Fearghal Óg Mac an Bhaird, recalling the island on which
the pilgrimage was based, identified particular features of the island: the church,
the penitential beds, the tree beneath which St Patrick sat, the cave and the lake.
He used his recall of the place to reaffirm his devotion to St Patrick.[56] Again
the penitential poem 'Loch Derg aon Róimh na hÉireann', by Tuileagna son of Torna
Ó Maoil Chonaire, focuses on 'this cell where Patrick fasted' [don tigsin 'n-ar
throisg Pádraig], 'this lake-wave that will cure my wound'[i lochthobar chabhra
ar gcreadh] and the cave marking the entrance to purgatory which had been
the focus of the medieval pilgrimage.[57] Similar features can all be found in the
Fermanagh area. The medieval parish of Inniskeen, including parts of

54 Pádraig Ua Duinnín (ed.), *McGuidhir Fhearmanach* (Dublin, 1917), pp 25, 74.   55 Pádraig Ó Maolagáin,
'An early history of Fermanagh' in *Clogher Record*, i no. 3 (1955), pp 135–6; John Richardson, *The great folly,
superstition and idolatry of pilgrimages in Ireland* (Dublin, 1727), pp 3–4.   56 Shane Leslie, *St Patrick's Purgatory*
(London, 1932), pp 168–71.   57 Leslie, *St Patrick's Purgatory*, pp 168–72. For an analysis of the poetry see
Tadhg Ó Dushláine, 'Lough Derg in native Irish poetry' in *Clogher Record*, xiii (1988–9), pp 76–84.

Derryvullan and Derrybrusk, for instance, had a strong topographic and place-lore connection with St Patrick in the sixteenth century. According to the register of Clogher, compiled from older traditions in the early sixteenth century, St Patrick spent the night in the area on his way south

> And coming to a valley next Curcha, seeing that there was a beautiful piece of level ground between clear streams of water he ordered his disciples to pitch his tent and decided to spend the night there, and rested that night, according to his custom, lying on a bare stone with another stone under his head, from which tent that church is up to the present day called, not incorrectly, Pobul Patraic in the Irish language. The stones mentioned, consecrated by the saint's touch, are now placed in front of the church, which have miraculously given and still indeed give health of body to many.
>
> [qui veniens ad vallem iuxta Curcha vidensque ibi pulchram terrae planiciem inter rivulos aquarum limpidissimos suis praecepit discipulis suum tentorium extendi, ibique decernens pernoctare et prout moris ipsius erat faciens [lectum] super nudum lapidem, aliumque lapidem capite subponens ibidem illa nocte pausavit, a quo siquidem tentorio ecclesia illa usque in hodiernum diem hibernice idiomate Pobul Patraic non immerito vocitatur. Lapides quidem supradicti tactu ipsius sanctissimi consecrati extra frontem ecclesiae nunc positi, quam plurimis sanitatem corporis contulerunt prout et nunc conferant miraculose.][58]

The physical stones which Patrick touched made tangible the presence of the saint in the region and other parishes in the diocese, such as Donagh in county Monaghan, likewise had holy wells named after the saint by local tradition.

III

It seems likely, given the circumstances, that the attack on Pilib Mág Uidhir at Domnach Magh da Claine was, in fact, the ambushing of a local pilgrimage site where people had gathered at a sacred space in honour of a saint on the patron's feast day. In that context Pilib's reaction to that attack tells us a good deal about his understanding of the role of the cult of saints in sixteenth-cen-

58 Nicholls, 'Register of Clogher', pp 400–1.

tury belief. According to the annals the real hero of this story was not Pilib but Patrick: 'And the name[s] of God and Patrick was [were] magnified through that.' [Ocus do moradh ainm Dé 7 Padraig trit sin.][59] This is not a phrase frequently used in the annals although it does occur in some other instances. It is a phrase rather more commonly associated with hagiographical writing. In the late fifteenth-century compilation of saints lives in the Book of Lismore the phrase, or phrases similar to it, occur eight times and in the early sixteenth-century life of St Colum Cille written by Maghnus Ó Domhnaill in 1532 it also occurs a number of times.[60] It is repeated frequently in the vernacular life of St Máedóc of Ferns written in Cavan, probably in the early sixteenth century, and in an early sixteenth-century text, the Book of Fenagh, written in Leitrim and containing a life of St Caillin.[61] Perhaps most significantly the phrase can also be found a number of times in the sermon lives of St Patrick that were circulating in the late fifteenth century.[62] Thus the context in which the annalist wished this story to be read was hagiographical rather than historical. Its aim was not so much to record an episode in a feud between two families but rather to demonstrate the power of the saint in a secular context. This may explain why the story was preserved in the annals. The composition of the sixteenth-century life of St Colum Cille suggests that the original life of the saint as recorded in the manuscript tradition was considerably expanded using stories from oral tradition and motifs from other texts.[63] The effect of this sort of expansion was to localise a national figure and to appropriate his or her power to a particular locality. The outcome of the process was certainly well known by the early seventeenth century when the Franciscan scholar John Colgan recorded in the beginning of his hagiographical work, the *Acta Sanctorum*, that his hagiographical researches had uncovered twelve St Brigits, fourteen St Brendans and 120 St Colmans all with distinct birthplaces and family connections.[64] A few years earlier a more credulous Geoffrey Keating had found twenty-two St Colum Cilles, twenty-five St Ciarans, thirty-two St Aodhans and fourteen St Brigits.[65] It may well be that the compiler of the Ulster annals saw in

59 *AU*, iii, pp 486–7.   60 Whitley Stokes (ed.), *Lives of the saints from the Book of Lismore* (Oxford, 1890), pp 49, 58, 61, 77, 95, 121, 196, 204, 208, 223, 243, 266; A. O'Kelleher and G. Schoepperle (eds), *Betha Colaim Chille* (Illinois, 1918), pp 436, 454.   61 Charles Plummer (ed.), *Bethada náem nErenn* (2 vols, Oxford, 1922), i, pp 190–290, ii, pp 177–281; W.M. Hennessy and D.H. Kelly (eds), *Book of Fenagh* (Dublin, 1875, reprint Dublin, 1939), pp 116–19.   62 For example, Whitley Stokes (ed.), *Three Middle Irish homilies* (Calcutta, 1877), pp 6, 11.   63 Joseph Szövérffy, 'Manus O'Donnell and Irish folk tradition' in *Éigse*, viii (1955–7), pp 108–32.   64 John Colgan, *Acta sanctorum veteris et majoris Scotiae seu Hiberniae sanctorum insulae* ... (Louvain, 1645, rept Dublin, 1948), sig. biv.   65 Geoffrey Keating, *Foras feasa ar Éirinn*, ed. David Comyn and P.S. Dinneen (4 vols, London, 1902–14), iii, pp 108–13.

this story of the events at Domnach Magh da Claine a chance to enhance the cult of Patrick, which as has been seen above was locally popular, with a piece of local lore to enhance the local significance of the national saint.

The importance of St Patrick to this story is clear from Pilib's reactions to the attack on the church. The annalist noted 'And the son of Mag Uidhir said felicitously, auspiciously that he would not allow the church of Patrick to be burned and incited his people to act well.' [Ocus mac Még Uidhir go sona, senamail d'á rádh nach léigfedh sé tempoll Padraig do loscadh 7 a muin-ntir do brosdughudh docum maithe do dhenum.][66] Exactly how he did that is not explained although it can be presumed that it took the form of some kind of public utterance. The practice of an oration to armies before battle certainly has precedents in classical literature but it also features in Irish set-tings. Before the battle of Knockdoe in 1504 the earl of Kildare was reputed to have spoken to his troops in an oration of encouragement.[67] In a native Irish context the life of Aodh Ruadh Ó Domhnaill contains a speech, probably composed by the author, put into the mouths of the Irish commanders before the battle of the Yellow Ford in 1598 and from this source was included by the Four Masters in their annals.[68] What was said at Donagh is not recorded, and the possibility must be allowed for that nothing was said, but the literary con-vention of an oration was observed. It is difficult to guess what might have been spoken. One strong possibility is that religious tradition might have been drawn on to promise supernatural support or protection. This was not uncom-mon. One Galway merchant, Thomas Lynch, reported from Donegal in 1539 that the friars used exactly such supernatural urgings to war. According to Lynch, the friars

> do preache dayly that every man ought, for the salvacion of his sowle, fight and make war ayenste Our Soverayne Lord the Kinges Majestie and his trewe subjectes; and if any of theym which soo shall fight ayenste His said Majestie, or his subjectes, dy in the quarrell his sowle, that shall be dedd, shall goo to Heven, as the sowle of Saynt Peter, Pawle and others which soffered death and marterdom for Godes sake.

Lynch, remonstrating with this view, was 'caste oute from the church ... for an heretike' and he was, perhaps wisely, 'gretly affraide'.[69]

---

66 *AU*, iii, pp 484–7. 67 *Cal. Carew MSS, Book of Howth*, pp 184–5. 68 Paul Walsh (ed.), *Beatha Aodha Ruaidh Uí Dhomhnaill* (2 vols, Dublin, 1948–57), i, pp 176–9; *AFM*, vi, pp 2066–71 repeats this. For other examples *AFM*, v, pp 1670–1, 1614–15. 69 *State Papers, Henry VIII*, ([London], 1834), iii, p. 141.

In the context of Mass on a patronal festival the religious tradition that was most likely to be relevant was the reading of a life of the local saint, in this context probably St Patrick.[70] By the early sixteenth century there were certainly a number of sermon lives of Patrick in circulation that would have provided the necessary material.[71] The most obvious event in the life of Patrick which might have relevance here is the story of his servant Benignus, recorded by two of Patrick's earliest biographers, Bishop Tírechán and Muirchú. In the longer version by Muirchú Patrick at Tara challenges the druid Luchet Máel to a test of strength in the presence of King Laoghaire. A house was built, half of dry wood and half of green wood. Benignus, wearing the druid's garment, was placed in the half of the house made of dry wood and the druid, wearing Patrick's garment, was placed in the other half and the house set on fire. The druid was burnt, leaving only Patrick's garment while Benignus was unharmed.[72] Significantly this story entered the oral tradition, although this may be a later occurrence than the events at Domnach Magh da Claine.[73] It may be that this was the story which inspired the subsequent description of events but there are also stories in the lives of more local Fermanagh saints that have some similarities to events at the church and may have been used. The fifteenth-century life of St Molaise of Devenish, copied in Fermanagh, probably at Devenish, in the early sixteenth century, contains a story in which Molaise and his monks while eating supper saw the roof of the house on fire. On the saint's instructions they did not abandon the house but stayed inside it. Divine intervention ensured that although the roof collapsed no one was injured. On another occasion Molaise extinguished the fire in the house of a local king by extending his arms, a common motif in Irish hagiography.[74] Another possible local source from which stories of protection from fire may have been drawn was the life of St Lasair, a disciple of Molaise, which was certainly in circulation in west Fermanagh in the early seventeenth century.[75] In one story the house in which Lasair was chanting psalms was set on fire by raiders but she was untouched by the fire.[76]

70 The Register of Clogher, written in the early sixteenth century, contains a hymn in praise of St Macartan and an office life compiled by the bishop of Clogher, Patrick O Cuilinn, which both seem to have been intended for use on patronal festivals. Nicholls, 'The register of Clogher', pp 423–31. 71 Stokes (ed.), *Three Middle Irish homilies*; Kathleen Mulchrone (ed.), *Bethu Phátraic* (Dublin, 1939); Stokes, *Lives of the saints*; P. de Brún (ed.), *Catalogue of Irish manuscripts in King's Inns Library, Dublin* (Dublin, 1972), p. 21. 72 L. Bieler and F. Kelly (eds), *The Patrician texts in the Book of Armagh* (Dublin, 1979), pp 94–6, 130, translated in Liam de Paor, *Saint Patrick's world* (Dublin, 1993), pp 155–6, 186–7. 73 Dáithí Ó hÓgáin, *The hero in Irish folk history* (Dublin, 1985), pp 8–10. 74 O'Grady (ed.), *Silva Gadelica*, i, pp 22–3; ii, pp 22–3. 75 Lucius Gwynn (ed.), 'The life of St Lasair' in *Ériu*, v (1911), pp 73–103; Brendan Jennings, *Michael O Cleirigh chief of the Four Masters and his associates* (Dublin, 1936), p. 71. 76 Gwynn, 'Life of St Lasair', pp 74–9.

Whether or not stories of local saints were invoked by Pilib Mág Uidhir to instil courage in his followers is merely speculation but what does seem clear from the historical record is that the honour of St Patrick was deemed to have been infringed by the attack. Although nothing has survived to help us understand precisely what role Pilib expected St Patrick to play, aspects of the image of the saint in south-west Ulster in the sixteenth century are well known. In particular, stories of Patrick were incorporated into the early sixteenth-century life of St Colum Cille compiled in the 1530s by Maghnus Ó Domhnaill in south Donegal. The Patrick presented in this work was, above all, a wonder-working saint who could make a ford appear in a river, could cause an abundance of fish to appear, could banish evil spirits. Most significantly Patrick was represented as a protector who blessed his friends and cursed his enemies, particularly those who refused to accept the faith he preached.[77] Again in the motif of protector Patrick was portrayed as a judge of the Irish at the end of the world, an idea drawn from a much older tradition, but as Colum Cille reputedly explained

> Lucky is he that shall be a follower of Padraic [and other saints of Ireland] on that day, and woe to him that shall not. And well for him which in that time may boast to Padraic of service done him touching the keeping of his feast day solemnly and with prayer, and with almsdeeds and fasting to do him honour; for Padraic shall be the advocate and the judge of all the men of Erin in the Day of Doom.

> [Mogenar bias do réir Padruic 7 naem eli Erenn isin ló-sa, 7 as mairg bíass dá n-aimhréir, 7 is madhngenair gá mbeith re maidhem ar Padruic an uair-si serbhis do denamh dó leith re na fheil do denamh go honórach 7 re hurnaigthe 7 re déirc 7 re troscad do denamh 'na onóir, oir is é bus aighne 7 bus breithemh d'Erindchaib uile a llo an bratha].[78]

In short, Pilib Mág Uidhir and his followers in the church of Domnach Magh da Claine would have looked to St Patrick as a powerful protector, working miracles and wonders to protect his people. In return, the people were defenders of the saint's honour as in Maghnus Ó Domhnaill's hagiography.

A slightly later story in the Annals of Ulster, dated 1537, provides a parallel situation which may indicate Pilib's desired outcome following the attempted

---

77 O'Kelleher and Schoepperle (eds), *Betha Colaim Chille*, pp 12–14, 16, 20, 114–18. For a further discussion of the attributes of the traditional saint, Bernadette Cunningham and Raymond Gillespie, ' "The most adaptable of saints": the cult of St Patrick in the seventeenth century' in *Archivium Hibernicum*, xlix (1995), pp 82–7. 78 O'Kelleher and Schoepperle (eds), *Betha Colaim Chille*, pp 114–15.

church burning. In this later event the Dublin government raided the lordship
of Ó Conchobhair Fhaighle and set on fire a church where Ó Conchobhair
Fhaighle was present 'but it came through the prodigies and marvel of God that
themselves [his enemies] all were burned and the church was not burned.' [7
tainíg tre fertaibh 7 tre mhírbhulibh De gur'loisgedh iadsan uíle 7 nar'loisgidh
in tempoll.]⁷⁹ The late seventeenth-century history of the Uí Raghallaigh preserves a rather similar story, though less violent in its consequences, in which a
man who spoiled a church under the protection of St Máedóc, was struck dumb
as a result of prayers to the saint.⁸⁰ Divine intervention, through a saint, was not
simply understood as being for protection but also for revenge and the next
essay shows how supernatural events could be seen as a judgement on an individual. Indeed Pilib had good parallels for this. According to the Annals of
Ulster for 1484 two of Pilib's brothers had been agents of divine retribution.
In this story some of the sons of Cú Chonnacht Mág Uidhir who had been

> disrespectful to the church of [St] Tigernach, namely of Daire Maelain,
> and to churches besides, were slain in the night, through vengeance of
> God and Tighernach, in Daire Maelain itself.
>
> [co heasonorach re heaglus Tigernaigh, idon, [D]aire-Maela[i]n 7 risna
> heaglusaibh archeana, do marbadh isin oidhche, tre ínneachadh De 7
> Tighernaigh, a nDaire-Maela[i]n fein].⁸¹

If Pilib intended that St Patrick's honour was to be promoted and defended
at Domnach Magh da Claine, in return he expected the marshalling of divine
aid in his dynastic feud with Réamonn. The record of Pilib and his family in
equally dubious activities in churches was not expected to count against him
in a world where spirituality was tough and practical. Dealing with the saints
as friends of God was a two-way relationship in which powerful forces could
be marshalled to a particular cause through appropriate devotional practices.

III

The victor of the skirmish at Donagh, Pilib Mág Uidhir, lived another sixteen
years after those events. However, there are progressively fewer references to

79 *AU*, iii, pp 616–17. 80 James Carney (ed.), *A genealogical history of the O'Reillys* (Cavan and Dublin, 1959),
pp 31, 81. 81 *AU*, iii, pp 288–9.

him, or his family, in the annals after the burning at Donagh. This retreat from the limelight suggests perhaps that they were being squeezed out of influence. Only once, in 1518, does Pilib himself feature again.[82] The circumstances are confusing. Two hostages, Aodh Balbh Ó Néill the son of Con Ó Néill and brother of the leader of the Tyrone family, and Aodh Mac Gaffraigh who seems to have been a dependant of Pilib Mág Uidhir's, were held by Aodh's uncle at Clappy Island in Lough Erne. In 1518 they were freed following a raid led by Pilib, although an entry in the Annals of the Four Masters states that Aodh Ó Néill was ransomed for fifteen horses.[83] Ó Néill's nephew, Cathal, was killed by Pilib on that occasion, though why Pilib became involved in internal Uí Néill politics is unclear. It may have been a last ditch attempt to bolster the family position. If so, this was probably also the motive behind a raid in 1520 against the family of Pilib Ó Raghallaigh of the north eastern part of Cavan.[84] After seizing their prey the Mág Uidhir party were ambushed on their way back to Fermanagh and some thirty were killed or drowned, including Pilib Mág Uidhir. Ironically for one who had stoutly defended the honour of the saints in 1508 the date on which he was killed was 4 April: the feast of St Tigernach, one of the principal saints of the diocese of Clogher.

82 *AU*, iii, pp 530–1.   83 *AFM*, v, pp 1342–3 and note l.   84 *AU*, iii, pp 532–5.

5

A world of wonders: marvels and prodigies in the diocese of Elphin, 1588

When Brian Mac Diarmada and his scribes came to assemble the entry for the year 1588 in the Annals of Loch Cé they included a story which seems on the face of it to be rather strange.

> There was a wicked heretical bishop in Elphin, and God performed great miracles upon him. And his place of residence was in the Grainsech of Machaire-Riabhach; and a shower of snow was shed for him, and a wild apple was not larger than each stone of it; and not a grain was left in his town; and it was with shovels the snow was removed from the houses; and it was in the middle month of summer that shower fell.

> [Easpacc mallaighthi heregda do beth a nOilfinn, ocus do rinne Dia ferta fele air; ocus asi áit a raibhi a thigedas a nGrainsigh in Machaire riabaigh; ocus do cuiredh cith snechta dó, ocus nir mó fiadh ughall na gach cloch de; ocus nir fagbad grainne na baile, ocus is re sluasdib do cuirthi an snechta sin o na tigtib; ocus as a mí medoin tsamrad do cuiredh an cioth sin.][1]

Stories of wonders were relatively common in the Irish annals for the sixteenth century and earlier. The Annals of the Four Masters recorded under 1574 a story rather similar to that recorded for Elphin

> On the calends of May [1 May] this year a shower of hail fell, after a strange and wonderful manner, for some saw nothing in it but what belonged to such showers in general; while there were others whose good strong houses it swept away, and whose flocks and herds it

1 *ALC*, ii, pp 484–5.

smothered. The fields of green corn, which had been sown a quarter or half a year before, were left by this shower bare and barren plains, without corn or blade. The same shower left upon the shins of those on whom it fell lumps the exact size of one of the hail-stones.

[Cioth cloichshneachta do ffhearthain hi callainn Maii na bliadhna so, bá hexamhail iongnath fearthain an cheatha íshin, uair bátar dronga in nErinn na ro mhachtnaidh é acht amhail nach cioth naile, Batar drong naile ó ro tógbait tige trebar dhaingne, 7 o ro bháidhit ceathra, 7 innile. Na guirt geamhair ro bhaoí ar na síoladh ráithe no leaithbli-adhain rias an tan sin ro ffáccaibh an cioth sin ina leargaibh loma gan ioth gan fheór iad. Ro fhagbhaidh an ciot cédna bheós cudroma gach cloiche dá ccuireadh do mhioll mhaothghurm for na luirgnibh fris a mbeanadh.][2]

For the years before 1588 the Annals of Loch Cé themselves had recorded a cluster of wondrous events. In 1586 the annals noted that 'The stream of the Shannon turned back to Lough Ree and it was twenty-four hours in that order in the presence of all who were in Athlone.' [Sruth na Sionna do filleadh tarais dochum Locha Righ, ocus a bheith ceithre huaire fiched ar an ordubh sin a fiadnuise aroibhe an Ath Luain uile.][3] More significantly for our story the annal-ists noted in the following year, 1587, 'A shower of hail fell in Machaire Connacht within a week after Lammas, and a small apple was not bigger than each stone of that snow and it destroyed much corn.' [Cith cloichsneachta do chur a Machaire Connacht a ccinn tseachtmuine iar Lughnasadh, ocus nir mo min uball na gach cloch dont sneachta sin, ocus arbhar imda do milledh do.][4] In a later instance in April 1635, Conall Mac Eochagáin scribbled a note in the margin of a fifteenth-century manuscript miscellany which he then owned:

A great wonder, 1635: a shower of hail fell in Fir Ceall in Ballycowan and in the Cealla and in the border of the plain of Durrow on the Feast of the Annunciation of Mary, that is, the 25th of March of this year, and every stone of it was the size of four inches in circumfer-ence. A hen was killed in Ballykilmurry, and her two legs were broken by one piece of it. Two scald crows were killed by it in Baile Chodag. Every stone went two inches in the earth, and what fell in the water went to the bottom like a natural stone. And some of them at the time

2 *AFM*, v, pp 1678–9. 3 *ALC*, ii, pp 474–5. 4 *ALC*, ii, pp 480–1.

of the shower struck a woman on the head, even under her hood, and wounded her, and her head was sore for a week from it. And a peasant whose feet were struck by the stones became covered with blisters. I am Conall Mac Geoghegan.

[Iongnadh mor 1635. Anno domini 1635, Cioth cloichshneachta do fhearadh i bhFearaibh Ceall .i. i mBaile meic Abhain ⁊ is na Ceallaibh ⁊ i leithimeal Mhuidhe Dermuidhe la fheil Muire na sanaisi .i. in 25 la do mhi Mharta na bliadhnasa ⁊ ba meidighthir cheitri hordlaithe timcheall gach cloiche dhe, cearc do mharbhadh i mBaile mic Giolla Muire ⁊ a da cois do bhrisi do chloich dhe, da fhinnoig do mharbhadh leis i mBaile Codag, gach cloch do dhul da ordlach i ttalamh ⁊ an meid do thuiteadh san uisge dhul a n-ichtar amhuil chloich eile, ⁊ cuid aca do bhuain i ccend mhna i n-aimsir in cheatha fa na fhiled fein, a gortughadh ⁊ a cend bheth seachtmhuin tinn uadha, ⁊ bodach ar bheanadur cuid do na clochaibh da chosaibh bheth lan do ballsgoidib uile. Misi Conall Mag Eochagain.]⁵

Such descriptions of wonders were clearly intended to leave readers pondering their significance.

It would be tempting to dismiss the more incredible of such stories as fanciful imaginings if there were not independent confirmation for some of them. Of direct relevance is a piece of evidence from an independent source which confirms the events which the annalists recorded for 1587. On 12 August 1587 Thomas Le Strange in a postscript to a letter addressed to the Irish lord deputy, Sir John Perrot, recorded

I have bene credebly enformed of a straunge thinge which was don upon Sonday last within a myle of Roscoman to a town called Olfine. Ther fell hayle stones as bige as a mans fist and hath distroyed most parte of the corne for a myle in breadth and viij myle in length to the said towne of Olfine and killed two men of Geordge Mc Peters and as Geordg himself saith the milk that came from the kyne that tyme doth so smell that no man was able to abide it.⁶

Le Strange's evidence is of importance since it comes from a standpoint very different to that of the annalists. Le Strange was a recent arrival in Connacht,

5 BL, Add. MS 30512, f. 15v, extract printed in Robin Flower, *Catalogue of Irish manuscripts in the British Library*, (3 vols, London, 1926), ii, p. 471; translated by Paul Walsh, 'Curiosities from the annals' in *Irish Book Lover*, xix (1931), pp 38–9. 6 PRO, SP63/130, no. 65.

appointed deputy governor of the province in 1588, and at his death in 1590 the annalists commented 'there was not in Connacht a foreigner more to be deplored by Connacht than he.' [oir ni roibhe a Connacht mac Goill bhudh mo do sgel do Connacht na e.][7] In instances where the annalist's version of events agrees with evidence from such a witness it seems likely that the substance of the account was correct.

There is one particularly significant difference between the other annalistic accounts of wonders in the 1580s and the entry for 1588 linked to the bishop of Elphin. Most accounts of wonders in the sixteenth-century annals are written as discrete entries in terse annalistic prose and draw no moral from the events. This was not because morals could not be drawn from such wonders. The description of hail in 1587, for instance, could well have been interpreted as a divine intervention in response to turbulent events which the annalist had noted earlier in the entry for the same year. In 1587 it was recorded by the Annals of Loch Cé that two of the sons of Eoghan Ruadh son of Cormac Mac Diarmada were hanged at Knockvicar by Captain Green O'Mulloy and George, the son of Peter Nugent.[8] It is interesting to note that according to the report of Thomas Le Strange quoted above, it was two of the men of George McPeter Nugent who were killed by the hailstones. The case for divine retribution could easily have been made by the annalist yet the wondrous death of the men responsible for the hanging was not mentioned in the annals, and no connection was made between the untimely death of two of the Clann Diarmada and the strange natural phenomena recorded in the same year.

In contrast to this, the annalistic entry relating to the bishop of Elphin in the following year, 1588, does not merely report another wondrous hail shower but also draws a moral from it. The annalist portrayed the hail shower as divine punishment for the actions of the Church of Ireland bishop of Elphin, John Lynch. This narrative linking of cause and consequence is not the only unusual thing about this annalistic entry. That John Lynch, bishop of Elphin, was described as 'heretical' [heregda] is particularly unusual. The word is not used by the annalist about any other New English Protestant which prompts the question of why it should have been used in this case. Its use is more curious given that the annalist previously seems not to have had any difficulty with Lynch's appointment. Under the year 1584 the Loch Cé annalist simply noted without comment 'John son of James Lynch was made bishop in Elphin and Andrew O Cridhain was removed.' [Eásboc do denamh

7 *ALC*, ii, pp 510–11. 8 *ALC*, ii, pp 478–9. For the identifications of the individuals see Paul Walsh, *Irish chiefs and leaders* (Dublin, 1960), p. 299.

do Séan mac Semais a Línsi a nOilfinn in bliadain sin, ocus Aindriu O Cridhain do chur ar ccúl.][9]

It is tempting to categorise the unusual 1588 entry on the protestant bishop of Elphin as simply a fabrication or a credulous retelling of a half-heard legend. Certainly when the Annals of the Four Masters were compiled for the year 1588 the story was omitted. Given the Four Masters' interest in ecclesiastical stories this seems a curious omission and it may suggest that the story was not well known outside Elphin. Alternatively it may be that the events of 1588 did not happen at all but rather that the wonder recorded in the previous year was reused as part of a narrative device to make a particular point relating to the bishop. The wording of parts of the 1588 entry, for instance, are almost identical to the wording used in 1587. However, even if the story of mysterious hailstones in 1588 is not a factual record of events, to dismiss it as a fabrication would be to miss the point. The 1588 account had a meaning for the annalist who wrote it and to understand that meaning is to begin to re-imagine the mental world of the people of sixteenth-century Roscommon. If we are to understand why the annalist should have told this possibly imaginary story we need to pay particular attention to its context, both political and religious.

I

The medieval Irish annalists had a fascination with a wide variety of wonders and used them in their historical compilations. Wonders, such as that described in the 1588 story of the bishop of Elphin, were part of the grammar of prose writing. They were tropes that the annalist could fall back on to express a hidden meaning. Upsets in the world, whether political or religious, were paralleled in disturbances in the natural order. Thus the obituary of Ruaidhrí Mac Diarmada, considered in the next essay, recorded his death in conjunction with stories of disturbances in the natural order. Again in a literary context many of the stories common in this part of Connacht in the sixteenth century used wonders as an integral part of their narrative technique. Two collections of such tales are known to survive in manuscripts from this area, including British Library, MS Egerton 1782 from the early sixteenth century and the Glenmasan manuscript dating from about 1500 now in the National Library of Scotland. The stories in both, some of considerable antiquity, are replete with marvellous episodes.[10] One tale, *Eachtra an mhadra mhaoil*, appears in its earliest form in British

9 *ALC*, ii, pp 458–9. 10 BL, Egerton MS 1782 and National Library of Scotland MS 72. 2. 3. [Glenmasan

Library Egerton MS 1782 a manuscript that was evidently compiled by the learned family of Ó Maoil Chonaire in county Roscommon in the second decade of the sixteenth century.[11] This story turns on wonders.[12] It is a variant on a werewolf story, one of the wonders of Ireland listed in the twelfth century by Giraldus Cambrensis, which is highly episodic and relies on shape-changing marvels for its effect.[13] Even the setting of the opening on 'the plain of wonders' [Máigh na nIongnadh] is significant. Wonders, such as the one described by the annalist here were part of the symbolic world within which the inhabitants of the diocese of Elphin in the sixteenth century lived. However, most stories of wonders occurred in religious contexts, and had a particular role in hagiographical writing where they served to mark out special events as divinely approved or censured.[14] One indication of the importance of this type of literature is the early sixteenth-century collection of religious tracts made for Máire daughter of Eoghan Ó Máille.[15] Although she was from Mayo the compilation was made in Donegal where she lived with her husband, Ruaidhrí Mac Suibhne Fanad, and is now usually known as *Leabhar Chlainne Suibhne*. Among these tracts are a large number of apocryphal works characterised by stories of marvels, such as the wonders on the night of Christ's birth.[16] Descriptions of similar wonders appear in a text known as the *Liber Flavus Fergusiorum*, written in Roscommon in the middle of the fifteenth century and probably still in circulation there in the late sixteenth century. The stories in this manuscript include not only the wonders of the night of Christ's birth but the fifteen wondrous signs of the day of Judgement and miraculous signs which appeared in the Temple in Jerusalem, including a great light which shone for one and a half hours and a cow which was delivered of a lamb.[17]

MS] were both written in this area in the early sixteenth century.   11 For discussion of provenance and dating of this manuscript see Flower, *Catalogue of Irish manuscripts in the British Library*, ii, pp 259–61.   12 R.A.S. Macalister (ed.), *Two Irish Arthurian romances* (London, 1908), pp 2–73.   13 J.J. O'Meara (ed.), *The first version of the topography of Ireland by Giraldus Cambrensis* (Dundalk, 1951), pp 53–6. John Carey, 'Werewolves in medieval Ireland' in *Cambrian Medieval Celtic Studies*, no. 44 (2002), pp 37–72; a werewolf story also appears in the sixteenth-century Book of Howth, *Cal. Carew MSS, Book of Howth*, pp 161–2.   14 Raymond Gillespie, *Devoted people: belief and religion in early modern Ireland* (Manchester, 1997), chapter 6 discusses some of the functions of wonders in this religious mind set.   15 RIA, MS 24 P 25 (*Leabhar Chlainne Suibhne*).   16 For a description of the religious contents of the manuscript Paul Walsh (ed.), *Leabhar Chlainne Suibhne* (Dublin, 1920), pp xliv–lviii.   17 RIA, MS 23 O 48. See also *Catalogue of Irish manuscripts in the Royal Irish Academy*, pp 1242–54. For discussion of the date and provenance of the manuscript see Edward Gwynn, 'The manuscript known as the *Liber Flavus Fergusiorum*' in *Proceedings of the Royal Irish Academy* xxvi, sect C (1906–7), p. 15. An edition of the infancy narratives is now available in Martin McNamara, et al. (eds), *Apocrypha Hiberniae 1, Evangelia Infantiae* in *Corpus Christianorum, Series Apocryphorum* 13 (Turnhout, 2001).

In the case of the annalists of Loch Cé it is possible to understand something of the range of supernatural tropes which the compilers had at their disposal to convey to contemporaries the disorder that had been injected into contemporary events. A notebook belonging to Pilib Ballach Ó Duibhgeannáin, one of the scribes of the Annals of Loch Cé, has survived. It dates from the years 1579 to 1584, and is thus almost contemporary with the Annals of Loch Cé.[18] This Ó Duibhgeannáin notebook may be regarded as a gathering of stories and other source material that might be useful to an annalist. Some of the contents are unsurprising: lists of the kings of Ireland; extracts from the *Leabhar Gabhála*; notes on the computation of the ages of the world; synchronisation of the ages of the world with the colonisation of Ireland, kings of the world and biblical personages; historical notes on Clann Mhíleadh and the battle of Clontarf. In addition to these historical notes of obvious value to an annalist, Ó Duibhgeannáin also recorded randomly in his notebook, presumably for later reference, at least two different types of wonder stories. The first related to what might be described as 'fixed' wonders or strange abnormalities in the landscape. He recorded a popular list of twenty-two 'wonders' of Ireland including marvellous wells that petrified material placed in them or that rose and fell as local lakes did, rocks that generated rain, islands, including Inisglora, where no body would decay, a mill pond that gave leprosy, the grave of a dwarf, a grave at which women involuntarily shrieked, werewolves, and a set of windows at Clonmacnoise.[19] Such lists of wonders were not uncommon in the area. The list of the wonders of Ireland in Ó Duibhgeannáin's notebook is very similar to that in the early fifteenth-century Book of Ballymote which was in the hands of a Connacht learned family in the late fifteenth century.[20] The scribe of Ballymote claimed to have taken his exemplar from an older manuscript known to him as the Book of Glendalough.[21] Another early sixteenth-century manuscript, British Library, MS Egerton 1782, compiled at least partly within the Mac Diarmada lordship, by the learned family of Ó Maoil Chonaire, contains a similar list of wonders.[22]

In addition to these nationally known wonders there were also more locally identifiable and more permanent wonders. Perhaps most common of these was the phenomenon of the holy well of which the diocese of Elphin seems to

---

18 NLI, MS G1. 19 NLI, MS G1, ff 58–62. 20 See Tomás Ó Concheanainn, 'The Book of Ballymote' in *Celtica*, xiv (1981), pp 15–25, for discussion of the scribes and the background of the manuscript. 21 The wonders are also recorded in the Book of Lecan and the Book of Uí Mhaine. For an edition of the text taken from the Books of Lecan and Uí Mhaine see J.H. Todd (ed.), *Leabhar Bhreathnach annso sis: The Irish version of the Historia Britonum of Nennius* (Dublin, 1848), pp 193–219. 22 BL, Egerton MS 1782, ff 125v.

have had quite a few. Some sixty-eight wells can be identified in county Roscommon from a variety of sources, of which twenty-three have dedications to saints.[23] While there is no clear documentary evidence of miracles at wells in Elphin, in the neighbouring diocese of Kilmore an early seventeenth-century list of churches and their dedications survives and records a number of holy wells described as either 'tobar mór miorbuilech' or 'fons miraculosus' [miraculous well].[24] Such wondrous features in the landscape were usually underpinned by hagiographical stories of how a saint in the locality had struck the ground and created a well. Stories of this type occur several times in the early sixteenth-century life of Colum Cille compiled by Maghnus Ó Domhnaill in Donegal. Saints might also manifest themselves through the landscape in other miraculous ways. According to one witness in 1641 at the cathedral at Elphin there were indentations in a rock where the native Irish 'said that St Patrick left the print of his knee', presumably while praying.[25] This gave the place a particular association with the saint so that in 1527 the annalists could record that Mor, daughter of Maelechlainn Mac Caba, was buried in Elphin 'under the protection of God and Patrick' [fá dhíden Dé ocus Phádraic] even though the church was dedicated to the Blessed Virgin Mary.[26]

Interesting as these permanent wonders in the landscape were, even more important in a historical context were the ephemeral wonders such as the abnormal weather the Loch Cé annalist described in 1588. Pilib Ballach Ó Duibhgeannáin's notebook is full of such natural wonders, interspersed among notes of a religious, historical or topographical nature. Some relatively unspectacular wonders were recorded in the notebook as having Irish locations, including a shower of hailstones at Cashel such that the horses swam at Cashel market.[27] However, Pilib Ballach was also interested in wonders further afield. He noted the story of two monstrous women washed ashore on the coast of Scotland and also recorded an account of strange happenings in Gascony in the year 1558.[28] Descriptions of unusual natural phenomena from more exotic oriental locations were also incorporated, such as foodstuffs in foreign lands that were sweet by day and sour by night. The description of the wonders of India included a description of an island in which there were two winters and

23 Breandán Mac Aodha, 'Tobarainmneacha i gContae Ros Comáin: réamhshuirbhé' in *Journal of the Old Athlone Society*, ii (1978–85), pp 136–8. These are also listed by parish in Francis Beirne (ed.), *The diocese of Elphin* (Dublin, 2000). 24 Canice Mooney (ed.), 'Topographical fragments from the Franciscan library' in *Celtica*, i (1946–50), pp 65–7. 25 The original of this deposition (TCD, MS 830, f. 28) is torn but a contemporary copy exists in TCD, MS 831, f. 217; see also pp 126–7 above. 26 *ALC*, ii, pp 262–3. For another example from 1543 see *AConn*, pp 730–1. 27 NLI, MS G1, f. 27r. 28 NLI, MS G1, ff 65r, 80v.

two summers each year with 'every fruit twice in the year' [gach uile thoradh fa dhó sa mbliadhuin], another two islands where stars were never seen, islands full of gold and silver mines.[29]

Wonders such as extremes of weather could be seen as omens or carry predictions. Thus the Annals of the Four Masters linked the drying up of part of the Liffey in 1452 with the death of the earl of Ormond in that year,[30] and Ó Duibhgeannáin's notebook recorded a number of prognostications based on natural phenomena.[31] Moreover, direct connections could be made between wonders and political events. Occasionally, the ephemeral wonders in the notebook are explicitly connected to dated events such as the shower of fish that fell three days before the death of An Calbhach Ó Domhnaill in 1566.[32] In another instance there was an implied connection between the record of an abnormal birth, of a 'two-headed four-legged baby', and the killing of Maghnus king of the Lochlannaigh in AD 1103. Ó Duibhgeannáin's notes also appear to link the finding of the inscription from the Cross of Christ in Rome in 1412 with two miraculous occurrences in Ireland: a speaking statue of Our Lady and the changing of water into wine when a woman was drawing water from a well on the eve of Epiphany. It is not made explicit whether the story he records of a pig giving birth to a white lamb, a famine in summer, and severe frost at Christmas 1435 were to be linked with the record of the capture of Niall Garbh Ó Domhnaill in the same year.

The significance of the various wonders that attracted the attention of the annalists and others, lies not in their existence or veracity but in when and where the annalists chose to incorporate them into their historical text. Relatively few natural wonders are recorded in the sixteenth-century Annals of Loch Cé. By contrast, the Annals of the Four Masters noted a great wind which destroyed churches in 1547, a shower of fish in Tirconnell in 1566, a wonderful shower of hail which destroyed houses and fields in 1574 and a wonderful star, possibly a comet, in 1577.[33] None of these specific happenings feature in the Annals of Loch Cé. Those wonders that are included in the sixteenth-century portion of the Loch Cé annals appear in two clusters. The first is in 1581–2. The annalist described a fiery bolt that destroyed a castle, the spire of the church of Killoscobe in Sligo, horses and cattle and at least one man, and also the fact that a cuckoo called on Christmas night 'and that was a great wonder' [ocus fa mór ant ingnad sin].[34] The recording of the first event may well have been due

---

29 NLI, MS G1, ff 27v, 88v–89r.   30 *AFM*, iv, pp 980–1.   31 NLI, MS G1, ff 11, 11v.   32 NLI, MS G1, f. 74r.   33 *AFM*, v, pp 1500–1, 1608–9, 1678–9, 1700–1; this latter was Halley's comet.   34 *ALC*, ii, pp 444–5, 456–7.

to local circumstances since the man killed by the fiery bolt, Sean Ruadh Mac an Fhiledh may well have been related to Domhnall Mac an Fhiledh who was one of the scribes who compiled the Loch Cé annals.

The second cluster of wonders is in 1586–8 and comprises the story of the Shannon turning backwards, a shower of hail in 1587 and the story of the hail directed against the bishop of Elphin in 1588 with which we began.[35] This clustering of wonders in the late 1580s requires explanation. The noticing and recording of wonders was probably of greatest importance at times of political tension and change. The recording of the exceptional hail shower in association with the story of the bishop of Elphin, and also the other wonder stories of about this date, may thus be related to the political tensions of the 1580s in Connacht. The late 1580s were difficult years in Connacht. At an economic level the annals noted that these were bad years. The Loch Cé annalists noted that 1585 was a very wet year, the Annals of the Four Masters similarly noting 'There was much rain in this year so that the greater part of the corn of Ireland was destroyed' [Iomatt fleachadh is in mbliadhain si co ro milleadh urmhor arblia Ereann], and 1587 saw a great mortality of cattle and destruction of corn.[36] By 1588, however, the worst of this had passed and the annalists recorded the harvest of 1588 as very plentiful.[37] There may have been tensions generated within Elphin by a change of lord. The chief of the Mac Diarmada lordship, Tadhg, died in 1585 to be succeeded by Brian, the compiler of the annals of Loch Cé. These two branches of the family were not on good terms having quarrelled over the succession to the lordship after the death of Brian's father in 1568. By 1570 Brian's branch of the family and that of Tadhg were in open warfare and this continued sporadically for a number of years.[38] However, if the succession to the Mac Diarmada lordship was not smooth, this was swamped by the internal political disputes of the MacWilliam Burke family in Mayo after 1585 which created considerable instability in the province of Connacht. Such internal dissension within lordships inevitably resulted in an increase in the numbers of gallowglasses in the area and in 1586 the forces of the president of Connacht and Scots mercenaries clashed at Ard na Rí, a major battle at which the annalists claimed 2,200 were killed.[39] The third factor which served to increase the political tension in the area was the appointment of Sir Richard Bingham as president of Connacht following the death of Sir Nicholas Malby in 1584. Bingham's appointment was marked by a significant escalation

35 *ALC*, ii, pp 474–5, 480–1, 484–5. 36 *ALC*, ii, pp 466–7, 478–9; *AFM*, v, pp 1826–7. 37 *ALC*, ii, pp 488–9. 38 *ALC*, ii, pp 406–9. 39 *ALC*, ii, pp 472–5. Colm Ó Lochlainn (ed.), 'Ár ar Árd na Riadh' in *Éigse*, v (1946–7), pp 149–55.

of military activity in Connacht. This was partly a result of the problems created by the MacWilliam Burke succession, but also Bingham's adoption of a more militaristic style of government than that of his predecessor, Sir Nicholas Malby. Bingham was not a man much liked by the annalists. As the Loch Cé annalist noted of him 'he made a bare, polished garment of the province of Connacht' [do rinne breid slatach sairthech do choiged Chonnacht].[40] It was these circumstances that forced the MacCostello family to make major adjustments to their traditional political alliances by engaging Theobald Dillon as their protector and ally as described in an earlier essay. Bingham's period of government coincided with the spread of royal taxation, especially the composition of Connacht, which the annalists saw as eroding the culture of lordship and reducing the status of the local lords.[41] It is hardly surprising that the annalist of Loch Cé should have been particularly sensitive to the appearance of abnormalities in the natural world which may have given some indication of what lay ahead in a period of rapid and fundamental political realignment. This may well help to explain why they were predisposed to record a story about the bishop of Elphin and the hailstones as big as apples in 1588.

II

If political tensions were one variable in mobilising stories about wonders then religious change, clearly on the annalist's mind in the 1588 case, was another. The singling out of the 'heretical' bishop for special descriptive treatment suggests that some sort of religious motivation influenced the construction of this entry in the annals. The bishop in question can only be John Lynch who had been nominated to the see of Elphin in November 1583 and would hold it for almost twenty-eight years until he resigned in August 1611. Lynch was not the first Church of Ireland bishop to hold the see of Elphin. He had three predecessors, Conach Ó Siadhail (1541–51), Roland Burke (1551–80) and Thomas Chester (1582–3). The annals give no hint that nature conspired to complain at their appointment and to expect that it would do so in the case of John Lynch would be naive.

    Evidence on Bishop John Lynch's background and beliefs is scant and contradictory. In 1591 Sir Turlough O'Brien, lord of the two north-western baronies of Corcomroe and Burren in Thomond, or County Clare, wrote an account of religious affiliations and practices in Connacht. He described John Lynch in these terms:

40 *ALC*, ii, pp 494–5.   41 *ALC*, ii, pp 466–7.

ffor the Bushopp of Ullfyne called John Lynch after being a ffriere and next one of the vicares of the Cathedrall church of Gallway in the providence of the lord beganne his conversion by studienge Calvyns institucons of the Christian religion then preachinge the reourma- con according to the truth of the gospell was preferred to this Bishoppricke now much or in a manner alltogether declined from prof- ittinge his dioceners keepinge his most residen[ce] in Gallway exter- nally benefitting his wife & cheeldren wch sort I hartelie feare yt he with dive[r]s others of his rancke in that contrey may mary them selves from the lord preferringe yt societye to the spirituall and everlasting coniunction to Christ our treue spowse.[42]

Despite this description, however, Sir Turlough O'Brien thought sufficiently well of Lynch to name him as one of those who should spearhead the preach- ing campaign of reform in Connacht, partly because he was one of the few Church of Ireland clergy who could preach in Irish.[43] A rather different view of Lynch was provided by a later commentator, Walter Harris, in his early eigh- teenth-century revision of Sir James Ware's seventeenth-century treatise on Irish bishops. Harris noted that Lynch had been born in Galway and was educated in New Inn Hall in Oxford. After his appointment as bishop of Elphin

by alienations, fee farms and other means so wasted and destroyed it [the bishopric] that he left it not worth 200 marks a year. It is said he lived a concealed and died a public papist.[44]

Harris's piece of folklore about Lynch's religious allegiance is perhaps sur- prising given the annalists' clear statement of his 'heresy' and Turlough O'Brien's apparently clear picture of a convinced Protestant and reader of the works of John Calvin. Yet it is not entirely improbable. Lynch had been educated at Oxford in the way in which pre-reformation clergy were trained. As such he specialised in canon law, gaining his degree in 1555.[45] For this generation, trained in this way, some attachment to traditional Catholic beliefs was inevitable. The form of attachment varied. For some, as we shall see below, this took the form

---

42 SP63/162, no. 91, printed in Bernadette Cunningham (ed.), 'A view of religious affiliation and practice in Thomond, 1591' in *Archivium Hibernicum*, xlviii (1994), p. 19. 43 Cunningham (ed.), 'A view of religious affiliation and practice in Thomond, 1591' p. 21. 44 Walter Harris, *The whole works of Sir James Ware concern- ing Ireland* (3 vols, Dublin, 1739), p. 634. 45 Joseph Foster, *Alumni Oxoniense, 1500–1714* (4 vols, Oxford, 1891), *sub* John Lynch.

of adopting merely outward conformity. In other cases it may well have been different. In 1615 it was reported that the wife and family of Bishop Roland Lynch of Kilmacduagh were all Catholics and other bishops shared the same fate. At the level of Church of Ireland clergy there was also a problem of recusancy among the native clergy who had conformed. For those in Connacht there were particular problems since the main power broker, and probably John Lynch's patron, the earl of Clanricard was a Catholic and less than enthusiastic about encouraging the spread of reformed doctrine.[46]

If Turlough O'Brien's evidence on the belief system of John Lynch is somewhat problematic it does provide further clues concerning Lynch's background which may help explain the annalists' account of strange happenings during his episcopate. It is clear that John Lynch was from Galway and his patronymic John FitzJames indicates his father was James. That he studied in Oxford would suggest that he was from one of the wealthy families of the civic elite. However, there are a number of families in mid sixteenth-century Galway that would fit this description. One piece of evidence that would confirm his linkage with the Galway civic elite is O'Brien's comment that he had been one of the vicars in the collegiate church of St Nicholas in Galway. Evidence from 1585 suggests that he had been warden of the college and that he had pawned some of the college plate.[47] Although he was not attached to that institution as early as 1551 when Edward VI granted a new charter to a warden and eight vicars as the body corporate of the Royal College of Galway, he may have been elected later.[48] The charter had given the mayor and corporation powers to elect and remove the wardens and vicars. This stipulation was contested under Mary, with an appeal to Archbishop Bodkin of Tuam, but the issue seems to have been clarified in an agreement with the corporation, probably in 1557. This stipulated that 'the said Mayor and Counsaill shall have the ellection, chossinge and admittinge of the Wardyn yerly and the election of all such prests or clerkes or anny man elles to serve in the church and Colladge'.[49] If Lynch became a priest of this church he owed his preferment to patronage within the corporation.

This relationship is worth pursuing since it may have created other important relationships that affected Lynch's position as bishop of Elphin. In the late sixteenth century the town of Galway's most important set of political

---

46 Alan Ford, *The protestant reformation in Ireland, 1590–1641* (Frankfurt am Main, 1985), pp 32–3. 47 James Hardiman, *The history of the town and county of the town of Galway* (Dublin, 1820) p. 243, note w. 48 Hardiman, *History of the town and county of the town of Galway*, appendix, pp xxvi–xxix. 49 J.T. Gilbert (ed.), 'Archives of the town of Galway' in Historical Manuscripts Commission, *Tenth report*, appendix, pt 5 (London, 1885), p. 387.

relationships was with the powerful earls of Clanricard. Patronage links within the corporation could lead to wider connections and there are hints that this was indeed the case. In March 1582 Sir Henry Sidney, the Irish lord deputy, on a tour of Ireland arrived at Galway and summoned the elderly Riccard Burke, second earl of Clanricard, and other powerful personalities from the county of Galway to him. In particular Clanricard brought his two sons, Ulick and John Burke, who had been intermittently in rebellion since 1576 over succession to the earldom, to Galway. There Sidney 'committed them, and in the chief church of the town had a sermon preached of them and of their wickedness by a countryman of their own called Linch, sometimes a friar at Greenwich, but a reformed man, a good divine and a preacher in three tongues, Irish, English and Latin'.[50] That Lynch had some links with Clanricard seems likely, as otherwise the irony of the chastising of Clanricard's sons 'by a countryman of their own' would have been much less effective. There is one late piece of evidence which supports this suggestion. In August 1606 John Lynch, while still bishop of Elphin, granted to Henry Lynch of Galway a substantial part of the episcopal property of the see of Elphin for ninety-nine years at a low rent.[51] By 1613 Henry Lynch, according to the bishop's successor, held most of the land of the bishopric 'paying nothing at all or no proportionat rent to bear up the dignity of the bishop'.[52] While it is possible 'that the grant to Henry Lynch was simply a commercial transaction it is much more likely that John Lynch was alienating ecclesiastical property to one of his relatives, possibly a nephew. If this connection is valid it helps to fix bishop Lynch in the heart of the Galway patriciate since Henry Lynch was son of Nicholas Lynch fitzStephen fitzArthur who had been mayor of Galway in 1561. More importantly Henry Lynch served as the fourth earl of Clanricard's estate agent in the early seventeenth century and was a close friend and confidant of the earl.[53]

Bishop John Lynch's probable links with the successive earls of Clanricard help to situate him in the politics of the diocese of Elphin in the late sixteenth century and help to explain the annalists' dislike of him. In the 1580s Ulick Burke, third earl of Clanricard, had been consolidating his position within Connacht. He did so by capitalising on the growing authority of the Connacht president as his father had done. The eventual triumph of Ulick Burke in 1582, following a prolonged internal dispute within the Clanricard lordship, was proof of that. Ulick was responsible for the murder of his brother John in 1582

50 *Cal. Carew MSS, 1575–88*, pp 352–3.   51 *Cal. pat rolls Ire., Jas I*, p. 277.   52 *Cal. S.P. Ire., 1611–14*, p. 346.   53 Bernadette Cunningham, 'Clanricard letters' in *Journal of the Galway Archaeological and Historical Society*, xlviii (1996), pp 162–208.

and the Annals of Loch Cé were clear that this was 'an ugly treachery' [fell granna] and claimed the like had not been seen since the fratricide of Naoise, one of the three sons of Uisnech.[54] Like other local lords, Ulick had used the presidency to settle old scores such as those with the MacWilliam Burkes of Mayo. Inevitably this associated him with Bingham in the years 1585–8. In 1586, for instance, the annalists noted that the earl of Clanricard was part of Bingham's force in Connacht which hanged three children linked to the Mayo Burkes and also hanged a number of the followers of Ó Flaithbheartach. Again in 1586 he was associated with George Bingham, a man for whom the annalists had scant respect and whose murder they regarded as a great service to the people of Connacht.[55] For such reasons Clanricard and his supporters might expect, at best, a luke-warm welcome in the diocese of Elphin in the mid-1580s and the protestant bishop of Elphin could have been perceived as representative of the religious divisiveness of Bingham's programme of reform.

The diocese to which John Lynch was appointed was not a particularly valuable or significant prize in the confessional battles of the sixteenth century. The religious houses in the area were left unsuppressed into the 1570s and in 1574 friars still held on to some houses in the area.[56] Financially the diocese was not a wealthy one. In 1525 the see was taxed at sixty-six florins in the papal records and the bishopric was said to be worth £103. 18s. in 1585.[57] In the main it was left alone. After the death of Andrew Ó Craidhéin in 1594 no Catholic bishop was associated with the diocese until the Franciscan Boetius Egan was provided to the see in 1625. Egan's 1631 report on the state of the diocese suggests that much of the ecclesiastical structure had collapsed. There were forty Catholic priests, although Egan claimed in a 1637 report to Rome that there had been only thirteen before his appointment.[58]

The progress of the reformed church in the diocese was equally slow. In 1613 it was complained that there were about thirty parishes in the diocese without a minister and most of the church lands had been alienated.[59] This was, perhaps, a little bleak. Admittedly forty-eight of the forty-nine rectories in the diocese in 1615 were impropriate but there were nineteen clergy, of whom eighteen

54 *ALC*, ii, pp 454–5. For the wider context see Bernadette Cunningham, 'Political and social change in the lordships of Clanricard and Thomond, 1569–1641', unpublished M.A. thesis, National University of Ireland, Galway, 1979, pp 108–30. 55 *ALC*, ii, pp 472–3, 516–17; *Cal. Carew MSS, 1575–88*, p. 432. 56. PRO, SP63/29 no. 87 and a shorter version of this in TCD, MS 656, ff 165v–7 which has some material not in the PRO version. 57 Canice Mooney, 'A short history of the diocese of Elphin' in Beirne (ed.), *The diocese of Elphin*, p. 37. 58 John Hagan (ed.), 'Miscellanae Vaticano-Hibernica' in *Archivium Hibernicum*, iii (1914), pp 359–65; P.F. Moran (ed.), *Spicilegium Ossoriense* (3 vols, Dublin, 1874–84), i, pp 214–17. 59 *Cal. S.P. Ire., 1611–14*, p. 346.

were resident, although most of these were reading ministers rather than preach-ers.[60] This rather depressing situation had arisen despite a promising start. In 1551 Roland Burke was appointed to the see of Elphin. Earlier, in May 1534, Burke had been appointed bishop of Clonfert by the pope but his consecration was delayed until 1537. In 1536 Henry VIII appointed a rival, reformed candidate to the see of Clonfert, Richard Nangle, the former vicar general of the Augustinians in Ireland. Nangle did not survive long and by 1539 he had been expelled from the see.[61] An explanation for Nangle's isolation in the east Galway diocese of Clonfert is not hard to find. Roland Burke was the son of Redmond Burke of Tynagh and therefore a cousin to Ulick Burke, first earl of Clanricard, the main power-broker in east Galway. Nangle on the other hand had no local support. Nangle soon fled to Dublin and in 1541 the crown, as well as the papacy, recognised Burke as bishop of Clonfert.[62] Roland Burke, in marked contrast to Nangle, could have relied on similar familial support networks in his subse-quent appointment at Elphin, even though there is no evidence that the six-teenth-century earls of Clanricard lent their support to the state church. At any rate, none of these administrative ecclesiastical changes impacted on the issue of belief. According to his late-seventeenth-century Catholic biographer, also named John Lynch, Roland Burke lived and died a Catholic and after his death in 1580 Burke left a field at Tynagh to endow four priests to recite the divine office which was stated to include masses for his soul.[63]

A rather similar story can be reconstructed around the succession to the Catholic see of Elphin in the mid-sixteenth century. In May 1542 Rome appointed the Augustinian friar Bernard Ó hUiginn to the vacant see of Elphin. He made his way to Elphin but finding no real power base there he retreated to the continent by 1544. By early 1553 he was back in his diocese again but remained no more than a year. Vested interests, again in the person of Roland Burke with his Clanricard connections, ensured that the outsider would gain little control.[64] As the papal nuncio, David Wolfe SJ, succinctly put it in 1561 'The said Bernard was a good and religious man in himself, but he was not acceptable to the people' [Questo Bernardo è stato uomo da bene e religiso quanto a se stesso, ma non era grato al popolo].[65] By this point Ó hUiginn had resigned as Catholic bishop

---

60 BL, Add. MS 19836. 61 *State papers, Henry VIII*, iii, pp 50–1, 123. 62. James Morrin (ed.), *Calendar of patent and close rolls of chancery in Ireland, Henry VIII to 18th Elizabeth* (Dublin, 1861), p. 82. 63 John Lynch, *De praesulibus Hiberniae*, ed. J.F. O'Doherty (2 vols, Dublin, 1944), ii, p. 314. 64 F.X. Martin, 'Confusion abounding: Bernard O'Higgins, OSA, bishop of Elphin, 1542–1561' in Art Cosgrove and Donal McCartney (eds), *Studies in Irish history presented to R. Dudley Edwards* (Dublin, 1979), pp 38–84. 65 Martin, 'Confusion abound-ing', p. 81, trans. p. 69.

of Elphin and the Dominican, Andrew Ó Craidhéin, of the Sligo merchant family, was appointed his successor in 1562. Ó Craidhéin's power base lay in the northern part of the diocese leaving Burke to draw the episcopal revenues from the southern part for the next eighteen years.

When Roland Burke died on 20 June 1580 it seemed that local power politics would play a part in the nomination of his successor as Church of Ireland bishop of Elphin. However, an extended vacancy ensued before a successor, Thomas Chester from London, was nominated in May 1582.[66] Chester's tenure of the see was short. The annalists noted his death under 1582 'a Saxon bishop who was in Elphin died in the middle month of the summer: his name was Thomas Chester; and in Cill-Liathain he died.' [Espog Saxanach do bi a nOilfinn dég a mí medoin int samradh. Tomas Sestar a ainm, ocus a Cill Liathain do fuair bas.][67] It seems likely that the annalist got the year wrong. Chester was still alive in December 1582 although the relevant documents had not been issued to allow his appointment.[68] Indeed he may never have been consecrated as the annal entry implies, simply stating that he was a bishop and not describing him as bishop of Elphin. It is probable that he died in June 1583 in Killathain, County Galway. His successor, John Lynch, was nominated in November 1583. What happened in the two gaps in the succession to Elphin in 1580–2 and again in late 1583 is unclear but it may be important for an understanding of the annalist's story. The annalist believed that one Andrew Ó Craidhéin, the Catholic bishop of Elphin, had been appointed Church of Ireland bishop of Elphin noting under the year 1582 'The bishopric of Elphin was given to Andrew O Craidhén by the council of Erinn at Dublin.' [Esbagoidecht Oilefinn do tabairt dAindriu O Craidhéin do comairle na hErend a nAth Cliath.][69] The story was not improbable as the contemporary case of the Dominican Eoghan Ó hAirt, Catholic bishop of Achonry, shows. In 1585 Ó hAirt, who had spent time at the Council of Trent with Ó Craidhéin and had travelled with him to Rome, was captured. In June 1585, the archbishop of Armagh, John Long, wrote to Secretary of State Walsingham noting that

> Owen O'Harte, bishop of Achaensis, alis Achadensis, committed unto me by his Lordship [the lord deputy] to be conferred with … is brought by the Lord's good direction to acknowledge his blindness, to prostrate himself before her Majesty, whom he afore agreed to acurse in religion, so persuaded as I doubt not of great goodness to

66 PRO, SP63/92, no. 65.   67 ALC, ii, pp 452–3.   68 PRO, SP63/98, no. 101.   69 ALC, ii, pp 454–5.

insue by his means, he hath renounced his bishoprick and, no doubt, void of all temporising is thoroughly persuaded that the man of sin sitteth at Rome under pretence of the seat of God.[70]

What followed is uncertain but in July 1585 an 'Owen O'Harte', together with an 'Andrew O Creane', was appointed as one of the commissioners appointed to create counties in Connacht where none existed.[71] In September 1585 he was one of the parties to the Sligo indenture for the composition of Connacht where he was described as 'Oyen Bishop of Aythkonry' and in October 1585 he signed a letter to the lord deputy 'Euegenius Achaden ep[iscopu]s'.[72] Despite his position as a Catholic bishop, it certainly seems that it was intended that Ó hAirt should be appointed by the crown to the Church of Ireland see of Achonry, which had been vacant since 1561, although there is no evidence that the appointment was formalised. Given Ó hAirt's subsequent career it seems unlikely that he renounced the Catholic see of Achonry. A seventeenth-century Catholic source places him there in the 1590s.[73] Moreover in 1587 he was one of four bishops credited with promulgating the decrees of the Council of Trent in Ulster as he was supposed to have done for Connacht in 1566.[74] Clearly something other than doctrine lay behind Ó hAirt's dealings in 1585. It seems most likely that the key issue was the temporalities of the diocese. This was an issue which Ó hAirt took seriously and even seems to have compiled a register of property belonging to the see.[75] As a Catholic bishop Ó hAirt had no title to the temporalities of the see which were held by his Church of Ireland counterpart. What the government and Ó hAirt may have been trying to negotiate, using the composition of Connacht as a way of doing this, was a continuation of the early sixteenth-century arrangements in Connacht whereby a bishop with local authority would be appointed with few questions as to his theological orthodoxy. In this case the arrangement seems to have broken down due to the intervention of Sir Richard Bingham and Ó hAirt was forced to flee to Munster in 1586.[76]

The Dublin government may have sought to negotiate a similar arrangement with Andrew Ó Craidhéin in 1581–2. It clearly did not work. A passage in John Lynch's late seventeenth-century biography of Ó Craidhéin hints at what may

70 W.M. Brady (ed.), *State papers concerning the Irish church in the time of Queen Elizabeth* (London, 1868), p. 97.   71 *Fiants Ire., Eliz.*, no. 4732.   72 A.M. Freeman (ed.), *The compossicion booke of Conought* (Dublin, 1936), pp 125, 132, 177.   73 L.F. Renehan, *Collections on Irish church history* (2 vols, Dublin, 1861), i, p. 275.   74 Renehan, *Collections on Irish church history*, i, pp 139, 435; Lynch, *De praesulibus Hiberniae*, ii, p. 340.   75 Liam Swords (ed.), 'A sixteenth-century register of Achonry' in *Collectanea Hibernica*, nos 39–40 (1997–8), pp 7–22.   76 Lynch, *De praesulibus Hiberniae*, ii, p. 341.

have gone wrong. The biographer Lynch recorded Ó Craidhéin's appointment as Catholic bishop of Elphin in 1582 and his return to Ireland. Lynch noted

> He was allowed to exercise his episcopal office for some time without great annoyance, till being summoned to take the oath of the queen's supremacy he declared that he would never defile himself by such a sacrilegious oath. He was then deprived of his see which was given in 1584 to an apostate religious who had consented to take the oath of supremacy. Being now exposed to constant vexations Andrew took himself to the convent of Sligo where he lived privately at the same time maintaining the Catholic cause.

> [Quo in episcopatu dum officio suo citra multam obicem aliquandiu fungeretur, ad principatum in ecclesia reginae iuramento asserendum vocatus, tali se sacrilegio contaminare prorsus renuit. Proinde dignitate motus et ab apostata religioso, qui ecclesiae primatum reginae iuramento deferre non dubitavit ac Andreae 1584 propterea sufficiebatur, assidue vexatus, ad conventum Sligoensem se recepit, privatam exinde vitam inter sui ordinis religiosos agens, fidem tamen catholicam subinde quibus poterat persuasionibus, quantam per apostatam aemulum licebat, accerrime propugnans.][77]

It is clear that Ó Craidhéin had managed to link two ideas which previously had been kept separate: religious orthodoxy and ecclesiastical authority. This opened the way for the annalist to take the unusual step of using the language of heresy when describing bishop John Lynch. It is only possible to speculate why the annalist may have chosen to use this word in this context. It may well be that he had encountered it in the context of gathering information on Lynch's experience in Elphin. It may even be that it came from papal documents. It is not known whether Ó Craidhéin referred to Rome any offer of the see of Elphin made to him by the Dublin administration but it is not improbable that he would have done so. He certainly had contact with Rome after his return to Ireland in 1562 and according to his biographer, John Lynch, he possessed two papal letters dated 1575 and 1579 which suggests some on-going contact with Rome.[78] If Ó Craidhéin had contact with Rome in the early 1580s and the annalist encountered such documents, the language of those documents could have been the stimulus for him to use the term 'heretic' in his description of

77 Lynch, *De praesulibus Hiberniae*, ii, p. 291.   78 Lynch, *De praesulibus Hiberniae*, ii, p. 291.

Lynch. It is clear that the failure of the government to reach some form of agreement with Ó Craidhéin in Elphin led to the appointment first of Chester, and then Lynch. Neither the annalists nor the later biographer seem to have regarded Chester as significant. The brief episcopate of Thomas Chester is ignored when the annals note under 1584 that John son of James Lynch replaced Andrew Ó Craidhéin as bishop of Elphin.[79]

What happened next is difficult to reconstruct. Whether Lynch ever went to his diocese is not known but there is at least one indication that he intended to move there from Galway. In 1588 John Lynch, bishop of Elphin, was said to hold the dissolved Dominican house at Elphin and the eighth of a quarter of land adjoining with the tithes together with a half quarter of land in Ó Flannagain's country.[80] Acquiring the Dominican house with such a small amount of land makes little sense unless it was intended as a residence, the medieval episcopal residence at Kilteashin having been long since destroyed.[81] If this was the case it seems that Lynch spent little or no time there. The annalist's story is clear that his residence was 'Grainseach in Machaire riabaigh' which can be identified as the Grange of Maghaire Riabhach or Grange in the parish of Lackagh in Clare barony, County Galway. This property was part of the lands of the dissolved Cistercian house of Abbeyknockmoy in County Galway and, significantly, in 1578 a reversionary lease of the property had been granted to Lynch's old patron, Galway corporation. That lease, for fifty years, would have commenced in 1582 on the expiration of a lease for twenty-one years granted in 1566.[82] A plausible reconstruction of the events from these fragments may look like this. After Lynch's appointment as bishop of Elphin in 1584, an event which drew no adverse comment from the annalist, he planned to move to the diocese and acquired some monastic property to build a house. He may even have gone there but whether he did or not he, like his Catholic predecessor Bernard Ó hUiginn, was found unacceptable. This may have been due to his links with Clanricard or possibly because he tried to assert control over the temporalities of the diocese in a way that his absentee predecessor, Roland Burke, had not done. Given his involvement in the composition of Connacht and the delineation of church land which was attempted in the composition inquisitions, this is likely. As a result of his actions he was forced to retreat back to Galway and was provided with a house at Grange by his former patrons, Galway corporation, on their newly acquired land. The souring of relations in Elphin, which these events probably entailed, led to the annalist's depiction of

79 *ALC*, ii, pp 458–9.   80 *Fiants Ire., Eliz.*, no. 5151.   81 *ALC*, i, p. 431.   82 *Fiants Ire., Eliz.*, nos 969, 3463, Breandán Mac Giolla Choille (ed.), *Books of survey and distribution: iii, county of Galway* (Dublin, 1962), p. 104.

local events as part of a providential design. It may well be that the local nature
of the circumstances surrounding the wondrous hail shower meant that its significance was rather limited and hence was not recorded by the Four Masters
in the seventeenth century.

III

The story of the wondrous shower of hailstones in Elphin in 1588 is not a
simple one. Indeed it may describe something that never happened. It is per-
fectly possible that the annalist was using a motif from a well-stocked mind or
notebook to present a particular message. Whether or not the wonder actually
occurred the message was clear. The marvel in the story signalled the religious,
political and social tensions that had emerged in Connacht society in the 1580s.
Economic and political problems combined with military ones to produce a
potentially explosive situation. At such times wonders came to have a particular significance because interpretations of divine providence or judgement could
be read into natural phenomena.

    That the focus of this story of strange happenings should be a bishop,
about whom the contemporary records are sometimes contradictory as to
whether he was a Catholic or a Protestant, hints at the complexity of local relationships arising from increasing polarisation on the issue of religion. Issues
of ecclesiastical authority and religious orthodoxy had become intertwined following on from a failure to make a traditional style settlement of the see of
Elphin after the death of Roland Burke. It seems that in 1588 all these tensions
came together in a way that had not happened before, and John Lynch proved
unacceptable to the people as bishop of Elphin. The bishop's particular difficulties may have been compounded by wider issues, not least Bingham's military campaigns in the province. Further afield, the appointment of Sir William
Fitzwilliam as lord deputy in that year was not welcomed by the annalists either,
noting 'he effected not a particle of good but injured all that was from Athlone
to Erne.' [gan en red maithesa do denam do, acht araibi o Atha Luain co hEirne
do milledh do.][83] One victim of such tensions was the unfortunate Church of
Ireland bishop of Elphin, until then tolerated by the annalists. In such ways,
and in such episodes, were social and religious attitudes redefined.

83 *ALC*, ii, pp 486–7.

6

Remembering Ruaidhrí Mac Diarmada: memory and memorialisation in Roscommon, 1568

Death was always an important marker of change in sixteenth-century Gaelic lordships. It impacted on the personal relationships that were disrupted by the loss but it also had wider social and political implications. Since will-making seems to have been uncommon in this society death gave rise to potential for disputes over the effects of the wealthy.[1] The death of a lord also posed a challenge for the whole lordship since it created a political vacuum which needed to be filled. The possibility of a dispute over succession was a serious consideration. The death of Ruaidhrí Mac Taidhg Mic Ruaidhrí óig Mic Diarmada in 1568 was no exception. His death is unusual, however, in that we know a great deal about its effect on one man in particular, his son Brian Mac Diarmada. Brian was the man who arranged for the Annals of Loch Cé to be compiled, and he personally ensured that the obituary of his father was part of that historical record. Under the year 1568 the Annals of Loch Cé preserve an obituary for Ruaidhrí Mac Diarmada (fig. 14). Written in a small neat hand, the main scribal hand of the preceding years, it is not the usual kind of annalistic obituary but a more comprehensive record of the man's life and death

> A cold, stormy, year of scarcity was this year; and this is little wonder, for it was in it Mac Diarmada died, i.e. Ruaidhri, the son of Tadhg, son of Ruaidhri Og, i.e. king of Mag-Luirg, and Airtech, and Tir-Tuathail, and chief lord over the whole territory of Clann-

---

1 Evidence is unclear on this point. Fynes Moryson in the early seventeenth century was certain that wills were uncommon (Graham Kew (ed.), 'The Irish sections of Fynes Moryson's unpublished itinerary' in *Analecta Hibernica* no. 37 (1998), p. 109) but Sir John Davies was equally clear that the Irish did make wills and used civil and common law practices in probate (Hiram Morgan (ed.), '"Lawes of Irelande": a tract by Sir John Davies' in *Irish Jurist*, n.s. xxviii-xxx (1993–5), p. 312). For one early seventeenth-century Clare will in Irish see James Hardiman (ed.), 'Ancient Irish deeds and writings' in *Transactions of the Royal Irish Academy*, xv (1826), pp 85–7.

14 Obituary of Ruaidhrí Mac Diarmada. From BL, Add. MS 4792

Maelruanaidh, and some more of the districts and fair territories of Connacht, both ecclesiastical and lay; a king who spent and defended Cruachan with its fair borders, and the rest of the province of Connacht; a king compared to whom no king that came of his sept before him, up to Maelruanaidh Mór, obtained as much wealth and high sovereignty in territory and in church. And hence it was to praise him after his death the poet uttered these words, to illustrate his bounty, his intelligence, and his generosity, when he said, the productive vine branch of the poets and doctors; the fragrant fruit tree of the learned and gamesters; the sheltering tree of guests and strangers; the triumphant ever-shady tree of the brughaidhs and biatachs; the generating furnace of prowess and honour; the golden ridge-pole of generosity; the bounteous, decisive, truly learned prince; the defensive column of the right and justice of the Clann-Maelruanaidh, in accordance with their privileges and old books; a Cormac Ua Cuinn-cet-chathaigh in knowledge, skill, and sciences; the Cuchulainn of the territory of Connacht in contending against, and triumphing over, enemies and pirates; the rewarding, generous, Guaire of the race of Muiredhach Muillethain; the Laech-Liathmhaine of Leth-Cuinn for generosity, truth, and bounty; a man who preserved his fame, his name, his repute, his charity, his humanity, and his good intelligence, from the age of infancy to the time of his death, and even at the hour of death, free from satire or reproach, censure or malediction, rebuke or envy; who spent his sovereignty and great lordship, his wealth and large property, according to the desire of his own great heart. But though it would be excessive to relate, and copious to completely illustrate, and though the most learned could not calculate, the power of his sovereignty over the districts and fair territories throughout the greater part of Connacht, both ecclesiastical and lay, he left not the value of one groat of inheritance; but he earned the blessing of patrons and ecclesiastics, poets and doctors, the poor and widows, strangers and orphans, the infirm and pilgrims, martyrs, and victims of heavy sickness, guests and exiles, for himself, and for his posterity, and heirs. He obtained, moreover, prodigious bounty and gifts from the elect Trinity, viz, illness without pain, without oppression, without anguish, without horror, and the command of his own sense, memory, reason, and understanding, until he experienced pure penance, and great penitence for his faults after spending nearly eighty years. And three score years of this period he was abbot in Trinity-Island on Loch-Cé, and on Loch-uachtair, and nineteen years chief lord over all the territories of the Clann-Maelruanaidh; and the half of every year of these he spent in an encampment on Machaire-Connacht, in despite of many of the Foreigners and Gaeidhel of Erinn, and of all other neighbours; (or it was forty-two years, perhaps, Mac Diarmada spent in that manner); and the place in which his fortified camp was wont to be during that time was near Sceithin-na-cend, and near Fuaran-Gar and near Imaire-Maighe-hAi, and on each side of them. But the disease from which there is no escape, and which cannot be avoided, attacked him, and he died after communion, after Mass, and after precept, on Maundy Thursday, on Carraig-Mic-Diarmada; and his body was nobly, honourably, interred in the abode of the saints, and the bed of the patrons, i.e. in Trinity Island, as he himself had ordered that he should be buried in the sepulchre of the preceding abbots, to exhibit, and manifest, his wisdom and knowledge, and to renounce pride, and to magnify the honour of the church after him. His soul afterwards journeyed to the general Pasch without end or limit in saecula saeculorum. Amen.

It was for him, therefore, the author composed the stanza,

> Sixty-eight years, certain to me,
> Five hundred, and a thousand years,
> From the birth of Christ, a long record,
> To the death of Ruaidhri Mac Diarmada.

Moreover, Mac Diarmada's country was made a harp without music, and a church without an abbot, after the death of Ruaidhri Mac Diarmada, for numerous evils came after his decease, viz the ruin and destruction of the power which the Clann-Maelruanaidh possessed up to that time. Their ardour and spirit were blunted; their brughaidhs, and biatachs, and widows were impoverished; their patrons, and professors, and airchinneachs were expelled, and many of their princes and nobles were annihilated and slain.

[Bliadain fhuar ainfinech esbadach an bhliadain si, ocus as beg ant ingnad sin, oir is innti adbath Mac Diarmada .i. Ruaidhri Mac Taidhg mic Ruaidri óig .i. rí mhoighe Luirg ocus Airtigh ocus tire Tuathail, ocus airdtigerna ar crich chlainni Mhaolruanaidh go huilidhi, ocus araill do criochaib ocus do caom thuathaib Connacht, a gcill ocus a tuaith; rí ro chaith ocus ro chossuin Cruachan co na caomoireraibh,

ocus cúiged Connacht airchena; ri nac bhfuair aon rí dá dtainig da
aicme roime riam, go Maolruanaidh mór, oired inmhe ocus ard
fhlaithis ris a tuaith ocus a negluis; conadh dia mholadh a haithli a
bháis ro raidh an fili na focail se, dfhoillsiughad a einigh ocus a aithne
ocus a eslabra fair, conebirt, Geg iothmar fhínemhna na néigius ocus
na nollaman, Craobh cumra chnuaiss na gcliar ocus na gcerrbach, Dóss
diona na ndámh ocus na ndeoraidh, Bile buadha buan fhoscaidh na
mbrughaid ocus na mbiattach. Indeoin forais an engnuma ocus an
einigh; féige forórdha na féle, an flaith fial foirglidi fireolach; colamhan
cosanta cirt ocus córa clainni Mhaolruanaidh do reir a sochair ocus a
senleabhar. Cormac ua Cuinn cet cathaigh dfhios ocus deolus ocus
dealadhnachaibh; Cuchulainn criche Connacht re cosnum ocus re
cathbhuadha ar bhídhbadaibh, ocus ar bhith dhanaraibh; Guaire duas-
sach degh oinigh tslechta Muireghaigh mhuillethain; Laoch
Liathmhuine Leithe Cuinn ar fhéile, ar fhirinne, ar oinech; fer do
coiméid a chlú ocus a ainm, ocus a áiremh, a dheirc ocus a dhaonnacht
ocus a dheghaithne, o aois naoidhentacht go hionmhaidh a éga, ocus
a nam an égai feissin, gan aoir gan imdergad, gan égnach gan escuine,
gan oirbire gan athiomrádh, ro chaith a ríghe ocus a ro flaithes, a shaidh-
bhres ocus a shior inmhe, do réir mhenman a mhór croidhe bhud-
héin. Acht chena, ger bhádhbhal re fhaisnéis ocus ger lionmar re lán-
foillsiugad, ocus gidh nár bhéidir a ríom re na ro eolchaib treissi a
thigernais ar na criochaib ocus ar na caomthuathaib ar fedh urmhóir
Chonnacht a cill ocus a tuaith, ni ro fhágaibh luach én bhuinn
doighrecht, acht amháin ro thuill bennachtain ocus buidechus érlomh
ocus egoilsech, fhiledh ocus ollaman, bhocht ocus bhaintreabtach,
dheoraidh ocus dhíllechtadh, anbhfann ocus oilithrech, aossa martra
ocus mórghalair, aoidhed ocus ionnorptach, dhó féin ocus dá iarsma
ocus dá oighredhaib. Fuair fós tabartus ocus tidhlucadh
tromadhbail on Trinóid thoghaide tre persanaigh .i. galar gan accair
gan anbfhorlonn, gan ghuaiss gan gráin, a chiall ocus a chuimne, a
ressún ocus a rothuicsi féin ar a chommus, go bhfuair aithrighe iodhan
ocus aithrechus adhbail ina chionaid, iar gcaithemh ochtmhodha bliadhan achtmad suaill, ocus trí fichid bliadan dibhsin na ab ar oilén na
Trinóide for Loch Cé ocus for Loch uachtair, ocus bliadhuin is lugha
nó fiche na airdtigerna ar criochaib clainni Mhaolruanaidh go huilidhi,
ocus leth gach aon bhliadna dhibhsin a bfhoslongport ar machaire
Chonnacht, daimhdheoin moráin do Ghalloib ocus do Ghaoidhealaib
Erenn ocus gach comarsan áirchena; nó gomad dá bhliadain ocus dá

fichet ro chaith Mac Diarmada ar an ordugadsin; ocus issé ionad inam-
bidh a fhoslongport ar an bfhedhsin go gnathach .i. um sgeithín na
gcend ocus um fhuarán nGar, ocus um iomaire moighe hOi, ocus ar
gach taobh dhíbh. Acht chena rodiormuis an teidhm tar nach dtíaghar,
ocus ar nach eidir iomgabáil fair, co bfhuair bass comna iar naiffrenn
ocus iar bproigept, Dardaoin mandáil ar cairrig Mic Diarmada, ocus
gurrus ádhlucadh a corp go huasal onorach a nadhbha na naom ocus
a niomdha na nérlum .i. for oilén na Trinóide, amail ro ordaig fein a
chur a nadhlucad na nab roime, do admháil ocus do fhoillsiugad a
egna ocus a eoluis, ocus do dhiultagad don diomus, ocus do mhédugad onóra na hegluisi na dhiaidh. Ro asgnám a anum íarsin ar an
gcaisc gcoitchinn gan chrich gan fhoirchend in sécula seculorum,
Amen; coinidh dó ro ráidh ant uchdar an rann,

> Ocht mbliadna sescu derbh dham,
> Cuig ced is míle bliadan,
> O ghein Crist, oiris fada,
> Báss Ruaidhrí Mic Diarmada.

Acht chena, do righnedh cruid gan chéis ocus ceall gan abad, ocus tír
gan tigerna, do thír Mic Diarmada ahaithle bháis Ruaidhrí Mic
Diarmada, óir tangadar uilc iomdha iar na ég .i. díth ocus dilghend
Chlainni Mhaolruanaidh fo na nert conuige sin. Ro maoladh a menma
ocus a meisnech; ro bochtaighed a brughada ocus a biattaigh ocus a
baintreabhthaigh; ro hionnarbad a hérloim ocus a hollamain ocus a
hoirchinnigh; ro mughaigedh ocus ro marbad morán dá macaibh righ
ocus deghdhaoinibh.][2]

The story is long, complex, seemingly turning back on itself at a number of
points, deploying both prose and syllabic verse. It is clearly very important.
Death, as the obituary recalled was inevitable, it was 'the disease from which
there is no escape' [an teidhm tar nach dtíaghar]. During life individuals were

2 *ALC*, ii, pp 396–405. The obituary is in the same hand in both manuscripts. Although not the hand of
Brian Mac Diarmada, there can be little doubt that he had a direct input into its form and content. In
addition to the text as given in the printed edition, the Dublin manuscript of the Annals of Loch Cé
includes thirteen lines of encomiums in the same hand, (TCD, MS 1293, f.134), which are not found in
BL, Add. MS 4792. These were clearly planned as an integral part of the entry for that year, as the manuscript text divides into two columns to accommodate them; they are not 'in the margin' as Hennessy suggested (*ALC*, ii, p. 398, n.1). Each phrase repeats the initial word 'fear' (man) and contains a sequence of
eulogistic adjectives descriptive of Ruaidhrí's personal characteristics, conveying the sense of an intelli-
gent, kind and likeable leader.

conscious of their own mortality, although the annalists rarely adverted to the fact in their historical compilations. In a notebook kept by Pilib Ballach Ó Duibhgeannáin, one of compilers of the Annals of Loch Cé, a quatrain on death is recorded which was probably well known since it also features in a late fifteenth-century Butler manuscript

> Whether morning or evening,
> on land or at sea,
> though I know I shall die,
> alas, I know not when.
>
> [In ba maiden in ba fuin
> in ba for tir no for muir,
> Ach ri fetar radad d'héc
> mor i[n] bed ni fetar cuin.][3]

Pilib Ballach also noted down a quatrain on the same theme from the early sixteenth-century life of St Colum Cille by Maghnus Ó Domhnaill which also occurs in the sixteenth-century life of Máedóc of Ferns

> Three little sods that cannot be shunned,
> As they say in the proverb;
> The sod of his birth, the sod of his death,
> And the sod of his burying.
>
> [Tri fodain nach sechantar,
> mar aderid a mor-fhocuil:
> fód a gene, fód a bais,
> 7 fod a adhnacail.][4]

The same notebook recorded further verses on the theme of the inevitability of death, including another also found in the Butler manuscript

> Do not swear
> by the sod on which you stand.

3 NLI, MS G1 f. 73v; Myles Dillon, 'Laud 610' in *Celtica*, vi (1963), pp 150–1.   4 NLI, MS G1, f. 73; A. O'Kelleher and G. Schoepperle (eds), *Betha Colaim Chille* (Illinois, 1918), pp 102–3. The date of composition is, of course, much earlier as this quatrain occurs in Adamnán's life of Colum Cille; Charles Plummer (ed.), *Bethada náem nErenn* (2 vols, Oxford, 1922), i, p. 236, ii, p. 229

You shall be over it but a short time:
for a long time you will be under it.

[Ná luidh na luidh
an fod for atai:
gairit bia fair
fada bia fai.]⁵

Death was an ever-present reality in this world and remembering lives and deaths
was an important function of the annalistic record which served as a creator
and preserver of social memory.

In this case remembering the life and death of Ruaidhrí Mac Diarmada
was clearly of importance to his son. Ruaidhrí had been lord of the Mac
Diarmada lordship since 1549 and earlier entries in the annals had traced his
career from the time of his inauguration, discussed in the first story in this
volume. After his death, according to the annals, 'Another person i.e.
Toirdhelbhach, the son of Eoghan Mac Diarmada, was made king in his place,
with the consent of the church and laity, of ecclesiastics and ollamhs.' [Araill
eli .i. Toirrdhealbach Mac Eoghan Mic Diarmada do riogad ina ionad, do thoil
chille ocus tuaithi, eglaisi ocus ollaman.]⁶ The portrayal of the fate of the lordship after the death of Brian Mac Diarmada's father does not suggest that the
annalist approved of the succession despite its legitimacy. By 1570 his branch
of the family and that of Toirdhealbach Mac Diarmada were in open warfare.⁷
Remembering the older rule was clearly an important validation of Brian's own
claim to the lordship and to his succession to the position of lord by 1585.

Remembering a death also had a religious imperative. As a later obituary
of Ruaidhrí's grandson, Brian Óg, scribbled at the back of the manuscript of
the Annals of Loch Cé noted,

for every doctor and divine says that when the life is pure, so is the
death; and if the death is good and pure, that one will obtain the suitable reward beyond.

[oir adber gach doctuir ocus gach diadaire an tan as eatal an betha
gurab amlaid an bas, ocus mad maith ocus mad andocc an bas go
bfuighe an focraig tall amail as techta do.]⁸

5 NLI, MS G1, f. 72v; Dillon, 'Laud 610', pp 152–3. 6 *ALC*, ii, pp 404–5. 7 *ALC*, ii, pp 406–9. 8 *ALC*,
ii, pp 518–19.

A story in the mid fifteenth-century Connacht manuscript *Liber Flavus Fergusiorum*, also contrasted the good and bad deaths and their rewards: heaven or hell.[9] The same manuscript also offered help in the form of an office for the dying in a question and answer format.[10] Ruaidhrí Mac Diarmada's death had been a good one. It had taken place on an auspicious date in the Christian calendar, the Thursday of Holy Week, and he had been fortified not only by hearing Mass and the sermon [precept] but also by communion, and by implication confession, which was required at Easter.

These rituals marked Ruaidhrí's physical detachment from the world but not his complete departure from it. As the obituary portrayed it he had gone on a journey 'ar an gcaisc gcoitchinn' [to the general Easter] or to the general resurrection which was believed to occur at the end of time. The journey to resurrection was through the otherworld of purgatory. At least part of this, the *limbus patrum* where the prophets and patriarchs who had died before the coming of Christ waited, was well known through the text known as the 'Harrowing of hell'. This described how Christ, after his entombment, descended into hell and freed its inhabitants who previously had no access to Christian salvation. One of the compilers of the Annals of Loch Cé had certainly encountered this text and had copied extracts in his notebook; another version circulated in the *Liber Flavus Fergusiorum*.[11] Moreover, the supposed location of an entrance to purgatory at Lough Derg in south Donegal probably heightened awareness of the tradition in north Connacht.[12] Purgatory was perceived, at one level, as a separate, distinct place but at another level there were connections between purgatory and the everyday world. Stories circulated of returns from the spirit world to seek revenge, to give counsel or to finish some piece of business. Most crucially what was done in the natural world was seen as affecting the supernatural one. Masses and prayers for the dead were deemed to shorten the period the deceased would spend in purgatory, although a note derived from St Ambrose in Pilib Ó Duibhgeannáin's notebook proclaimed that hearing one Mass devoutly when alive was better than a thousand Masses said for one's soul after death.[13] Those who had died relied on the prayers of

---

9 Carl Marstrander (ed.), 'The two deaths' in *Ériu*, v (1911), pp 120–5. For the provenance of the manuscript see Edward Gwynn, 'The manuscript known as the *Liber Flavus Fergusiorum*' in *Proceedings of the Royal Irish Academy*, xxvi, sect. C (1906–7), p. 15; *Catalogue of Irish manuscripts in the Royal Irish Academy*, pp 1254–73. 10 RIA, MS 23 O 48, f. 22v. 11 NLI, MS G1, ff 81–7; William Gillies (ed.), 'An early modern Irish "Harrowing of hell"' in *Celtica*, xiii (1980), pp 32–55. 12 For the tradition see Michael Haren and Yolande de Pontfarcy (eds), *The medieval pilgrimage to St Patrick's Purgatory* (Enniskillen, 1988). 13 NLI, MS G1, f. 44v.

the communion of saints since they could no longer intercede for themselves. Remembering the dead through Masses and prayers, and encouraging others to remember the dead as part of the community through memorialisation, was therefore an important part of daily life with a well-established social, cultural and religious grammar of remembering. This concern with commemoration may help to explain why Brian Mac Diarmada's obituary for his father is so long and complex. It is not typical of the other obituaries in the annals, but a contextualisation of its form and content can offer insights into attitudes towards life, death, and eternity, among those who lived in late sixteenth-century Connacht.

I

Annalistic obituaries were usually short, pithy, and formulaic, often exploiting a series of rhetorical devices.[14] Among the early sixteenth-century examples in the Annals of Connacht, that for Cathal Mac Diarmada in 1530 was typical of an obituary for a particularly noteworthy person:

> Cathal son of Ruaidri Mac Diarmada, the captain who of all his contemporaries most harassed and harried his enemies and foes and was the best patron of poets and exiles and poor people and the men of every art, died.
>
> [Cathal Mac Ruaidri Meic Diarmada, cenn fedhna is mo do bhuaidhir 7 do bhúainmill da bhidhbadaib 7 da escaraid a comaimsir fris et dob ferr do cenn damh 7 deorad 7 deibhlenn 7 d'aos gaca cerde archena, d'ecc.][15]

More straightforward and concise was the obituary for Diarmait Mac Donnchadha in the following year, 'Diarmait son of Sean son of Aed son of Maelruanaid, the most generous and the noblest of the posterity of Maelruanaid Mac Donnchada, died' [Diarmait mac Seain meic Aodho mec Maoilruanaidh, duine dob eile 7 dob firuaisle do slicht Maolruanaid Meic Donnchada, d'eg.][16] Such short entries clearly served a particular function. They were inserted to ensure that the subject of the obit was remembered and that

---

14 Wilson McLeod, 'The rhetorical geography of the late medieval Irish chronicles' in *Cambrian Medieval Celtic Studies*, no. 40 (Winter 2000), pp 57–68.   15 *AConn*, pp 672–5.   16 *AConn*, pp 676–7.

his most noteworthy past exploits were commemorated, but they are devoid of personal comment and involvement by the author.

Unsurprisingly there is much more personal emotion in the 1568 obituary for Brian Mac Diarmada's own father but it is still a formal, restrained, text. There is nothing about Brian's personal grief and, indeed, the relationship between the annalist and the subject of the obituary is never made explicit. In another instance, however, Brian recorded a much more personalised obituary, intruding himself and his grief into the text. When in 1581 Calbhach Ó Conchobhair, Brian's friend and brother of his future wife died, Brian included in the Annals of Loch Cé a long and emotive obituary

> and the death of this only son of Domhnall O'Conchobhair, and of Mor, daughter of O'Ruairc, is one of the great woes of Erinn; and there never came of the race of Brian Luighnech a man of his years a greater loss than he, and it is not likely that there will come. And this loss has grieved the hearts of Connacht, and it has especially grieved the poets and doctors of the province of Connacht; and it has divided my own heart into two parts. Alas! alas! wretched is my condition after my comrade and companion, and the person who was the choicest and dearest to me in the world. I am Brian Mac Diarmada, who wrote this on Carraig-Mic-Diarmada; and I am now to be compared to Oilill Olum after his sons, when they had been slain along with Art Enfhir, son of Conn Ced-chathach, in the battle of Magh-Mucraimhe, by Maccon, the son of Macniadh, son of Lughaidh; or to Deirdre, after the sons of Uisnech had been killed in treachery in Emhain-Macha, by Conchobhar, the son of Fachtna Fathach, son of Rossa Ruadh, son of Rudhraidhe; for I am sad, sorrowful, distressed, dispirited, in grief and anguish. And it is not possible to reckon or describe how I am this day, after the departure of my companion from me, i.e. the Calbhach, and the last day of the month of March he was interred in Sligo.

> [ocus is do sgélaib mora na hEirenn ant én mhac sin Domnaill I Conchubair ocus Moire ingine I Ruairc; ocus ni táinic do shlicht Briain Luighnigh riamh fer a aosa bud mo do scel na é, ocus ni doig co ticfa; ocus do chráidh in sgél sin croidheadha Connacht, ocus co hairithe do chráidh se éiges ocus ollumhain cuiged Connacht, ocus do comhroinn se mo croidhe féin na da chuid. Uch, uch, is truagh mar taim a ndeoigh mo cheile ocus mo companaigh, ocus an ti ba tocha

ocus do ba tairisi lem ar bith. Misi Brian mac Diarmada do sgribh sin
ar carruig Mic Diarmada, ocus is samhalta me anois re hOilioll olom
andiadh a cloinne, ar na marbad a bhfochair Airt einfir mic Cuinn ced
cathaigh a cath mhuighe Mucruimhe le Mac Con mac Maicniadh mic
Luighech, no re Deirdre tareis cloinne hUisnech do marbad a bhfeall
a nEamuin Macha, le Concubar mac Fachtna fathaigh, mic Rosa ruaidh
mic Rudhraidhe. Oir atáim gu dubach dobronach dibragoidech
domhenmnach, a ndubhaighe ocus a ndoghaillsi; ocus ní hetir a ríomh
na a innisin mar atáim aniu andiaidh mo companaigh do dhul uaim
.i. an Calbach, ocus an la deigenach do mhí Mhárta do hadhlaicedh a
Sligech é.][17]

Such personal involvement with the subject, including the use of the first person
singular, was a new departure in such obituaries. It may be that there was a particularly close personal bond, perhaps that of foster-brother, which would
explain, in part, the unconventional form of this obituary. Part of the explanation may also be the fact that Brian Mac Diarmada was not trained in the
techniques deployed by the learned class for the writing of history or poetry
but equally what we may well be seeing here is a hint of European sensibilities
appearing in the relatively rare example of a piece of prose written, or at least
contributed to, by an amateur writer. Given the tensions which Connacht society experienced in the late sixteenth century, some of which have been more
fully explored in other essays in this volume, it would be highly likely that some
of these might have manifested themselves in the form of literary innovations.
The greater emphasis on narrative in the later annals, the increased length of
many entries and the more personal tone of some entries may all be part of
this process. In the case of Brian Mac Diarmada's obituary for his father the
tone and motifs adopted were more formal as might befit the dignity of the
obituary of a chief.

II

It is evident from the general pattern of the late medieval annals that the composition of each obituary was guided by rules. Typical elements included reference to the person's genealogical connections, secular and ecclesiastical status,

17 *ALC*, ii, pp 434–7.

specific personal or political attributes and the manner of death and burial. Other contemporary literary forms also provided ground rules for memorialisation. The *marbhna*, or poetic lament, written after the death of a lord fulfilled the same political/literary purpose as the annalistic obituary in a highly structured way. In many respects the obituary drafted by Brian Mac Diarmada for his father is an adaptation of the poetic lament.[18] Indeed the syllabic verse quoted in the annalistic entry may well be derived from the formal lament written on Mac Diarmada's death. The *marbhna*, '*Teasda Éire san Esbáinn*', written on the death of Aodh Ruadh Ó Domhnaill in 1602, for instance, comprises a sequence of well-structured parts.[19] It opens with a lament for Aodh stressing the loss Ireland had suffered so that 'Ireland is a ship without a rudder' [Arthrach gan sdiuir Banbha Breagh]. The second part of the poem is historical, setting Aodh into a much wider context. This draws on both classical precedents and the world of early Irish history and in doing so attempts to universalise the significance of Aodh. The final element of the poem is a celebration of Aodh himself, listing his victories and linking his departure to the collapse of the fortunes of the Irish. A *marbhna* for the Roscommon poet Muiris Mac Torna Uí Mhaoil Chonaire, who died in 1645, contains a similar three part structure. '*Máthair na horchra an éigsi*' first expresses grief for the loss of the poet, then seeks to universalise that experience by claiming that the loss of Muiris will have severe repercussions on the poetic world of Ireland, and finally there is a celebration of the poet's specific attributes.[20]

Not all the surviving poetry of lamentation conforms exactly to this model. Apart from this formalised and structured *marbhna* there were less formal types of lament including the *caoine* and the *feartlaoi*, all of which fulfilled different functions.[21] The non-syllabic verse in the annalistic obituary may derive from such a poem. One lament by Fionnghuala iníon Dhomhnaill Uí Bhriain on the death of her husband Uaithne Mór Ó Lochlainn, who died in 1617, begins with lamentation and moves into a historical perspective by citing her husband's

---

18 Katharine Simms, 'The poet as chieftain's widow: bardic elegies' in Donnchadh Ó Corráin, Liam Breatnach and Kim McCone (eds), *Sages, saints and storytellers* (Maynooth, 1989), pp 400–11. 19 P.A. Breatnach (ed.), 'Marbhna Aodha Ruaidh Uí Dhomhnaill' in *Éigse*, xv (1973–4), pp 34–50. For other similar compositions see R.B. Breatnach (ed.), 'An elegy on Donal O'Sullivan Beare' in *Éigse*, vii (1953–5), pp 162–81; Paul Walsh (ed.), *Gleanings from Irish manuscripts* (2nd ed., Dublin, 1933), pp 29–48 on Niall Garbh Ó Domhnaill. 20 Réamann Ó Muireadhaigh (ed.), 'Marbhna ar Mhuiris Mac Torna Uí Mhaolchonaire' in *Éigse*, xv (1973–4), pp 215–21. 21 P.A. Breatnach, 'The poet's graveside vigil: a theme of Irish bardic elegy in the fifteenth century' in *Zeitschrift für Celtische Philologie*, xlix–l (1997), pp 50–63. The *caoine* was the most commented on by English observers, D.B. Quinn, *The Elizabethans and the Irish* (Ithaca, 1966), pp 24–5, 83; Kew, 'The Irish sections of Fynes Moryson's unpublished itinerary', p. 110.

genealogy but has little to say about his achievements. Instead, it contains
Fionnghuala's appeal to the fourth earl of Thomond for help after her husband's death.[22] Such a late example may not be typical of what had gone before
but in one poem of the 1550s lamenting the death of the Baron Delvin, the
poet, William Nugent, explicitly declared that he would not deal with the
caithréim or battle achievements of the deceased. This comment suggests that
such a description was normal but could be omitted.[23] Again a lament by
Diarmuid mac an Bhacaigh Ó Clúmháin for Ó hEadhra, probably of the late
fifteenth century, conforms only occasionally to the normal thematic pattern.[24]
It seems therefore that mourning opened a range of literary possibilities from
the formal to the more informal and provided a range of options for the selection of themes and topics in the composition of an obituary.

The prose obituary for Ruaidhrí mac Diarmada in the Annals of Loch
Cé is rather less organised than the formal *marbhna* but it shows many of the
same traits and draws on similar sources for its motifs. It appeals to the past
and lists his achievements within the context of a lament at both the beginning and the end of the text. It also appears to draw on other annalistic obituaries for some of its stock of heroic analogies and literary terminology. He
was, for instance, praised for his generosity to poets, which the first essay in
this volume argued was necessary to the formation of cultural capital necessary for a good lordship. Over a third of the 163 obituaries recorded in the
Annals of Loch Cé between 1500 and 1590 highlighted generosity as an important attribute of the deceased and about 10 per cent identified poets as important to the deceased and another 10 per cent of obituaries recorded the deceased
as charitable. Again the highlighting of Ruaidhrí's religious sensibilities was
in line with almost a quarter of the other obituaries in the late sixteenth-century Loch Cé annals. The similarities with other annalistic obituary writing
does not stop with general attributes but extends to the language used. The
phrase 'his body was nobly, honourably interred' [ádhlucadh a corp go huasal
onorach] echoes numerous obituaries in the Annals of Connacht, not least
that of Cathal Croibhdhearg in 1224, and implies an honourable burial ritual
appropriate to a king.[25] Comparison with traditional heroes are more common
in eulogistic verse than in the prose annals, but there are precedents in the late
medieval annals for likening the subject of the obituary to Cú Chulainn, Guaire

22 'A nainm an Spioraid Naoimh h'imrighe, 'Uaithne', L.P. Ó Murchú (ed.) 'Caoineadh ar Uaithne Ó Lochlainn,
1617' in Éigse, xxvii (1993), pp 67–77. 23 'Brónach Goill Bhanba dá éis', Eamonn Ó Tuathail, 'Nugentiana' in
Éigse, ii (1940), p. 11. 24 'Bráidhe ón éigsi a n-Eas Dara', Lambert McKenna (ed.), The book of O'Hara (Dublin,
1951), pp 314–21. 25 AConn, pp 4–5, 80–1, 100–1, 210–11, 214–15.

and others. Ruaidhrí Mac Diarmada's depiction as the Cú Chulainn of Connacht is matched by the Annals of Connacht description of Toirdhealbhach Ó Conchobhair Ruadh, king of Connacht who died in 1425, as the Cú Chulainn of his times, and that of Cathal Óg, son of Mac Raghnaill, in the same annals as the Cú Chulainn of Conmaicne in 1524.[26] In each instance the Connacht annalists were appropriating to themselves a heroic figure with traditional Ulster associations, seemingly ignoring, in their search for heroic analogies, the traditional rivalry between Connacht and Ulster that stories of Cú Chulainn represented.

It is clear that these analogies were not random affairs. When the early sixteenth-century annalists wrote obituaries for Aodh Dubh Ó Domhnaill in 1537 they explicitly compared him to Brian Bóroimhe.[27] On the face of it this seems a strange comparison to make but it become more comprehensible in the light of the fact that Aodh Dubh's mother was from the Ó Briain family of Clare. It seems that it was through this route that Maghnus Ó Domhnaill had a copy of the twelfth-century Uí Bhriain propagandistic text *Cogadh Gaedhel re Gallaibh* in the 1530s.[28] In most cases the stock of motifs were drawn from local tradition. When Ruaidhrí Mac Diarmada's generosity is likened to that of Guaire Aidne, a seventh-century king of Connacht, the analogy echoed an obituary for an earlier Ruaidhrí Mac Diarmada who had died in 1421, and also a long and elaborate memorial for Aodh Dubh Ó Domhnaill who died in 1537.[29] Elsewhere in the same obituaries where Aodh Dubh was likened to Conn Cétchathach for his warlike activities, Ruaidhrí Mac Diarmada was compared with Conn's grandson, Cormac ua Cuinn Chétchathaigh, on account of his knowledge and skill.[30] The fact that the forename Cormac was a traditionally popular one in the Mac Diarmada family may partially explain Brian Mac Diarmada's choice of heroic analogy here. Whether or not this is the case it is evident that the analogies reflect the literary milieu of the area. Stories featuring these characters appear in manuscripts copied in the area from the mid-fifteenth century. Some of the same kind of heroic analogies are also found in the obituary of Calbhach Ó Conchobhair, close friend of Brian Mac Diarmada.[31] While in the seventeenth century the Counter Reformation clergy

26 *AConn*, pp 468–9, 654–5. The motif of Mac Diarmada as Cú Chulainn appears in a poem of the 1590s, Lambert McKenna (ed.), *Dioghluim dána* (Dublin, 1938), p. 304.   27 *AU*, iii, pp 614–15; *AConn*, pp 704–5. 28 O'Kelleher and Schoepperle (eds), *Betha Colaim Chille*, pp 6–7.   29 *AConn*, pp 454–5, 704–5.   30 *AConn*, 704–5; *ALC*, ii, pp 398–9. Curiously, these heroic analogies are omitted from the corresponding obituary of Aodh Dubh Ó Domhnaill in the Loch Cé annals, *ALC*, ii, pp 306–9.   31 Stories featuring these figures appear in BL, Egerton MS 1782; NLI, MS G1; RIA, MS 23 O 48 and National Library of Scotland, MS 72.2.3 [Glenmasan MS] all of which can be associated with this area.

would try to reduce the status of these heroic figures, by minimising their powers, they still held powerful sway in the world of traditional religion during the sixteenth century.[32]

The 1568 entry for Ruaidhrí Mac Diarmada in the Annals of Loch Cé has all the standard elements of an annalistic obituary. It includes a summary genealogy, a statement of the extent of his political jurisdiction, and a reference to his secular and ecclesiastical importance. His dual status as a man of note in secular and ecclesiastical spheres is emphasised. His particular attributes are elaborately recorded, and the manner of his death and burial are described. In addition to these standard features, the entry includes some unusual elements: the opening reference to the adverse weather that marked the year of his death, and the closing section which stressed the loss suffered by the Mac Diarmada lordship as a consequence of his death. Whereas it was more usual for annalistic obituaries to refer to the appointment of a successor as the most significant consequence of the death of a chief, and thereby infer a certain continuity in the history of the family and the lordship, the obituary for Ruaidhrí Mac Diarmada did not entirely conform to this pattern. Instead, it described the consequences of the death for the bereaved in a manner more akin to a formal bardic elegy.[33] By departing from the usual annalistic formula and incorporating instead the sentiments of a poetic elegy, the focus was directed almost exclusively on the deceased person rather than the broader context of the lordship. Rather than simply affirming the status of the lordship by reference to Ruaidhrí's successor, it drew attention instead to the extent of the catastrophic loss, where all that was left was the memory of this once great leader. Although the succession of Toirdhealbhach Mac Eoghain Mhic Diarmada was recorded in a final sentence, the Mac Diarmada lordship was depicted in the obituary as one whose significance now relied on the commemoration of the illustrious life and virtuous death of a noble and heroic ancestor.

There are significant parallels between the structure of the obituary for Ruaidhrí Mac Diarmada and that in the Annals of Connacht for Cathal Croibhdhearg Ó Conchobhair, king of Connacht who died in 1224.[34] The pathetic fallacy of the opening lines of each obituary serves to emphasise the exceptional loss of a significant leader, though the more far-fetched claims in the obituary for the Ó Conchobhair king of Connacht are not used for Mac

---

32 For example Keating's insistence that the deeds Fianna were the result of imagination and they were not superhuman, Geoffrey Keating, *Foras feasa ar Éirinn* ed. David Comyn and P.S. Dinneen (4 vols, London, 1902–14), ii, pp 326–7, 330–1.   33 Breatnach, 'The poet's graveside vigil', p. 51.   34 *AConn*, pp 2–5 and *ALC*, i, pp 268–9.

Diarmada.[35] The statement of political status which follows is also more circumspect in the case of Mac Diarmada, and while he could not be portrayed as king of Connacht, his kingly status was repeatedly asserted in phrases beginning with the word 'king' [rí], which imitates the form of the obituary of Cathal Croibhdhearg. Although it is nowhere explicitly stated that he was king of Connacht, Ruaidhrí Mac Diarmada was portrayed as defender of Crúachu, symbolic heart of the kingdom of Connacht. The noble and honourable burial of the 'king' in a monastery with which he had a particular connection again paralleled the earlier king of Connacht and affirmed his personal patronage of the church as well as the sanctity of his own soul.

The inclusion of citations from poetic compositions was not a regular feature of annalistic obituaries, but it occurs in both the obituaries of Cathal Croibhdhearg and Ruaidhrí Mac Diarmada. Such verses emphasised the social importance and high political standing of the subject of the obituary. Their inclusion may have been designed to heighten the emotional impact of the obituary by recalling the social setting of the oral performance of a commemorative elegy. While there are also significant differences between the Loch Cé obituary of Ruaidhrí Mac Diarmada and the obituary of Cathal Croibhdhearg Ó Conchobhair with which the Annals of Connacht opens, the extent of the similarities are sufficient to suggest that the obituary of the illustrious king of Connacht had been read closely by and influenced the thinking of the compiler of the annalistic entry on the death of Ruaidhrí Mac Diarmada, 'king of Moylurg'.

III

One important aspect of the career of Ruaidhrí Mac Diarmada which the annalistic entry celebrated but which other literary forms, such as the *marbhna*, rarely touched on was religion. To attempt to reconstruct the religious beliefs of Ruaidhrí Mac Diarmada in any detail would be an impossible. The obituary certainly attributes Christian virtues to Ruaidhrí. For instance it records that his wish to be buried among the canons at Loch Key was as a result of the renunciation of pride. This implies that his choice of burial place signified equiva-

35 The obituary of Cathal Croibhdhearg in *ALC* does not make the same explicit connection between the adverse weather and the death of the king, and in this and other features the version of the more condensed and standardised obituary of Cathal Croibhdhearg found in *ALC* could not be said strictly to provide a model for Brian Mac Diarmada's obituary of his father.

lence of status with any member of that religious community and renunciation of any claim to higher temporal status as a lord. Pride, according to a note in Pilib Ó Duibhgeannáin's notebook, was one of the three reasons why God would choose to shorten a sinner's life.[36] This kind of simple spirituality was based not on doctrine but on the avoidance of sins affecting the whole community (pride being one of the Seven Deadly Sins) and prompting social grace through the Seven Works of Mercy (also carefully noted in Ó Duibhgeannáin's notebook).[37] However, other attributes recorded in the obituary, such as generosity to the poor, strangers, pilgrims, guests, and the sick, were somewhat more ambiguous. As the first essay in this volume suggests generosity was an important political attribute. Moreover, generosity was not just a Christian virtue but by this date were also associated in the popular mind with ancient secular heroes. The annalist's obituary had likened Ruaidhrí to Guaire, a Connacht hero whose main claim to fame was his reputation for extraordinary generosity. The analogy with Guaire's generosity was as much an allusion to heroic virtue as to a specifically Christian one.[38] To define holy living in terms of Christian virtues would be to place the power of definition in the hands of churchmen. The annalist's understanding of Ruaidhrí's fate is perhaps closer to that which the Jesuit William Good encountered in Limerick in the late sixteenth century when he noted that the Irish 'suppose that the souls of such that are deceased go into the company of certain men ... touching whom they retain fables and songs as of giants Fin MacHyule, Oscar MacOshin'.[39] Christian heaven understood in this way could accommodate secular heroes as well as saints.

One way of trying to understand the religious aspects of Ruaidhrí's obituary is through the record of his burial. The selection of a burial place was clearly of some importance. The basic desire to know and commemorate the location of a grave so that it could be visited was one element. How frequent the custom of visiting graves was is not known but in one commemorative Sligo poem of the late fifteenth or early sixteenth century the poet speaks of standing beside Ó hEadhra's grave. Though partly a literary device, the visit to the grave is portrayed as an event that took place some time after the funeral. In another early seventeenth-century poem of lamentation Eoghan Mac an Bhaird indicates that women visiting the graves of deceased men was normal

---

36 NLI, MS G1, f. 44. This text corresponds to item 1 in Brian Ó Cuív (ed.), 'Tréidhe sa nua-Ghaeilge' in *Éigse*, ix (1959–60), p. 180.   37 NLI, MS G1, f. 44.   38 Maud Joynt (ed.), *Tromdámh Guaire* (Dublin, 1931) which on linguistic grounds is probably fifteenth century, Keating, *Foras feasa ar Éirinn*, iii, pp 61–5 130–1. For other references to Guaire in the literature see Máirín O'Daly, 'Mesce Chúanach' in *Ériu*, xix (1962), pp 75–80.   39 William Camden, *Britannia* (London, 1610), p. 147.

practice. Mac an Bhaird's poem, 'A bhean fuair faill ar an bhfear', contrasts the soli-
tude of Nuala Ní Dhomhnaill at the Roman grave of her father with the large
number of mourners that would have accompanied her on visits to the grave
if it were in Ireland.[40]

On occasions the choice of burial place could be unconventional. The
Annals of Loch Cé recorded under 1581 the death of an eminent cleric, Brian
Caech Ó Coinnegáin

> and the place of burial which he selected for himself was i.e. to be
> buried at the mound of Ballintober. And we think it was not through
> want of religion Brian Caech made this selection, but because he saw
> not the service of God practised in any church near him at that time.
>
> [ocus isi roimh annlaicthe do thogh se fein dó .i. a adhlucadh ag dumha
> Baile an Tobair, ocus isé mhesmaoid nach o droch creidemh do rinne
> Brian Caoch an togha sin, acht mar nach bfhacaidh sé seirbhis De da
> dénamh a néin eaglais na fhochair san aimsir si.][41]

The selection of a fairy mound as a burial place was not a decision to be taken
lightly. Such fairy mounds were dangerous places. A local tradition recounted
in Pilib Ó Duibhgeannáin's notebook claimed that those who believed in the
presence in fairy mounds of the Tuatha Dé Danann would be damned.[42]
Ballintober appears to have had both pagan and Christian associations however, and when Diarmaid Ó Conchobhair Donn was buried in Ballintober in
1589 the annalist noted that he was interred 'under the protection of God and
Brigid' [fa diden De ocus Brigdi.][43] Choosing to be buried in consecrated ground
associated with a monastic house or church was part of the salvation strategy
of a Christian person. Many individuals appealed to patron saints whom they
hoped would be patrons and intercessors for them at the last judgement. Thus
in one poem of the late sixteenth-century, 'Ceanglam re chéile, a Chormuic', Irial Ó
hUiginn added a last verse which implored

> O John [the] Baptist, when this abode [the world] has passed away
> take me with thee; if, O my friend, I cling to thee my sin will be for-
> given in yonder abode [of heaven].

40 McKenna (ed.), Book of O'Hara, pp 314–15, 318–9; Eleanor Knott (ed.), 'Mac an Bhaird's elegy on the Ulster lords' in Celtica, v (1960), pp 162–5; Kew (ed.), 'The Irish sections of Fynes Moryson's unpublished itinerary', p. 110. For an earlier example see Lambert McKenna (ed.), 'Some Irish bardic poems' in Studies, xxxix (1950), pp 440–3. 41 ALC, ii, pp 436–7. 42 NLI, MS G1, f. 52v. 43 ALC, ii, pp 480–1.

15 The church on Trinity Island, Lough Key. Reproduced from
Francis Grose, *The antiquities of Ireland* (1791)

[A Eoin Baisde, beir mheisi
libh fa thásg an tigheissi;
badh réigh mh'fhala san tigh thall
ribh, a chara, dhá gceanglam.]⁴⁴

Deciding to be buried in ground attached to a monastery or church meant
choosing to be buried under the protection of a saint or saints associated with
that church. Thus, in 1527, the annalists could record that Mor, daughter of
Maelechlainn Mac Caba, was buried in Elphin 'under the protection of God
and Patrick' [fá dhíden Dé ocus Phádraic].⁴⁵ To choose to be buried outside
this context, as Brian Caech Ó Coinnegáin apparently did, meant cutting one's
self off from saintly intercession for one's soul.

     Ruaidhrí Mac Diarmada was buried on Trinity Island in Lough Key pre-
sumably in the graveyard attached to the house of Premonstratensian canons

44 McKenna (ed.), *Book of O'Hara*, pp 160–1.   45 *ALC*, ii, pp 262–3. For another example from 1543 see
AConn., pp 730–1.

there (fig. 15). This was an innovative choice for a lord of the Meic Diarmada since most of his predecessors had been buried in the Cistercian house of Boyle. The customary association with Boyle abbey was clearly of some antiquity since when Maelruanaid Mac Diarmada died near Carrick in 1522 he was 'buried in the sepulchre of his father and his grandfather in the monastery of Boyle.' [a ádhnacal a n-othurlighe a athar 7 a senathar a mainesdir na Buille.][46] The custom also continued. In 1560 Ruaidhrí, a cousin of the Ruaidhrí memorialised in 1568, died and 'he was buried in the tomb of his ancestors, i.e. in the monastery of the Boyle.' [ro hadhlucad a nothurlighe a shen é .i. a mainisdir na Buille.][47]

There may have been several reasons why Ruaidhrí Mac Diarmada chose to depart from family tradition and not be buried at Boyle. The effective partition of the lordship in 1538 left Boyle in the hands of the branch of the family which did not control Carraig Mhic Diarmada. However, this cannot have been a major consideration since Ruaidhrí himself had retaken the monastery in 1562.[48] More significant may have been the burning of the monastery in 1555.[49] How much repair work, if any, was carried out is not known but by 1569 the house was dissolved and granted to Patrick Cusack of Gerrardstown, County Meath.[50] The passage from sacred to secular uses may have given rise to concerns about the benefits to be obtained from burial in monastic ground and indeed the dangers of burial in ground which had been polluted by secular uses. The 1618 will of Mathew Archbold of Westmeath, for instance, clearly stipulated that he wished 'my body to be buried in the abbey of Multyfarnham if it be not polluted or the Franciscan friars from hence banished before my burial time and if so, as God forbid, I leave my body to be buried where the same shall seem most convenient.'[51] On a more practical level, it may not have been possible for the family to access the abbey of Boyle in 1568 in the way they would traditionally have done. However, if this was the case in 1568 it did not prevent the burial of Tadhg Mac Diarmada Ruadh at Boyle in 1582 and Aodh Mac Diarmada Ruadh in 1589.[52]

The main factor in relocating the Mac Diarmada family burial place from Boyle to the monastic house at Lough Key seems to have been the position which Ruaidhrí claimed as abbot of the Premonstratensian house there, the family having earlier claimed the title of abbot of Boyle. The precise significance of this is not stated. It seems likely that he was not in holy orders but was rather a commendatory abbot whose function was to hold the temporalities of a religious house during a vacancy. However, it seems unlikely that this

---

46 *AConn*, pp 644–5. 47 *ALC*, ii, pp 376–7. 48 *ALC*, ii, pp 384–5. 49 *ALC*, ii, pp 366–7. 50 *Fiants Ire. Eliz.*, no. 1455. 51 NA, RC 5/16, f. 66. 52 *ALC*, ii, pp 450–1, 496–7.

was ever formally sanctioned. In this case the vacancy lasted from the 1540s until Ruaidhrí's death in 1568 at which point the title passed to his son and successor, Brian, who in 1577 was described as 'superior of the monastery' [uachtaran na mainisdrech].[53] This situation may well have come about as a result of the attempts by local individuals to appropriate to themselves the income of the church. It did have the indirect consequence that the monastery on Holy Island does not feature on any of the lists of dissolved monastic houses in sixteenth-century Connacht and presumably continued to function under Mac Diarmada patronage. There is one reference to the drowning of the 'chief priest' [uasal shagart] of Trinity Island in 1578 and part of a structure that seems to have been the church was rebuilt in the previous year.[54] The obituary also claimed that Ruaidhrí was abbot of the Premonstratensian house at Lough Oughter in Cavan, presumably on the basis that this was a daughter house of Holy Trinity, even though this seems highly unlikely. Certainly in the 1540s that house had its own prior.[55]

It seems probable that the decision to be buried at the monastery of Holy Trinity shaped a good deal of the religious imagery which was used of Ruaidhrí by his son in the obituary. The dedication of the Holy Trinity house to the Trinity, of which it had an image important enough to be mentioned in the context of the burning of the house in 1466, meant that prayer to the Blessed Trinity would be an appropriate form of intercession for Ruaidhrí.[56] In this way his devotion to the Trinity was emphasised in the obituary. The rewards which he had already received from that devotion were spelt out. Ruaidhrí had been blessed with a good death which had not involved pain. He had retained command of his sense and reason until he had made his last confession and had done penance for his sins.

Other religious considerations were also important in the choice of a final resting place. By being buried in the midst of a religious community Ruaidhrí was hoping to benefit from the liturgical memory of that community. It is not known whether the religious community on Trinity Island kept a book in which the deaths of their members and benefactors were noted, as was done at the Augustinian house of Holy Trinity in Dublin.[57] However on the basis of practice elsewhere it seems likely that the community did remember its deceased

53 *ALC*, ii, pp 420–1. Exactly what this meant is unclear since there was also an abbot of Trinity Island in 1584, Eoghan Ó Maoilchiaráin, see Denis Murphy (ed.), *Triumphalia chronologica monasterii Sanctae Crucis in Hibernia* (Dublin, 1895), p. 235. 54 *ALC*, ii, pp 420–1. 55 Aubrey Gwynn, *The medieval province of Armagh* (Dundalk, 1946), p. 267. 56 *AConn*, pp 534–5. 57 J.C. Crossthwaite (ed.), *The book of obits and martyrology of the cathedral church of the Holy Trinity ... Dublin* (Dublin, 1844), reprinted in Raymond Refaussé with Colm Lennon (eds), *The registers of Christ Church cathedral, Dublin* (Dublin, 1998), pp 47–86.

brothers and patrons in Masses on an annual basis, or perhaps more frequently. Thus the community at Trinity Island could remember Ruaidhrí Mac Diarmada in their liturgies and he would also benefit from their prayers. Such memory and memorialisation was both social and liturgical.

Allowing monastic institutions to play such a large part in memorialisation was sometimes less attractive than it seems since it was often entered into under specific conditions. According to the obituary one of the reasons Ruaidhrí was buried on Trinity Island was 'to magnify the honour of the church' [do mhédugad onóra na hegluisi]. Exactly what this means is unclear. Certainly the presence of a lord of the family may have done something to increase the status of the monastic house but that would have conflicted with the afore-mentioned renunciation of pride. The reference to magnifying the honour of the church may imply a gift of land or other wealth from Brian Mac Diarmada to the community in return for the commemorative liturgical services of the canons. The family certainly gave land to other religious communities. According to the annals in 1543 Ruaidhrí Mac Diarmada bought confiscated church lands at Clonshanville and Kilnamanagh from the Dublin administration which he gave to the Dominican house at Clonshanville.[58] The motives for this transaction are not recorded but it may be significant that Ruaidhrí's wife, Sadhbh, had died the previous year and was buried in Athenry.[59] It is possible, perhaps likely, that the gift of land to the Dominican house was intended to fund the maintenance of some form of chantry where she would be remembered by the clergy. Such endowments were the price which lay men and women paid to monastic houses for the preservation of memory both social and liturgical *in saecula saeculorum*. It was, as the first essay has explored, a world of gifts as exchanges. A gift to the religious house would result in the counter-gift of prayer and the preservation of memory. In practice, the memorialisation might have continued until the land grant was absorbed into the wider land bank of the house or the community was dissolved. In this world forgetting was at least as significant as remembering.

IV

Brian Mac Diarmada's eulogy on his father recorded in the Annals of Loch Cé reveals a great deal about memory and memorialisation in sixteenth-century

58 *ALC*, ii, pp 338–9. 59 *ALC*, ii, pp 332–3.

Connacht. Unlike other parts of Ireland the inhabitants of Connacht were reluctant to erect dramatic funeral monuments to their dead. Only a handful of these can be identified from the late fifteenth or early sixteenth centuries. There are examples at Strade, where a tomb front contains the patron and images of the Magi, Saints Peter and Paul and Christ displaying His five wounds, and at Sligo Abbey where the tomb of the merchant family of Ó Craidhéin depicts St Dominic, St Catherine, St Michael and St Peter as well as an archbishop and Christ crucified.[60] The functions performed by these stone monuments, remembering the dead and representing the intercessions of their protectors, were more usually fulfilled in other less tangible ways in most of Connacht. Brian Mac Diarmada relied on a combination of tradition and innovation as well as marshalling the resources of the church to commemorate his father. Whether the obituary as it was recorded in the annals was intended for the personal use of the owner of the book who might read it in private or whether, as in the cases discussed in the story of the murder of Maghnus Ó Duibhgeannáin above, it was read to a wider audience on a fixed occasion each year we do not know. The repetitive sequence of alliterative encomiums recorded in a separate column parallel to the prose obituary of Brian Mac Diarmada may well have been intended for public reading.[61] It may equally be that this written form follows an oral pattern of thought, as in the case of the annalists' resort to proverbs.[62] In either case as a form of memorialisation the annalistic obituary proved to be at least as durable as a monument carved in stone.

60 John Hunt, *Irish medieval figure sculpture* (2 vols, Shannon, 1974), i, pp 201–2, 218.   61 TCD, MS 1293, f. 134.   62 *AConn*, pp 646–7, 738–9; *AFM*, v, pp 1768–9, 1804–5. Proverbs are also used by sixteenth-century hagiographers, Plummer (ed.), *Bethada náem nÉrenn: lives of Irish saints*, i, p. 248, ii, p. 241. For further literary examples see T.F. O'Rahilly (ed.), *A miscellany of Irish proverbs* (Dublin, 1922), pp 79–146.

7

Sir Nicholas Malby's obituary, 1584
outsiders in the sixteenth-century Irish annals

On 4 March 1584 Sir Nicholas Malby, second president of Connacht, died suddenly at his residence at Athlone.[1] He was about fifty years old, and had been in charge of the English provincial administration in Connacht for the previous eight years. The office of Connacht president had been established in 1569, on the initiative of Sir Henry Sidney, in recognition of the perceived need to have a local English presence to maintain order in regions beyond easy reach of the Dublin government. What is notable about Malby's death is not so much the event itself but rather the way in which the native Irish annalists chose to commemorate it. The compilers of the Annals of Loch Cé, for instance, wrote an obituary of Malby, a Yorkshire-born soldier, as part of their historical record. The annalist wrote

> Sir Nicholas Malby, who had been captain over Connacht, died the third day of the month of March; and there came not to Erinn in his own time, nor often before, a better gentleman of the Foreigners than he; and he placed all Connacht under bondage. And it is not possible to count or reckon all that this man destroyed throughout Erinn, and he executed many works, especially on the courts of the towns of Athlone and Roscommoñ.

> [Sir Nicalass Malbie do bi na caipdin os cind Connacht deg in tress la do mí Marta, ocus ni tanic a nErinn a comaimsir fris na go menic riam do Galloib, duine uasal bud ferr ina se, 7 do cuir se cuicced Connacht uili fo doeirsi; ocus ni fetur a rim no a áiremh gach ar mill in fer sin ar fedh Erenn; ocus do rinne sé moran oibrech ar cuirt baile atha Luain 7 rossa Commain do sunnradh.][2]

---

1 *Cal. S.P. Ire., 1574–85*, p. 498. 2 *ALC*, ii, pp 458–9.

When the Four Masters came to compile their Annals of the Kingdom of Ireland in the 1630s, they too found a place for Sir Nicholas Malby in their records.[3]

I

Why Nicholas Malby should have been commemorated in this way is rather curious. The honour of an obituary in the annals was usually reserved for prominent individuals from within Gaelic lordships, such as Ruaidhrí Mac Diarmada whose obituary was examined in the previous essay, together with important ecclesiastical personalities. Yet Malby was, in many ways, an archetypal New English colonist. As early as 1556 he was among those Englishmen willing to be associated with the proposed plantation of Laois. This interest proved short-lived and after some involvement in dubious speculative activities at home he concentrated on his military career. He gained military experience in France and Spain in the early 1560s, and then returned to Ireland after Sir Henry Sidney became lord deputy, and was appointed a sergeant-major in the English army in Ireland in 1567. He was employed in Ulster against Seaán Ó Néill and Somhairle Buidhe Mac Domhnaill, and was a highly-regarded English military commander. In 1569 he was sent to assist Sir Peter Carew against the Butlers in Leinster. Yet Malby was always interested in more than a military career. In 1571 he set off to London, armed with letters from prominent Dublin administrators, in the hope of acquiring some preferment.[4] He successfully applied for a grant of the office of the collector of the Customs of three ports in County Down. Later the same year he obtained a grant of the barony of Kinelarty as part of Thomas Smith's scheme for the plantation of the Ards peninsula. When that enterprise failed Malby again visited the royal court, in early 1576, this time seeking to surrender his patent for Kinelarty in exchange for land in fee farm elsewhere in Ireland.[5] It may have been as a result of this visit to London that he was named as chief commissioner of Connacht in succession to Sir Edward Fitton.[6] In October 1576 he was knighted at Athlone by Sir Henry Sidney, the Irish lord deputy.[7] For the next eight years he was to be the main agent of the Dublin administration in Connacht and was largely responsible for the successful implementation of the first composition scheme for Connacht from

3 *AFM*, v, pp 1814–27. 4 PRO, SP63/31, nos 13, 42. 5 *Dictionary of national biography*, s.n. 6 *Fiants Ire., Eliz.*, no. 2884. 7. W.A. Shaw, *The knights of England* (2 vols, London, 1906), ii, p. 77.

1577 to 1584. What characterised Malby's period as a Connacht administrator was his skill as a negotiator and his ability to broker deals among the factional interests within the province.

Aside from his official duties as governor of Connacht Malby devoted considerable energy to establishing himself as a significant landowner in County Roscommon. His twenty-one-year lease from the crown of the castle and lands of Roscommon along with extensive monastic lands in the region, made in November 1577, was changed in June 1579 to an outright grant of the land to him and his male heirs when he offered to build a walled town there. At the time, Malby's son, Henry, was still a minor and the grant of Roscommon included provision for the defence of the castle in the event of the holder being a minor.[8] He also obtained title to some monastic land in County Longford in 1579.[9] In the ensuing years Malby undertook the modernisation of the medieval castle at Roscommon, which he envisaged as the core of his estate. The lands he had acquired made him one of the largest landowners in the province. Malby's presence attracted numerous other English settlers to County Roscommon, and some of the soldiers who had previously served with him in Ulster became tenants on his Roscommon lands.[10] Some of his principal tenants were also appointed to offices in the provincial presidency.[11] In Malby's relatively short time in Connacht he had a significant impact on the province both through his role as president and through his activities in promoting the informal colonisation of Roscommon. The extent of his role in the province has not yet been assessed fully by historians, but it did not go unnoticed by his contemporaries.

II

The facts of Malby's career as colonist and government official make his inclusion in the annals exceptional. However, he was not the only Englishman mentioned in the late sixteenth-century Irish annals. From the mid-1570s other English soldiers and administrators merited similar attention from the Gaelic historians. The four Englishmen who served as presidents of Connacht in the late sixteenth century feature surprisingly prominently in the annals. Sir Edward

---

8. *Fiants Ire., Eliz.*, no. 3550.   9 *Fiants Ire., Eliz.*, nos 3550, 3582.   10 For the estates see T. Cronin, 'The Elizabethan colony in Co. Roscommon' in Harman Murtagh (ed.), *Irish midland studies* (Athlone, 1980), pp 107–20.   11 G.W. Lambert, 'Sir Nicholas Malby and his associates' in *Journal of the Galway Archaeological and Historical Society*, xxiii (1948), pp 1–13.

Fitton (1569–77), Sir Nicholas Malby (1577–84) and Sir Richard Bingham (1584–98) regularly came to the notice of the compiler of the Annals of Loch Cé. While those annals effectively terminate in 1590 (except for a few very brief later comments), Bingham's involvement in Connacht in the 1590s and his successor Sir Conyers Clifford who served briefly in 1599 are noticed in the seventeenth-century biographical narrative *Beatha Aodha Ruaidh Uí Dhomhnaill* and in the Annals of the Four Masters. The annalist of Loch Cé placed accounts of some of the military activities of the Connacht presidents during their lifetimes, as well as obituaries after their deaths, alongside accounts of similar activities by Gaelic leaders so that their annals comprised a composite historical record of late sixteenth-century Connacht politics.

The inclusion of an obituary of Malby as an English official in the Annals of Loch Cé may seem curious given the overall focus of the annals on local Gaelic personalities from within the Gaelic world. The annalists had previously displayed little interest in the activities of the English administration in Ireland. When kings and queens of England were mentioned the information about them was frequently inaccurate.[12] From the mid-sixteenth century the activities of English lords justice or lords deputy were occasionally noted, usually on issues of specific Connacht significance. The death of Thomas Radcliffe, earl of Sussex, was recorded incorrectly and without comment under 1582.[13] Sir Henry Sidney's position as lord deputy was recorded when the bridge over the Shannon at Athlone was constructed in 1567, the surrender of Roscommon castle to him by Ó Conchobhair was noted in 1569 and finally his death was entered under 1586 with the comment that he had been a 'good justiciary' [Giuistis maith].[14] Sir John Perrot, as lord deputy, was treated more briefly, entering the annalists' story only because he arrived in Ireland at the same time as Richard Bingham was appointed governor of Connacht and the death of his son was recorded in 1587.[15] Sir William Fitzwilliam's arrival in Ireland was noted unfavourably, and his visits to Connacht were briefly recorded.[16] The relative prominence accorded to individual presidents of Connacht, in contrast to their superiors, is an indication of the local effectiveness of the institution

---

12 For example under the year 1547 the annals noted the death of 'King Henry' and recorded the accession of his daughter, Mary, omitting Edward VI. The scribe Brian Mac Diarmada believed, wrongly, that this entry should have been in the previous year (*ALC*, ii, p. 350). The death of Edward was noted under 1553 with some chronological notes intended to fix the date of Henry VIII's death (*ALC*, ii, p. 362). 13 *ALC*, ii, 456–7. The annalist gives the earl's name in a Gaelicised form as 'Iarla O Susaic, .i. Tomas in uisgi'. Sussex died on 9 June 1583. 14 *ALC*, ii, pp 396–7, 468–9, 470–1. 15 *ALC*, ii, pp 458–60, 480–1. 16 *ALC*, ii, 482–5; 494–5; 500–1; 504–7.

of the presidency in the western province as compared with the remoteness of the Dublin government or the royal court. By contrast the Anglo-Irish annals composed within the Pale in the early seventeenth century by Thady Dowling, chancellor of Leighlin, record in more detail the comings and goings of royal officials over the same period.[17]

The Loch Cé annalist seemed unaware of the importance or status of the office of lord deputy. The annalist used the term 'guisdís' or justiciar to describe the holders of the office, a term that had been in use since the medieval period. He failed to differentiate between a lord lieutenant, lord deputy, or lord justice although the more politically informed Dowling certainly appreciated the difference between the gradations of the office. Dowling distinguished clearly between 'deputatis Hibernia' for lords deputy and 'justiciarii' meaning lords justice. The enhanced status of the earl of Essex was marked by his exalted title of 'locum tenens domine regine'. The viceroyalty was not the only national institution which the annals of Loch Cé failed to understand fully. The description of the meeting of parliament in 1585 was confined to one line and was, at best, confused. There was obvious uncertainty as to how this institution was to be described, the compromise being 'acta pairlimint' which suggests a basic misunderstanding of the difference between the institution and its end product. This is all the more curious because, according to the Annals of the Four Masters, Brian Mac Diarmada, the patron and part compiler of the Loch Cé annals was a member of that parliament.[18] In contrast the better-informed Annals of the Four Masters provided a clear account of the events of 1585, showing a much greater retrospective awareness of the functions of the parliament as an institution.[19]

The growing awareness of developments outside the immediate world of factional Gaelic politics in Connacht which the annalists display after the middle of the 1570s may be linked to the establishment of the presidency of Connacht in 1569 and the associated taxation arrangements which saw an increase in the number of provincial civil servants in the province. The opening of the bridge over the Shannon noted by the annalists under 1567 also made the province more accessible to administrators from Dublin. New English names appear in the Connacht annals with some regularity and, over time, their spelling more closely approximates to the English form. In 1567 Francis Cosby is mentioned (although in the context of an account of the massacre at Mullaghmast in

17 Richard Butler (ed.), *The annals of Ireland by Friar John Clynn and Tady Dowling* (Dublin, 1848).   18 *AFM*, v, pp 1832–3.   19 *AFM*, v, pp 1826–41.

county Kildare). In the 1570s names of Englishmen with links to the province appear more frequently, Captain Collier in 1570, Francis Cosby's son, Captain Harrant and Robert Savage in 1577. These men were in Connacht not simply as administrators but, (as in the case of Theobald Dillon discussed above), rapidly gained a stake in provincial life through a process of informal colonisation. Moreover the annalists became better informed about English affairs. The doings of the earl of Leicester, for instance, in his Spanish campaigns were duly recorded by the annalists in 1586 and his death was noted under 1588.[20] It appears that the increased presence of outsiders in Connacht enhanced the flow of news information into the province from outside.

III

To understand why the Loch Cé annalists not only became aware of the activities of these newcomers in Connacht politics but also how they reacted to them, it is important to look at innovative annalistic obituaries such as that for Sir Nicholas Malby. These entries reveal a great deal of how the people of Connacht perceived the newly arrived local English representatives of the monarch and particularly the successive presidents of Connacht. The earliest of the obituaries of English provincial presidents is that of Sir Edward Fitton, a native of Cheshire, who was appointed as first president of Connacht in 1569.[21] Though Fitton had been promoted to the office of Treasurer of Ireland at the time of his death, it was during his time as president of Connacht that he had come to the attention of Brian Mac Diarmada, for whom the Annals of Loch Cé were compiled. When Fitton died in 1577 he received an obituary in the Annals of Loch Cé

> The treasurer of Eirinn, i.e. Edward Fitton, died in Dublin, the last day of the middle month of summer; and there came not of the Saxon Foreigners, for a long time, one more to be lamented than he, as regards nobility and dignity.
>
> [Treisiréir na hErenn, .i. Edbhord Fitón, dfhaghail bháis a mBaile Atha Cliath an la deighionach do mi medhoin int samhradh, ocus ní thánic

re fada do Galloib Saxan sgél budh mó ináss, alleth uaisle ocus oir-
rdercuis.][22]

In many ways this was a very traditional obituary using language and ideas
which were often applied to native lords in the annals. The phrase 'nobility and
dignity' [uaisle ocus oirrdercas] appears in the obituary of Tadhg son of Brian
Ó Ruairc in the Annals of Loch Cé for 1560 and that for Maelruanaidh Mac
Diarmada, son of Tomaltach, in 1566. The same formula was again deployed
in other later obituaries.[23] The technique of using traditional language to inte-
grate these new political personalities into the existing social order in Connacht
was not confined to the obituaries. The terminology which the annalists applied
to the offices of the English provincial administration in Connacht was not
normally a direct borrowing into Irish of the terms which the office holders
used of themselves. Instead, the annalists used the traditional terminology of
leadership that had been current in late medieval Gaelic Ireland. In the case of
Sir Edward Fitton, first mentioned in 1570, it is true that the initial response
of the annalist was to adapt his official title into Irish referring to the holder
of the office as 'préisidens'. However, although this borrowed term continued
to be used occasionally, it was increasingly replaced with another, 'lord of the
province of Connacht' [tigerna choiged Connacht], an adaptation of the traditional title accorded to a native Irish lord.[24] Occasionally other titles were
used for the holder of the post but increasingly they had to be explained. Thus
when the annalist referred to Nicholas Malby as governor they decided to
explain the term by adding the Irish approximation 'governor, i.e. the lord of
Connacht' [guibhernoir, .i. tigerna Connacht].[25]

The Loch Cé annalists portrayed Fitton in their obituary as someone equivalent to a traditional Gaelic lord. By doing so, they effectively minimised the
sense of change or innovation which might otherwise have been indicated by
the inclusion of an English administrator. However, it may be that what the
annalists did not say was as important as what they did. It is possible to get a
sense of the limitations of the obituary in the Loch Cé annals as it might have
been read by contemporaries by comparing it with another obituary written of
Fitton, this time by his own family, and erected on a brass plaque in St Patrick's
cathedral in Dublin (fig. 16).[26] Two features in particular differentiate the Dublin

22 *ALC*, ii, pp 428–9. *AFM* noticed his death under the year 1579 without comment.   23 *ALC*, ii, pp 376–7,
390–1, 424–5, 446–7.   24 For example, *ALC*, ii, pp 414–15, 426–7, 440–1, 442–3, 460–1.   25 *ALC*, ii, pp
464–5.   26. For the text on the brass see Heather A. King, 'Irish memorial brasses to 1700' in *Proceedings of
the Royal Irish Academy*, xciv, sect. C (1997), pp 126–7, 139.

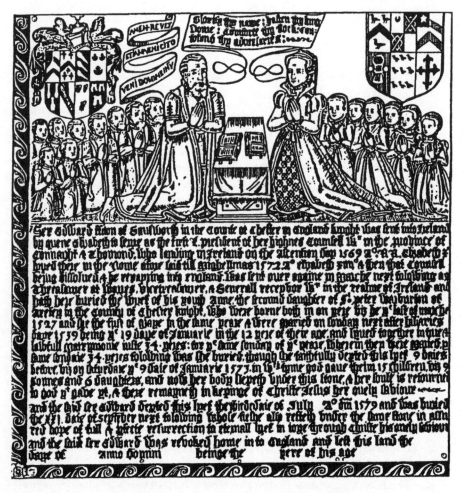

16 Memorial brass to Sir Edward Fitton and his family,
St Patrick's Cathedral, Dublin (from a rubbing by Heather King)

brass from the annalist's obituary. The first is the long description on the brass
which detailed Fitton's family. It gave details of his wife and her family connections and recorded their fifteen children who were depicted on the brass,
the nine boys being shown behind their father and the six daughters behind
their mother. Although some genealogical detail was normal in other annalistic obituaries in the annals, and served to place the individual within Gaelic
society, Fitton had no such ancestral connections within that world since he
and his wife were English. The second difference between the brass memorial
and the annalistic obituary in the representation of Fitton is the matter of reli-

gion. The annalistic entry made no mention of Fitton's religion despite the fact that very many such obituaries did record religious attributes, and one has been examined in the previous essay. Aodh, son of Cormac Mac Diarmada, for instance, was said to have died in 1549 after 'communion and sacrifice' [comna ocus tshacarbuic]; in 1551 Lochlainn Ó Maoil Chonaire died 'after triumphing over the world and the devil' [iar mbreith bhuaide o dhoman ocus o dheman.][27] Fitton's brass, on the other hand spoke of his 'assured hope of full and p[er]fect resurrection to eternall lyef in joy through Christe his onely saviour'.[28] What seemed to be a traditional obit for Fitton in the annals concealed as much as it revealed and despite the traditional attributes accorded to him on his death, Fitton was less part of that world of Connacht than might appear.

Sir Nicholas Malby's obituary in the annals of Loch Cé demonstrates a similar ambiguity about his position in that society. Despite apparent praise for Malby, the annalist was ambivalent about his subject. His attributes are summarised into two groups which contain opposing sentiments. The second of those two groups of attributes illustrates the tension clearly. On the one hand Malby was regarded as destructive, 'and it is not possible to count or reckon all that this man destroyed' [ocus ni fetur a rim no a áiremh gach ar mill in fer sin].[29] This was not an idea which the annalists used lightly or kindly. They used it of Jordan Buidhe MacCostello who died in 1561 after waging a fourteen year feud with the Mac Diarmada family: 'and this man was noble [and] destructive' [agus fa huasal aidhmillte an fer sin].[30] They used it again on the death of Cormac Mac Diarmada in 1552 'and this man was a great destroyer and evil-doer' [ocus fa mor in fer millte ocus uilc do ghenamh in fer sin]; who had also killed one of the sons of Ruaidhrí Mac Diarmada 'in treachery' [a feall].[31] To be regarded as destructive was not seen as a reason for eulogy or praise by the annalists. On the other hand Malby's building activities at Roscommon and Athlone were a cause for praise. The building activities of the patron of the annals, Brian Mac Diarmada, were likewise recorded as praise-worthy and the annalists also recorded other building works such as the construction of castles and the bridge at Ballinasloe as positive features.[32] Part of this attitude may stem from the sense of building for the corporate good as a pious work. Bequests for church buildings were common in late medieval Irish wills but some individuals left money for other community building projects which were to be seen as good works. Gerald Fitzgerald of Killmaoge in county

27 ALC, ii, pp 352–3, 358–9, 402–3.   28 King, 'Irish memorial brasses to 1700', pp 136–7, 139.   29 ALC, ii, pp 458–9.   30 ALC, ii, pp 378–9.   31 ALC, ii, pp 360–1.   32 ALC, ii, pp 356–7, 420–1, 422–3, 474–5.

Kildare, for instance, left money in his 1611 will for the construction of a bridge as a pious benefaction.[33] Again writing of the life of Francis Kirwan, Catholic bishop of Killala, before the rising of 1641 his late seventeenth-century biographer, John Lynch, praised his construction of bridges and causeways across bogs as pious works.[34] Thus Malby was perceived by the annalists as an ambiguous figure with both good and bad traits. He was a good gentleman but also '[he] placed all Connacht under bondage' [do cuir se cuicced Connacht uili fo doeirsi.][35]

Malby himself would have understood such a description, and was well aware that there were two aspects to his official functions within the province. Writing a letter from Athlone in July 1582, he defended his actions against criticism from within the provincial administration by asserting that his approach was one of 'good dealing with the honest sort and using correction to the evil disposed.'[36]

IV

The annalistic obituaries of Fitton and Malby therefore betray a complex story. Brian Mac Diarmada's annals recorded the lives of outsiders who were becoming increasingly prominent in Connacht society and whom the annalists saw as having a place in that world although not part of it. The place which Malby and Fitton occupied in local Connacht society was not well defined and in that lay its strength. In the factional politics of the province in the late sixteenth century, with Mac Diarmada and other lords under pressure from Ó Domhnaill to the north and with the continuation of internal disputes, many of the key players sought to recruit additional support for their positions. Some recruited Scottish mercenaries to aid their cause. Others looked to alternative sources of support. Thus, Fitton's first bout of activity as Connacht president, in 1570, was narrated in the Annals of Loch Cé as

> The President, i.e. Edward Fitton, came into Connacht this year, accompanied by the Queen's forces, together with the rising out of Connacht (as many of them as were obedient to him), viz., the earl

33 NA, RC5/3, f. 348. 34 John Lynch, *Pii antistitis icon sive de vita et morte Rmi D. Francisci Kirovani* (Maclovii, 1669, reprint Dublin, 1951), pp 43–4. For requests for prayers in return for bridge building at Holy Cross, County Tipperary, Peter O'Keefe and Tom Simington, *Irish stone bridges: history and heritage* (Dublin, 1991), p. 176. 35 *ALC*, ii, pp 458–9. 36 PRO, SP63/94, no. 32.

of Clan-Rickard, and all the race of Ulick-an-fhiona, and the Sil-
Cellaigh, and the Clann-Domhnaill of Sliabh-ruadh, and Captain
Collier, and Patrickin Cusack, and the rising out of Gaillimh, and
many more that we cannot enumerate, and all these went to take the
castle at Sruthair [Shrule]. Mac William Burk, with his kinsmen and
relatives, and the sons of Oliver Burk, assembled a large army of
Albanachs …

[In préisidens .i. Edbhard Fetón do thoighecht a Connachtaibh an
samradh sin, ocus armáil na bainrighna leis, maille re hérghe amach
Connacht an mhéid fa humhal dó dhibh .i. iarla clainni Ricaird ocus
slicht Uilleg an fiona uile, ocus siol gCeallaigh ocus clann Domhnaill
ant sleibhe ruaidh, ocus caiptín Coiléir ocus Paidricín Ciomsóg, ocus
eirghe amach na Gaillmhe, ocus morán ele nach roich linn dáiremh;
ocus tiaghaid sin uile do ghabháil chaisléin Sruthra. Mac Uilliam a
Búrc cona braithribh ocus cona chomhfogus, ocus clann Oilbhérus a
Búrc, do cruinniughad slúaigh mhoir dAlbanachuibh …].[37]

Unfortunately, the manuscript is incomplete at this point and so the narrative
ends in mid-sentence. However, there is sufficient description of the factions
involved in the capture of Shrule castle from the MacWilliam Burkes of Mayo
to allow us assess the annalist's perception of the event and of Sir Edward
Fitton's role therein. The Englishman was presented as the leader of one fac-
tion within the province, the most prominent of whom was Riccard Burke,
second earl of Clanricard, and his followers. Their supporters were a wide-
ranging but mixed group of locals and outsiders. The opposition on this occasion comprised MacWilliam Burke of Mayo and his followers, assisted by a
'large army' of Scots. The Annals of the Four Masters offers a more detailed
account of the military encounter which followed. Demonstrating a clear bias
in favour of the Mayo Burkes not evident in the contemporary Annals of Loch
Cé account, the Four Masters portrayed the outcome as inconclusive. They
argued that the Mayo Burkes won the day but, having decided not to remain
in the camp that night, the opposing forces were allowed to claim the victory
as theirs.[38] In the longer term, it was the earl of Clanricard who retained possession of the castle of Shrule, won from the Mayo Burkes with the assistance
of Sir Edward Fitton in 1570. Thus, the episode was just one of many examples where the actions of the English president of Connacht are best inter-

37. *ALC*, ii, pp 408–9.   38 *AFM*, v, pp 1640–9.

preted as being channelled by local political factions in pursuit of their own
local ambitions within the province of Connacht.

This factional reality may help to explain why Fitton and Malby were
treated with apparent generosity in the obituaries constructed by the Loch Cé
annalists. After the death of Tadhg, the grandfather of Brian Mac Diarmada
the compiler of the Annals of Loch Cé, the family resolved themselves into
two main branches, sliocht Eoghain and sliocht Ruaidhrí (to which the annalist Brian Mac Diarmada belonged). There was ongoing tension between the
two parties and the lordship was effectively partitioned in 1538, sliocht Eoghain
holding the lands around Boyle while sliocht Ruaidhrí were based at the traditional Mac Diarmada stronghold at Carraig Mhic Diarmada in Lough Key.[39]
By 1562 the feud had reached such a peak that sliocht Eoghain had engaged gallowglass mercenaries in a raid which lasted a week. The Loch Cé annalist, writing from the perspective of sliocht Ruaidhrí, described the destruction of the
Mac Diarmada stronghold, and the killing of a horseman, Murchadh, adding
'and it is not possible to reckon or tell all the steeds, cows, horses, and property of every other kind they destroyed.' [ocus ni heidir a riom na innisin gach
ar millsed dechaib ocus do bhuaibh, do chaiplibh ocus dá gach uile édail
airchéna.][40] Ruaidhrí employed Mac Suibhne mercenaries in retaliation. In 1565
both parties tried to extend their influence in Connacht through raiding neighbouring lordships in all of which Brian Mac Diarmada played a part.[41] A further murder in 1567 seems to have been part of the same cycle of violence.[42] In
1568 matters came to a head with the death of Ruaidhrí. The lordship passed
to Tadhg of sliocht Eoghain. How this change in the balance of power was
achieved in not described in detail. Following the obituary of the deceased lord,
discussed in the previous essay, the annalist simply noted 'another person, i.e.
Toirdhelbhach, the son of Eoghan Mac Diarmada, was made king in his place,
with the consent of the church and laity, of ecclesiastics and ollamhs.' [Araill
eli .i. Toirrdhealbach mac Eogain Mac Diarmada do riogad ina ionad, do thoil
chille ocus tuaithi, eglaisi ocus ollaman.][43] In reality the transfer of power was
a much more violent affair with the annalist recording further intervention of
Scots gallowglasses.[44] This dispute also seems to have become enmeshed in
wider Connacht politics, and the English provincial administration became
involved. In November 1571 Mac Diarmada's country was ravaged by the lord
deputy and in early 1572 it was reported by Fitton that the land lay waste.[45]

39 *ALC*, ii, pp 312–13; see above, fig. 4, p. 49. 40 *ALC*, ii, pp 382–3. 41 *ALC*, ii, pp 388–9. 42 *ALC*, ii, pp
396–7. 43 *ALC*, ii, pp 404–5. 44 *ALC*, ii, pp 406–9. 45 PRO, SP63/34, no. 29; SP63/35, no. 12.

Fitton reported to the lord deputy that he had indicted most of the freeholders of north Connacht, including Mac Diarmada, and some form of official
plantation seems to have been contemplated as part of the strategy for the
future government of the area.[46]

In this context it seems that Brian Mac Diarmada perceived that his best
chance of influencing the succession within the lordship lay in attracting the
support of the provincial president to his side. Shortly after Fitton's arrival in
1569 Mac Diarmada was pardoned for any outstanding offences and by June
1571 he had been appointed as seneschal of the barony of Moylurg which suggests he had already impressed Fitton at that date. In the same year he requested
Fitton's support to prevent Ó Domhnaill raiding his territory and Fitton
responded by sending a force to support Brian.[47] In 1577, together with Ó
Conchobhair Shligigh he appealed to Fitton's successor Malby for support
against Ó Domhnaill who was again raiding in the area.[48] He continued his
contacts with the Dublin administration and in 1578 was in Dublin with Ó
Conchobhair Shligigh.[49] In 1580 he was appointed as one of the commissioners, or justices of the peace, in Connacht by Nicholas Malby again suggesting
a link with the provincial administration.[50] It is clear that Brian Mac Diarmada
saw this contact as a valuable one and worth maintaining since in 1585 the annalist note that the third provincial president, Sir Richard Bingham, spent time at
Brian's house.[51] For Brian Mac Diarmada successive presidents of Connacht
were not merely names of provincial administrators but political allies in the
factional politics of Connacht.

Allying with the newcomer administration was not simply a military initiative, it also had propaganda overtones. Including obituaries of Malby and
Fitton in their annals was in part a propaganda coup, a declaration of what
support could be expected. Others tried a similar technique. In the 1570s, as
the Connacht presidency grew in influence, one of the power brokers in north
Connacht, MacWilliam Burke, revelled in his genealogical connection with the
Tudors. In a genealogical tract it was noted

> and the descendants of Elizabeth, daughter of the Brown Earl, is the
> queen of England i.e. Elizabeth that now is, 1578, so that it is through
> the blood of the children of William Burke she came to the crown.
>
> [agus ar sliocht Elysabeth inghean an Iarla Dhuinn atá bainrioghan

---

46 PRO, SP63/31, no. 12; SP63/35, no. 12; SP63/35, no. 23.   47 Fiants Ire., Eliz., nos 1289, 1817; ALC, ii, pp 412–13.
48 ALC, ii, pp 414–15.   49 ALC, ii, pp 422–3.   50 Fiants Ire., Eliz., no. 3667.   51 ALC, ii, pp 464–5.

Shaxan .i. Elysabeth so ann 1578; ionnus gurab ó fhuil Chlainne Uilliam Búrc do tháinic sí do chum na corónach.][52]

The same connection was also celebrated in the traditional form of a bardic poem, 'Ó Dhia dhealbhtar gach óige', which charted the descent of the MacWilliam Burkes from Charlemagne

The present woman Elizabeth is an odorous branch of the wood of Charles; as is each scion of her race, though the half is from Lionel.

[Eilísdábét an bheansa anois
cleath chubhra do choill t-Séarluis
mar tá gach cleath do cinél
gidh tá a leath do Leoinidhel.][53]

Such genealogical connections, real or imagined, had an important propaganda function and were a declaration that support could be marshalled from perhaps unexpected sources in local disputes. How those might be utilised was suggested in 1588, for instance, when the president, Sir Richard Bingham, seized Sligo castle from Donnchadh Ó Conchobhair Shligigh, who was by then Brian Mac Diarmada's father-in-law. In response, Ó Conchobhair Shligigh 'went to complain to Saxon-land' [do dol a ccosaid co Saxanaibh.][54] Complaining required a network of political alliances which could be as effective as military resources.

That the reaction to the expanding administrative structures and the growing numbers of personnel in the Connacht presidency was a traditional one is suggested by the description of the composition of Connacht first introduced in 1577. This taxation agreement, designed to finance the presidency was significant primarily because it created a formal administrative link between native and newcomer. Collectors of composition rent soon acquired an important role as brokers in local society. From the perspective of the Dublin government, the Connacht president was an agent of crown policy in the provinces; from the local perspective, the presidency was just one novel element in the complex web of political inter-relationships that comprised Connacht society. Whether in military, legal, or administrative matters, the way the presidency functioned in Connacht was determined not by Dublin's policy, but by the ways in which the local power groups within Connacht engaged with the presidency.[55]

52 Tomás Ó Raghallaigh (ed.), 'Seanchus Búrcach' in Journal of the Galway Archaeological and Historical Society, xiii (1927), pp 121–3.   53 Tomás Ó Raghallaigh (ed.), 'Seanchus Búrcach' in Journal of the Galway Archaeological and Historical Society, xiv (1928–9), pp 38–9.   54 ALC, ii, pp 486–7.   55 Bernadette Cunningham, 'Natives

The working of the presidency seems to have depended largely on the personal efforts of Malby to implement it, and to collect the rents due. That the first composition payments ceased with his death is significant. It implies that those local lords who paid the rent may have perceived it as a personal payment to Malby as an alternative local magnate, sealing an agreement between them under which they expected to benefit from the legal assistance and perhaps the military protection he could offer.[56] That the local elite in Connacht were open to such agreements, and were persuaded by Malby to pay what was essentially a tax to support the provincial administration is an indication that the holder of that office was regarded as a potential alternative to overlords such as the Burkes, earls of Clanricard, when protection and arbitration were required.

The differing ways in which the process known as the first composition of Connacht in 1577 were interpreted by its participants are worth exploring. The lord deputy, Sir Henry Sidney, in an attempt to stabilise power relations in Connacht in 1577 sought to reduce the authority of the principal native lords by entering into composition agreements with their followers. Under these agreements the traditional exactions of the native lords, usually in the form of military service from their followers, and the cess extracted by the Dublin administration to fund the English army in Connacht were replaced by an annual rent charge on specific tracts of land. In return the provincial administration assumed responsibility for the defence of the area. The aim of the agreements was to establish a new social order by undermining what was regarded as the excessive power wielded by the overlords by reducing the dependence of lesser lords on them.[57] In Mayo the way in which the MacWilliam Burkes used the agreement was rather different from its intended use. In the *Seanchus Búrcach* there is a passage describing, from the native side, the working of the composition agreement. The author, commenting on the fact that MacWilliam had been unable to collect his exactions from the barony of Gallen because of the inhabitants' unwillingness to pay, noted

> On that account Mac William Burk, i.e. John son of Oliver, went to prefer his complaint to the house of the Court against you, to Captain Malbie. And the Captain and Council, viz, the Archbishop of Tuam,

and newcomers in Mayo, 1560–1603' in R. Gillespie and G. Moran (eds), *A various country: essays in Mayo history, 1500–1900* (Westport, 1987), pp 24–43. **56** PRO, SP63/59, no. 71; SP63/86, nos 35–7; SP63/100, no. 44i; SP63/112, no. 79. **57** Bernadette Cunningham, 'The composition of Connacht in the lordships of Clanricard and Thomond' in *Irish Historical Studies*, xxiv (1984–5), pp 1–2.

and Master Bacon, and Justice Dillon, and Edward White made an order for him here, i.e. two beeves in lieu of every armed man, and two beeves in lieu of every horseman, and a beef for every kerne – and that is the same as two beeves in every quarter throughout his lordship, unless it is more than that. And they had reason for that, for they allowed not power of superiority with chief command to any man whatever about that time. And they did this for his board and maintenance, i.e. of Mac William. And Mac William has this order, written in English, from the hand of the Council.

[Ar an ádhbhar sin, do chuaidh Mac Uilliam Búrc, .i. Seán Mac Olibherus do chasaoid isteach go tigh na cúirte oraibh a ceann Chaiptín Mailbi; agus do rinne an Caiptín agus an Comhairligh .i. Ardeasbog Thuama, agus Máighistir Beachain, agus Giúistís Dilamhuin, agus Edubhard Faoit ordugha dhó annso .i. dhá mhart annsa bhfear eidigh, dá mhart annsa mharcach, agus mart annsa cheithearnach, agus is ion- nann sin agus dá mhart annsa cheathramhain ar feadh a thighearnais, ach muna mó é ná sin. Agus do bhí adhbhar aca chuige sin, óir níor leigeadar féin cumhacht uaisle le ceannais feaghnuigh do dhuine ar bith fa an am sin. Agus do rinneadar sin cun a bhuird agus arm a bheathuigh dhósan .i. do Mhac Uilliam, agus atá an t-ordugha sin sgríobhtha i mBéarla ag Mac Uilliam ó láimh na Comhairle.][58]

While the provincial government clearly intended that the composition arrange- ments should weaken MacWilliam's power they were used by MacWilliam to strengthen it. What had begun as an attempt to impose authority and social order on the localities was transformed so that the provincial government became a pawn in the negotiation of social authority within the MacWilliam lordship.

The composition scheme was greatly expanded in 1585. However, the con- temporary native reaction to the 1585 composition, as revealed in the Annals of Loch Cé, was rather different from that associated with the 1577 agreement. The 1585 agreement was not perceived as having the potential to strengthen local interests. Instead it was depicted in the annals as posing a challenge to the honour of the native lords. The Annals of Loch Cé described the 1585 com- position in the following terms,

58 Ó Raghallaigh (ed.), 'Seanchus Búrcach' in *Journal of the Galway Archaeological and Historical Society*, xiii (1927), pp 116–19.

A great tribute was imposed on Connacht by Saxons, i.e. an ounce of
gold on every quarter, both ecclesiastical and lay; and the lordship of
each Gaelic lord was lowered by them.

[Doeirchis mor do cur ar Connachtuib do Saxanchuib .i. uingi dór sa
cethramain itir cill ocus thuaith, ocus tigernus gach uile tigerna gaide-
alach dissleghad doib.][59]

Again, the language of the entry in terms of 'lordship' was not that of colonisation but rather that of traditional society. Indeed the annalist did not need
to invent any new terms for the process even though in the early seventeenth
century the Annals of the Four Masters would borrow from English the word
'composition' to describe the sort of deal introduced in 1585. The action of
taking tribute with the corresponding reduction in the political influence or
'lordship' of those from whom the tribute was taken was a well established part
of native economic and political life and was part of what was celebrated in
Malby's obituary. However, the negative view of the annalists does not reveal
the full story. In practice, the composition payments were paid annually through
to the mid 1590s, and this tangible evidence indicates that the deal must have
had extensive local support within Connacht.[60]

It is possible to see the reaction of at least one Connacht resident to the
presidency and composition in a poem of Tadhg Dall Ó hUiginn. In 'A theach-
taire théid ar sliabh' the poet is charged with what he regards as the composition
rent of others. The poet records that, in response,

I went to the courthouse to see if I could obtain right or justice.

[d'fios an bhfuighinn ceart nó cóir
go tigh cúirte do-chóigh mé.]

The court to which he appeals is clearly the presidency court since he relates
his appearance

Then as for the President, to whom I would go to relate my case,
with tears on my cheeks I used to make complaints to him, sternly
and bitterly.

He says, gruffly, that not by his will would a gage be taken from me;
that, however, I can give payment for it eventually.

59 *ALC*, ii, pp 466–7.   60 PRO, SP63/18, nos 48, 48 i.

[Dála an Uachtaráin ann sin,
chum a déinsi ag reic mo sgéal,
misi is mo dheór ar mo ghruaidh,
do-nínn casaoide chruaidh ghéar.

Adeir seision, lán do ghruaim,
nách béarthaoi geall uaim dá dheóin,
gidh eadh fós, is éidir dhamh
díol do thabhairt as fa dheóidh.][61]

The argument put forward by Ó hUiginn rested not on the question of payment of the composition rent but rather on the assertion that he had been
unjustly charged with more than his assessed payment. It is evident that he was
not opposed to the agreement itself. Indeed, his decision to utilise the administrative machinery of the provincial presidency to make his case affirms his
fundamental support for the political structure it represented. In practice,
despite the realisation that the jurisdiction of traditional lordships was being
undermined, the local support which the composition agreement received effectively guaranteed the success of the provincial presidency. It seems best to interpret Malby's acceptance by the annalist who wrote his Loch Cé obituary as an
appreciation that he was a liminal figure in Connacht politics. Although there
were contradictions inherent in his role, he was a power broker who could be
recruited to support particular factional disputes, and he could maximise his
influence by using disputes within families as political leverage. Malby's military activities in Connacht were low key, though the rivalries between Ulick
and John Burke, sons of the earl of Clanricard, attracted his attention in the
winter of 1576 and again from the autumn of 1580, until finally resolved in the
latter part of 1582.[62] In October 1577 he took Ó Conchobhair Shligigh's side
in a dispute against Ó Domhnaill, over Bundrowes castle. Malby was also intermittently involved in military exploits against Brian Ó Ruairc in Leitrim. In
Mayo he attempted to impose order on the rival factions of the Burkes and
successfully negotiated an agreement between rival contenders for the title
MacWilliam in 1580.[63]

This picture can be extended to understand more fully why Malby had
achieved this role in the locality. It is clear that the standards by which the

61 Eleanor Knott (ed.), *The bardic poems of Tadhg Dall Ó hUiginn* (2 vols, London, 1922–26), i, pp 156–8, ii, pp 104–5.   62 PRO, SP63/95, nos 27, 40; SP63/96, no. 37; SP63/98, no. 3.   63 PRO, SP63/71, no. 64; Bernadette Cunningham, 'Natives and newcomers in Mayo, 1560–1603', pp 32–3.

annalists judged the newcomers in Connacht were those of traditional Irish society and not those of a colonial world. Thus in 1589 the soldiers of Sir Richard Bingham were condemned by the annalist since 'there never came into Connacht such wicked people as were in that army; for there was not a man in the world to whom they were faithful in church or territory.' [ni thainic a Connacta riamh comholc a roibhe ar in sluagh sin, oir ni roibhe duine sa doman da rabhadar dileas a ccill na tuaith.][64] These were sentiments shared by Malby who had complained in 1581 that the soldiers he deployed in Connacht were 'the scum of their countries'.[65]

In contrast to the lower ranks of the soldiers, Malby, Fitton and their associates in the provincial administration were not unacceptable as political leaders in sixteenth-century Connacht. The inclusion of their obituaries in the annals makes clear that they were seen as important personalities in the region. They would only become unacceptable if they broke the norms of traditional society, and significantly disrupted the social hierarchy. Even individuals such as Sir Richard Bingham, whose time as Connacht president from 1584 to the mid 1590s was marked by a significant increase in military activity, was not seen primarily as an agent of English conquest or colonisation. Rather, Bingham's actions were perceived as disrupting the established social order within Gaelic society. Thus, according to the annalist, it was Bingham's aggressive actions which set the gentry of Connacht against Queen Elizabeth. The annalist was aware that a case could be made that such actions were illegal and not approved of by Dublin, 'When the justiciary of Erinn heard of that evil being inflicted on Connacht by the Binghams, he came with great anger and terrible fury, until he arrived at Galway' [Mar do chualaigh giustis na hErenn int olc sin do chur ar Connacht do Bingamachaib, tainic se go feirg moir ocus go londus nadhbail go rainig Gaillim.][66] In these circumstances the lord deputy was depicted as a rival to the provincial president and thus as another variable to be taken into account in the maintenance of the traditional political order within the province.

The view of the Connacht annalists was more contingent than a simple divide between natives and newcomers and they were prepared to adopt Sir Nicholas Malby and Sir Edward Fitton into their already complex political world. The native commentators were not unaware of the political problems present in late sixteenth-century Connacht in a climate of rapidly changing political allegiances. The Annals of Loch Cé, despite their understanding of the contribution which could be made by men such as Malby, reflect their

64 *ALC*, ii, pp 498–9. 65 PRO, SP63/81, no. 43. 66 *ALC*, ii, pp 494–5.

ambivalence about this changing balance of power. The ambiguity of Malby's
own obituary is one testimony to that. The same perspective is revealed in more
general observations recorded for 1584, the year of Malby's death, which claimed
'it is impossible to count, or reckon, or relate, all the injuries and oppression
the foreigners committed' [ni heidir a rim no a airoim no a faisneis cech ander-
rnatar Goill dolcaib ocus dainlettrom] and 'all Erinn was occupied by the
Foreigners this year, so that they put back the honour and nobility of the men
of Eirinn.' [Éire uile ar na gabáil le Gallaibh in bliadhain sin, innus ccur cuirset
oinech ocus uaisle fer nErenn ar gcul.][67] The precise context of these comments
is not revealed.

A better understanding of the ambiguities created by rapid political change
is provided by some of the late sixteenth-century poetry composed for Mac
Diarmada. One poem to Mac Diarmada written by Eochaidh Ó hEódhusa
probably in the latter years of the Nine Years' War captures something of the
essential contradictions of the situation. On the one hand Mac Diarmada is
portrayed as a warrior in a very traditional manner in '*Fód codarsna críoch Bhanbha*'.
He is a warrior in the tradition of the Táin, he lays low castles, harries the land
of the foreigners and attacks their heroes. However the very violence which the
poet celebrates is also the cause of Connacht's problems.

> The lords of the Goill, the Gaoidhil of Banba,
> it is customary for them to destroy the patrimony
> out of mutual hatred
> another part of her turmoil.
> ...
> Her English knights fear their chief
> the fear of the Gaill of the Gaoidhil
> there is nothing to restrain them anywhere
> Ireland has no rest between them.
>
> Yet all this sad plight is less sad
> than the state of Connachta,
> this fair-havened old-hazeled land,
> from the turmoil of Gaill and Gaoidhil.
>
> [Rioghraidh Ghaill, Gaoidhil Bhanbha,
> gnáth leo lot na hathardha

67 *ALC*, ii, pp 460–3.

re gomh croidhe dá chéile;
blogh oile dá haimhréidhe.

...

Eagla cniochtGhall re a gceanaibh
eagla Ghall ar Ghaoidhealaibh
's gan ghlas fa éineing orra
ní has d'Éirinn eatorra.

Gidh eadh ní hionann gach olc
is anbhuain fhairche Chonnocht,
achadh cuaingheal na gcall sean,
ó bhuaidhreadh Ghall is Ghaoidheal.][68]

Why the annalists should have regarded such internal fragmentation as natural
is unclear but one possible way of looking at this is suggested by the Connacht
annalists in the obituary of Aodh Dubh Ó Domhnaill in 1537. Having stressed
Ó Domhnaill's virtues, including the fact that he could have had the sovereignty of Ireland had he wished, the annalist commented

> but since he saw that the Gaels were becoming men of bad faith, trust-
> ing no man, unruly and froward, he made an alliance with the king of
> England, so that he was not oppressed by the might of the Galls but
> held sway in Leth Chuind without cavil after the manner of the men
> of Ireland.

> [et o'tconnairc se Gaoidhil Erenn ar ndul chunn michoinghill 7 chuinn
> nemhcreidemhna d'ennduine 7 iad anumal drochsmachta, do chengail
> se rann re Righ Saxan, innus nar luidh nert Gall air 7 co roibhe tren
> Leithi Coinn aige gan amharus do rer gnaith fer nGaoidel].[69]

Similar sentiments are reflected in a theological framework in the comments
of one Leinster scribe, Corc Óg Ó Cadhla. Writing in the margins of a medical tract he was transcribing in 1578, the year after the massacre at Mullaghmast
which all the annalists agreed was a terrible event, he complained of Elizabeth
I's religious reforms and the conduct of the English and noted

---

68 L. McKenna (ed.), *Dioghluim dána* (Baile Atha Cliath, 1938), p. 302, translated by McKenna in *Irish Monthly*,
xlix (1921), pp 327–8; in this instance we have used a revised translation kindly provided by Edel Bhreathnach.
69 *AConn*, pp 702–5.

It is a matter of surprise to me that God tolerates them so long in authority; except that He beareth patiently, and that His vengeance cometh slow and direct. An additional point: the Irish themselves are bad, and that Heaven hath provided them with castigation at another turn of history, we shall not discuss at length – for we should waste our ink and our paper with the thing we have suggested.

[is iongnadh liom a fhad fhuilinges Dia a gcennus iad, achd amháin gurob fada fhuilinges agus gurob mall direch a dhighaltus. Agus tuilledh eile .i. co bhfuilid Erinnaigh féin co holc agus co dtugadh a smachdughadh do nimh amhantur eile ni bhem da lenmhain a bhad, oir do chaithfimais ar ndubh agus ar bpaiper ris an ní adubhramar.][70]

That the internal divisions within the Gaelic polity were a punishment of God was an argument that would achieve much greater prominence in the early seventeenth century but it clearly contributed to a sixteenth-century sense of fatalism also.[71] The argument was most fully spelt out in a poem to Cormac Ó hEadhra of Sligo, who died in 1612. In 'Dia do chongnamh le Cormuc', Maol Muire Ó an Cháinte explicitly linked God's blessing with material success and therefore implicitly linked political failure with divine punishment.[72] Such a framework was central to the way in which Lughaidh Ó Cléirigh narrated the story of Aodh Ruadh Ó Domhnaill in his early seventeenth-century biography. While Aodh Ruadh was certainly portrayed as providentially chosen to lead his people, setbacks might be expected as a result of internal division by placing undue confidence in his own power rather than in the power of God.[73] Thus were problems theologised and in doing so a moral explanation for political problems could be found.

V

The explanations of how Sir Nicholas Malby's obituary came to be written in Brian Mac Diarmada's Annals of Loch Cé provide a useful corrective to the view of events in sixteenth-century Connacht from the windows of Dublin castle. It reveals a world of ambiguous social relationships as they evolved within

70 Paul Walsh, Gleanings from Irish manuscripts (2nd ed., Dublin, 1933), pp 159, 161. 71 Marc Caball, 'Providence and exile in early seventeenth-century Ireland' in Irish Historical Studies, xxix (1994–5), pp 174–88. 72 Lambert McKenna (ed.), The book of O'Hara (Dublin, 1951), pp 226–31. 73 For example Paul Walsh (ed.), Beatha Aodha Ruaidh Uí Dhomhnaill (2 vols, Dublin, 1948–57), i, pp 272–7.

pragmatic political positions rather than in the more theoretical framework of reform strategies. The same world from a different perspective is revealed in Sir John Harrington's 'Brief notes and remembrances'. Harrington had served in Connacht, Munster and Ulster under the earl of Essex in 1599 and concluded his experience with the observation

> They [the Irish] are abusive in their discourse and yet they do appeare in the upper sorte very kinde and hospitable to all new comers as I did well experience in this countrie even so much as if my own lands were here I would hazarde my dwellinge with them for life. I was often well entertaind, and in some sort got ill will for speaking in praise of their usage among our owne commanders, whom I often tolde that tho' I was sente oute to fighte with some, there did appear no reason for my not eatinge with others. I was well used and therefore am in dutie bounde to speake welle of the Irishrie.[74]

It may well be that Harrington and Malby's experiences were closer to the realities of everyday life before the outbreak of the Nine Years' War than has been assumed. That war shifted perspectives and in the 1630s when the Four Masters composed their obituary for Malby, with the benefit of hindsight they expressed a rather different view to that of the sixteenth-century annalists.

> Sir Nicholas Malby, governor of the province of Connacht, died at Athlone, about Shrovetide. He was a man learned in the languages and tongues of the islands of the west of Europe, a brave and victorious man in battles [fought] throughout Ireland, Scotland, and France, in the service of his sovereign; and this was a lucrative service to him, for he received a suitable remuneration from the Queen, namely the constableship of the town of Athlone, and the governorship of the province of Connacht, [which he enjoyed] for seven years before his death, and a grant in perpetuity of the towns of Roscommon and Ballinasloe, for himself and his heirs; but he himself had previously acquired Ballinasloe from the sons of the earl of Clanricard. Captain Brabazon held the place of Sir Nicholas until the arrival of Sir Richard Bingham in Ireland as Chief Commissioner of the province of Connacht, in the month of June the following summer.

---

74 John Harrington, *Nugae antiquae*, ed. Henry Harrington (3 vols, London, 1789), ii, p. 222.

[Sir Niclas Maulbi gobernóir chóiccidh Connacht décc in Áth Luain
fá initt, fear foglamtha i mbérlaibh 7 i tteangthoibh oilén iarthair Eorpa
esidhe, fear crodha cathbhuadhach seachnon Ereann, Alban, 7 na
Fraingce ag foghnamh dia phrionnsa, 7 ro badh seairbhís co somhaoín
dósomh indsin, uair fuair a dhiongmhala do dheaghthuarasdal on
mbainrioghain .i. Constablacht baile Átha Luain, gobernoracht chóiccidh Chonnacht fri sé seacht mbliadhan ria na bhás, síoruidheacht
Rossa comáin 7 beóil atha na sluaiccheadh dó feain 7 dá oidreadhaibh,
ina dheadhaigh acht amháin gur ab ó cloinn iarla cloinne Riocaird ro
chéd sholathair sé Bél Átha na Sluaiccheadh. Ionad Sir Nioclás ag
captin Brabusún go teacht Sir Risderd Bingam i nErinn ind árd chome-
ssoirecht chóiccidh Connacht i mí iun an tsamhraidh ar ccind.]⁷⁵

In the Annals of the Four Masters the eulogy was lengthier and more fulsome
in its praise than that in the earlier Loch Cé annals. A very definite change in
perspective is also discernible. Malby was perceived by the Four Masters as an
agent of Queen Elizabeth, and there was a clearer concentration on the office
he represented, even to the extent of naming his successors in that office. For
the Four Masters, writing in the wake of the Nine Years' War and the increasing centralisation of power in Ireland, the growth in influence of a regional
government official seemed a natural and well established process. Indeed, they
were concerned not just with the personalities but with the continuity and succession of the office, even mentioning the relatively uninfluential Sir Anthony
Brabazon's interim term of office as governor of Connacht. The world of the
early seventeenth century was quite different from the late sixteenth-century
world of Sir Edward Fitton, Sir Nicholas Malby, and Brian Mac Diarmada.
The pragmatic interaction between native and newcomer, which resonates in
the obituaries of Englishmen in the Irish annals, reflects the realities of late
sixteenth-century Connacht polities and was the key determinant of the changes
that were then underway.

75 *AFM*, v, pp 1814–27. Malby had reported the acquisition of the castle and lands of Ballinasloe and the
strategic bridge over the river Suck in a letter to the secretary of state, Sir Francis Walsingham, in December
1582, PRO, SP63/99, no. 32.

Bibliography

CATALOGUES AND REFERENCE WORKS

Abbott, T.K., and Gwynn, E.J., *Catalogue of the Irish manuscripts in the Library of Trinity College Dublin* (Dublin, 1921).

de Brún, Pádraig, *Catalogue of Irish manuscripts in King's Inns Library, Dublin* (Dublin, 1972).

Dictionary of national biography, ed. Leslie Stephen et al. (63 vols, London, 1885–1900).

Dillon, Myles, Mooney, Canice, and de Brún, Pádraig, *Catalogue of Irish manuscripts in the Franciscan Library, Killiney* (Dublin, 1969).

Foster, Joseph, *Alumni Oxoniense, 1500–1714* (4 vols, Oxford, 1891).

Gwynn, Aubrey, and Hadcock, R. Neville, *Medieval religious houses: Ireland* (London, 1970; reprint, Dublin, 1988).

Hayes, R.J. (ed.), *Manuscript sources for the history of Irish civilisation* (11 vols, New York, 1965; *First supplement*, 3 vols, New York, 1979).

Hogan, Edmund, *Onomasticon Goedelicum locorum et tribuum Hiberniae et Scotiae* (Dublin, 1910; reprint Dublin, 2000).

Kenney, James F., *The sources for the early history of Ireland: ecclesiastical: an introduction and guide* (New York, 1929; reprint Dublin, 1979).

Moody, T. W., Martin, F. X., and Byrne, F. J (eds), *A new history of Ireland, ix, maps, genealogies, lists* (Oxford, 1984).

Ní Sheaghdha, Nessa et al., *Catalogue of Irish manuscripts in the National Library of Ireland*, fascicules i–xiii (Dublin, 1967–96).

Ó Cuív, Brian, *Catalogue of Irish language manuscripts in the Bodleian Library at Oxford and Oxford College libraries, pt. 1, descriptions* (Dublin, 2001).

O'Grady, S.H., and Flower, Robin, *Catalogue of Irish manuscripts in the British Library* (3 vols, London, 1926–53; reprint Dublin, 1992).

O'Rahilly, T.F., Mulchrone, Kathleen, et al., *Catalogue of Irish manuscripts in the Royal Irish Academy*, fascicules 1–27 (Dublin, 1926–70).

Quin, E.G. et al. (eds), *Dictionary of the Irish language based mainly on Old and Middle Irish materials* (Dublin, 1913–76).

Shaw, W.A., *The knights of England* (2 vols, London, 1906).

Thom's almanac and official directory of the United Kingdom and Ireland, 1881 (Dublin, 1881).

PRIMARY SOURCES

Manuscripts

Dublin, National Archives
Chancery bills

Dublin, National Library of Ireland
D 10389–90
G1

Dublin, Royal Irish Academy
23 O 48 (476) *Liber Flavus Fergusiorum*
23 P 7 (688) Annals of the Four Masters, AD 1500–1616
C iii 3 (1220) Annals of the Four Masters, AM 2242- AD 1171
C iii 1 (1219) Annals of Connacht

Dublin, Trinity College
556
830
831
1282 (H. 1. 8) Annals of Ulster, AD 431–1504
1293 (H. 1. 19) Annals of Loch Cé
1301 (H. 2. 11) Annals of the Four Masters, AD 1334–1604
6404 Notebook of Sir James Ware

Edinburgh, National Library of Scotland
72.2.3 Glenmasan MS

London, British Library
Add. 4717 Annals of Clonmacnoise, in English translation
Add. 4792 Fragment of the Annals of Loch Cé, AD 1568–1590
Add. 18205
Add. 19836
Add. 30512
Add. 40766
Add. 47172 Entry book of the court of Castle Chamber
Add. 48015
Cotton Titus B XII
Cotton Titus B XIII
Egerton 136
Egerton 189
Harley 2048
Lansdowne 255

London, Public Record Office
SP63 State Papers, Ireland

Oxford, Bodleian Library
Rawl. B 489 Annals of Ulster

PRINTED PRIMARY SOURCES

Bergin, Osborn (ed.), *Irish bardic poetry* (Dublin, 1970).

Bieler, Ludwig, and Kelly, Fergus (eds), *The Patrician texts in the Book of Armagh* (Dublin, 1979).

Brady, W.M. (ed.), *State papers concerning the Irish church in the time of Queen Elizabeth* (London, 1868).

Breatnach, Pádraig A. (ed.), 'Marbhna Aodha Ruaidh Uí Dhomhnaill', *Éigse*, xv (1973–4), 34–50.

—, 'A poem on the end of patronage', *Éigse*, xxxi (1999), 85–8.

—, 'A seventeenth-century abridgement of *Beatha Aodha Ruaidh Uí Dhomhnaill*', *Éigse*, xxxiii (2002), 77–172.

Breatnach, R.B. (ed.), 'An elegy on Donal O'Sullivan Beare', *Éigse*, vii (1953–5), 162–81.

Butler, Richard (ed.), *The annals of Ireland by Friar John Clynn and Tady Dowling* (Dublin, 1848).

Calendar of entries in the papal registers relating to Great Britain and Ireland: papal letters, 1898–1304 [etc.], (London, 1893–).

Calendar of the Carew manuscripts, preserved in the archiepiscopal library at Lambeth, 1515–1624 (6 vols, London, 1867–73).

Calendar of the state papers relating to Ireland, 1509–1670 (24 vols, London, 1860–1912).

Camden, William, *Britain, or a chorographical description of the most flourishing kingdoms, England, Scotland and Ireland, and the islands adjoining out of the depth of antiquitie*. Trans. Philemon Holland (London, 1610).

Carney, James (ed.), *A genealogical history of the O'Reillys, written in the eighteenth century by Eóghan Ó Raghallaigh* (Dublin and Cavan, 1959).

Colgan, John, *Acta Sanctorum veteris et majoris Scotiae seu Hiberniae sanctorum insulae* (Louvain, 1645; reprint Dublin, 1948).

Crossthwaite, J.C. (ed.), *The book of obits and martyrology of the cathedral church of the Holy Trinity … Dublin* (Dublin, 1844).

Cunningham, Bernadette (ed.), 'A view of religious affiliation and practice in Thomond, 1591', *Archivium Hibernicum*, xlviii (1994) 13–24.

—, 'Clanricard letters: letters and papers, 1605–1673, preserved in the National Library of Ireland, manuscript 3111', *Journal of the Galway Archaeological and Historical Society*, xlviii (1996), 162–208.

Dillon, Myles (ed.), *Lebor na cert: the book of rights* (Dublin, 1962).

Doan, James (ed.), *The romance of Cearbhall and Fearbhlaidh* (Dublin, 1985).

Freeman, A.M. (ed.), *The compossicion booke of Conought* (Dublin, 1936).

Gilbert, J.T. (ed.), 'Archives of the town of Galway' in Historical Manuscripts Commission, *Tenth report*, appendix, pt 5 (London, 1885), 380–566.

Gillies, William (ed.), 'An early modern Irish "Harrowing of hell"', *Celtica*, xiii (1980), 32–55.

Giraldus Cambrensis, *The first version of the topography of Ireland*. Translated by John J. O'Meara (Dundalk, 1951).

Greene, David (ed.), *Duanaire Mhéig Uidhir* (Dublin, 1972).

Gwynn, Lucius (ed.), 'The life of St Lasair', *Ériu*, v (1911), 73–103.

Hagan, John (ed.), 'Miscellanae Vaticano-Hibernica, 1580–1631', *Archivium Hibernicum*, iii (1914), 227–366.

Hardiman, James (ed.), 'Ancient Irish deeds and writings', *Transactions of the Royal Irish Academy*, xv (1826), 3–95.

Haren, Michael (ed.), 'Vatican archives *Minutae brevium in forma gratiosa* relating to Clogher diocese', *Clogher Record*, xii (1985–7), 55–77.

Harrington, John, *Nugae antiquae*, ed. Henry Harrington (3 vols, London, 1789).

Harris, Walter, *The whole works of Sir James Ware concerning Ireland* (3 vols, Dublin, 1739).

Hennessy, W.M. (ed.), *The Annals of Loch Cé: a chronicle of Irish affairs from AD 1014 to AD 1590* (2 vols, London, 1871).

Hennessy, W.N., and Kelly, D.H. (eds), *Book of Fenagh* (Dublin, 1875; reprint Dublin 1939).

Historical Manuscripts Commission, *Eighth report* (London, 1881), appendix 2.

Hogan, Edmund (ed.), *The description of Ireland ... in anno 1598* (Dublin, 1878).

Hore, H.F. (ed.), 'Irish bardism in 1561', *Ulster Journal of Archaeology*, 1st ser., vi (1858), 165–7.

Inquisitionum in officio rotulorum cancellariae Hiberniae ... repertorium (2 vols, Dublin, 1826–9).

Irish fiants of the Tudor sovereigns during the reigns of Henry VIII, Edward VI, Philip & Mary, and Elizabeth I, with a new introduction by Kenneth Nicholls (4 vols, Dublin, 1994). (Reprinted from *Reports of the Deputy Keeper of the Public Records in Ireland*, 1875–1890).

Joynt, Maud (ed.), *Tromhdámh Guaire* (Dublin, 1931).

Keating, Geoffrey, *Foras feasa ar Éirinn*, ed. David Comyn and P.S. Dinneen (4 vols, London, 1902–14).

Kew, Graham (ed.), 'The Irish sections of Fynes Moryson's unpublished itinerary', *Analecta Hibernica*, no. 37 (1998), 1–138.

Knott, Eleanor (ed.), *The bardic poems of Tadhg Dall Ó hUiginn* (2 vols, London, 1922–6).

—, 'Mac an Bhaird's elegy on the Ulster lords', *Celtica*, v (1960), 162–5.

—, 'The flight of the earls', *Ériu*, viii (1915–16), 192–4.

Lynch, Anthony, 'Calendar of the reassembled register of John Bole, archbishop of Armagh, 1457–71', *Seanchas Ard Mhacha*, xv, no. 1 (1992–3), 113–85.

Lynch, John, *De praesulibus Hiberniae*. ed. J.F. O'Doherty (2 vols, Dublin, 1944).

—, *Pii antistitis icon sive de vita et morte R.D. Francisci Kirovani* (Maclovii, 1669; reprint Dublin, 1951).

Mac Airt, Sean (ed.), *Leabhar Branach: the book of the O'Byrnes* (Dublin, 1944).

Mac Airt, Seán, and Mac Niocaill, Gearóid (eds), *Annals of Ulster to AD 1131: text and translation* (Dublin, 1983).

Macalister, R.A.S. (ed.), *Two Irish Arthurian romances* (London, 1908).

—, *Lebor gabála Érenn: the book of the taking of Ireland* (5 vols, Dublin, 1938–56).

Macalister, R.A.S., and Mac Neill, J. (eds), *Leabhar gabhála: the book of conquests of Ireland: the recension of Micheál Ó Cléirigh* (Dublin, 1916).

Mac Giolla Choille, Breandán (ed.), *Books of survey and distribution: iii, county of Galway* (Dublin, 1962).

McKenna, Lambert (ed.), *Dioghluim dána* (Dublin, 1938).

—, *Aithdioghluim dána* (2 vols, London, 1939–40).

—, 'Poem by Eochaidh Ó hEoghusa', *Irish Monthly*, xlviii (1920), 539–44.

—, 'Poem to Mac Diarmuda of Magh Luirg', *Irish Monthly*, xlix (1921), 327–32.

—, 'Some Irish bardic poems', *Studies*, xxxix (1950), 440–3.

—, *The book of O'Hara* (Dublin, 1951).

McNamara, Martin, et al. (eds), *Apocrypha Hiberniae, 1: Evangelia infantiae*, in *Corpus Christianorum; series Apocryphorum* 13 (Turnhout, 2001).

Mac Neill, Charles (ed.), 'MS Rawlinson A 237', *Analecta Hibernica*, no. 3 (1931), 151–218.

Mac Niocaill, Gearóid (ed.), 'Disiecta membra', *Éigse*, viii (1955–7), 74–7.

Maps of the escheated counties of Ireland, copied at the Ordnance Survey Office, Southampton (Southampton, 1861).

Marstrander, Carl (ed.), 'Bídh crínna', *Ériu*, v (1911), 126–41.

—, 'The two deaths', *Ériu*, v (1911), 120–4.

Meyer, Kuno (ed.), *The instructions of King Cormac Mac Airt*, Todd Lecture Series, xv, (Dublin, 1909).

Mooney, Canice, 'Topographical fragments from the Franciscan library', *Celtica*, i, pt. 1 (1946), 64–85.

Moran, P.F. (ed.), *Spicilegium Ossoriense* (3 vols, Dublin, 1874–84).

Morgan, Hiram (ed.), '"Lawes of Irelande": a tract by Sir John Davies', *Irish Jurist*, n.s. xxviii–xxx (1993–5), 307–13.

Morley, Henry (ed.), *Ireland under Elizabeth and James the first* (London, 1890).

Morrin, James (ed.), *Calendar of the patent and close rolls of chancery in Ireland* (3 vols, Dublin, 1861–3).

Mulchrone, Kathleen (ed.), *Bethu Phátraic* (Dublin, 1939).

Murphy, Denis (ed.), *Annals of Clonmacnoise from the earliest period to A.D. 1408, translated into English by Conell Mageoghagan, A.D. 1627* (Dublin, 1896).

—, *Triumphalia chronologica monasterii Sanctae Crucis in Hibernia* (Dublin, 1895).

Murphy, Seán, 'The Sligo papers, Westport house, Co. Mayo: a report', *Analecta Hibernica*, no. 33 (1986), 15–46.

Murray, L.P. (ed.) [continued by Gwynn, A.], 'Archbishop Cromer's register', *Journal of the County Louth Archaeological Society*, vii (1929–32), 516–24; viii (1933–6) 38–49, 169–88, 257–74, 322–51; ix (1937–40), 36–41, 124–30; x (1941–4), 116–27, 165–79.

Ní Laoire, Siobhán (ed.), *Bás Cearbhaill agus Farbhlaidhe* (Dublin, 1986).

Ní Shéaghdha, Nessa (ed.), 'The rights of Mac Diarmada', *Celtica*, vi (1963), 156–72.

Nicholls, K.W. (ed.), 'The Lisgoole agreement of 1580', *Clogher Record*, vii (1969–72), 27–33.

—, 'The register of Clogher', *Clogher Record*, vii (1969–72), 363–431.

O'Brien, M.A. (ed.), *Corpus genealogiarum Hiberniae*, I (Dublin, 1962; reprint 1976).

Ó Cróinín, Dáibhí (ed.), 'A poem to Toirdhealbhach Luinneach Ó Néill', *Éigse*, xvi (1975–6), 50–66.

Ó Cuív, Brian (ed.), 'Tréidhe sa nua-Ghaeilge', *Éigse*, ix (1958–61), 180.

—, 'Bunús Mhuintir Dhíolún', *Éigse*, xi (1964), 65–6.

—, 'A fragment of Irish annals', *Celtica*, xiv (1981), 83–104.

—, 'The decline of poesy', *Celtica*, xix (1987), 126–7.

O'Daly, Aenghus, *The tribes of Ireland*, ed. John O'Donovan (Dublin, 1852).

O'Daly, Máirín (ed.), 'Mesce Chúanach', *Ériu*, xix (1962), 75–80.

Ó Doilbhín, Eamon (ed.), 'Ceart Uí Néill: a discussion and translation of the document', *Seanchas Árd Mhacha*, v (1969–40), 324–58.

O'Donovan, John (ed.), *Annála ríoghachta Éireann: Annals of the kingdom of Ireland by the Four Masters from the earliest period to the year 1616* (7 vols, Dublin, 1851; reprint, New York, 1966).

Ó Dufaigh, Seosamh (ed.), 'Cíos Mhic Mhathghamhna', *Clogher Record*, iv (1961–2), 125–34.

O'Grady, S.H. (ed.), *Silva Gadelica: a collection of tales in Irish* (2 vols, London, 1892).

Ó Lochlainn, Colm (ed.), 'Ár ar Árd na Riadh', *Éigse*, v (1946–7), 149–55.

—, 'Prince and poet: a poem to Art Mac Aonghusa', *Éigse*, ii (1940–1), 157–62.

O'Kelleher, A., and Schoepperle, G. (eds), *Betha Colaim Chille* (Illinois, 1918).

Ó Maolagáin, Pádraig (ed.), 'An early history of Fermanagh', *Clogher Record*, i, no. 3 (1955), 131–40; no. 4 (1956), 113–25; ii, no. 1 (1957), 50–59; no. 2 (1958), 280–92; no. 3, 458–67, iv, no. 1–2 (1960–61), 42–49, 163–73.

Ó Muireadhaigh, Réamann (ed.), 'Marbhna ar Mhuiris Mac Torna Uí Mhaolchonaire', *Éigse*, xv (1973–4), 215–21.

Ó Murchú, L.P. (ed.), 'Caoineadh ar Uaithne Ó Lochlainn, 1617', *Éigse*, xxvii (1993), 67–77.

Ó Raghallaigh, Tomás (ed.), 'Seanchus Búrcach', *Journal of the Galway Archaeological and Historical Society*, xiii (1926–7), pp 50–60, 101–37; xiv (1928–9), 30–51, 142–66.

O'Rahilly, Cecile (ed.), *Eachtra Uilliam: an Irish version of William of Palerne* (Dublin, 1949).

O'Rahilly, T.F. (ed.), *A miscellany of Irish proverbs* (Dublin, 1922).

Ó Raithbheartaigh, Toirdhealbhach (ed.), *Genealogical tracts*, I (Dublin, 1932).

Ó Riain, Pádraig (ed.), *Corpus genealogiarum Sanctorum Hiberniae* (Dublin, 1985).

O'Sullivan, William (ed.), *The Strafford inquisition of County Mayo* (Dublin, 1958).

Ó Tuathail, Éamonn (ed.), 'Nugentiana', *Éigse*, ii (1940–1), 5–14.

Pender, Séamus (ed.), 'The O'Clery book of genealogies', *Analecta Hibernica*, no. 15 (1951), xi–xxxiii, 1–198.

Piers, Henry, *A chorographical description of the county of Westmeath* (reprint Tara, 1981).

Plummer, Charles (ed.), *Vitae sanctorum Hiberniae* (2 vols, Oxford, 1910).

—, *Bethada naem nÉrenn: lives of Irish saints* (2 vols, Oxford, 1922).

—, *Miscellanea hagiographica Hibernica* (Brussels, 1925).

Radner, J. N. (ed.), *Fragmentary annals of Ireland* (Dublin, 1978).

Refaussé, Raymond, with Lennon, Colm (eds), *The registers of Christ Church cathedral, Dublin* (Dublin, 1998).

Richardson, John, *The great folly, superstition and idolatry of pilgrimages in Ireland* (Dublin, 1727).

Rochford, Robert, *The life of the glorious bishop St Patricke ... together with the lives of the holy virgin S. Bridgit and of the glorious abbot Saint Columbe* (St Omer, 1625).

Russell, Charles W. (ed.), 'On the agreement in Irish between Gerald, ninth earl of Kildare and the Mac Rannalds', *Proceedings of the Royal Irish Academy*, x (1869), 480–96.

Shuckburgh, E.S. (ed.), *Two biographies of William Bedell* (Cambridge, 1902).

Simington, R.C. (ed.), *Books of survey and distribution, i: county of Roscommon* (Dublin, 1949).

—, *Books of survey and distribution, ii: county of Mayo* (Dublin, 1956).

State Papers Henry VIII (11 vols, London, 1830–52).

Stokes, Whitley (ed.), *Three Irish glossaries* (London, 1862).

——, *Three middle Irish homilies on the lives of Saints Patrick, Brigit and Columba* (Calcutta, 1877).

——, *Lives of the saints from the Book of Lismore* (Oxford, 1890).

Sughi, M.A. (ed.), *Registrum Octaviani alias Liber Niger* (2 vols, Dublin, 1999).

Swords, Liam (ed.), 'A sixteenth-century register of Achonry', *Collectanea Hibernica*, nos 39–40 (1997–8), 7–22.

Todd, J.H. (ed.), *Leabhar Bhreathnach annso sis: the Irish version of the Historia Britonum of Nennius* (Dublin, 1848).

Todd, J.H., and Reeves, W. (eds), *The martyrology of Donegal: a calendar of the saints of Ireland* (Dublin, 1864).

Ua Cadhla, Cormac (ed.), 'Geinealaighe Fearmanach', *Analecta Hibernica*, no. 3 (1931), 62–150.

Ua Ceallaigh, Seán (ed.), *Trí truagha na scéaluidheachta: Oidhe Chlainne Tuireann, Oidhe Chlainne Lir, Oidhe Chlainne Uisnigh* (Baile Átha Cliath, 1927).

Ua Duinnín, Pádraig (ed.), *MeGuidhir Fhearmanach: the Maguires of Fermanagh* (Dublin, 1917).

Van Hamel, A.G. (ed.), *Lebor Bretnach* (Dublin, 1932).

Walsh, Paul (ed.), *Genealogiae regum et sanctorum Hiberniae, by the Four Masters, edited from the manuscript of Michél Ó Cléirigh* (Maynooth, 1918).

—, *Leabhar Chlainne Suibhne* (Dublin, 1920).

—, 'Bás Cearbhall agus Farbhlaidhe', *Irisleabhar Muighe Nuadhat* (1922), 26–45.

—, *Gleanings from Irish manuscripts* (2nd ed., Dublin, 1933).

—, *Beatha Aodha Ruaidh Uí Dhomhnaill* (2 vols, Dublin, 1948–57).

—, 'Curiosities from the annals', *Irish Book Lover*, xix (1931), 38–9.

Walsh, Reginald (ed.), 'Irish manners and customs in the sixteenth century', *Archivium Hibernicum*, v (1916), 17–19.

Ware, Sir James, *De Scriptoribvs Hiberniae* (Dublin, 1639).

SECONDARY SOURCES

Bannerman, John, *The Beatons: a medical kindred in the classical Gaelic tradition* (Edinburgh, 1986).

Beirne, Francis (ed.), *The diocese of Elphin* (Dublin, 2000).

Bhreathnach, Edel, 'Authority and supremacy in Tara and its hinterland, c.950–1200', *Discovery Programme Reports*, 5 (Dublin, 1999), 1–23.

Binchy, D.A., 'Lawyers and chroniclers' in Brian Ó Cuív (ed.), *Seven centuries of Irish learning* (2nd ed., Cork, 1971), 50–61.

Bourdieu, Pierre, *Outline of a theory of practice* (Cambridge, 1977).

Boyle, Alexander, 'Fearghal Ó Gadhra and the Four Masters', *Irish Ecclesiastical Record*, 5th ser, c (1963), 110–14.

Breatnach, Caoimhín. 'Rawlinson B 502, *Lebar Glinne dá Locha*, and *Saltair na Rann*', *Éigse*, xxx (1997), 109–32.

—, *Patronage, politics and prose: Cesacht Inghine Guile, Sgéala Muice Meic Dhá Thó, Oidheadh Chuinn Chéadchathaigh* (Maynooth, 1996).

—, '*Oidheadh Chloinne Tuireann* agus *Cath Maige Tuired*: dhá shampla de mhiotas eiseamláireach', *Éigse*, xxxii (2000), 35–46.

Breatnach, Pádraig A., 'The chief's poet', *Proceedings of the Royal Irish Academy*, lxxxiii, sect. C (1983), 37–79.

—, 'The methodology of seanchas: the redaction by Cú Choigcríche Ó Cléirigh of the chronicle poem *Leanam Croinic Clann nDálaigh*', *Éigse*, xxix (1996), 1–18.

—, 'The poet's graveside vigil: a theme of Irish bardic elegy in the fifteenth century', *Zeitschift für Celtische Philologie*, xlix–l (1997), 50–63.

Broun, D, *The charters of Gaelic Scotland and Ireland in the early and central middle ages* (Quiggin pamphlets, 2) (Cambridge, 1995).

Bruford, Alan, Gaelic folktales and medieval romances, *Béaloideas*, xxxiv (1966), 1–284.

Byrne, F.J. *Irish kings and high kings* (2nd ed., Dublin, 2001).

—, 'Senchas: the nature of Gaelic historical tradition: approaches to history' in J.G. Barry (ed.), *Historical Studies*, ix (Belfast, 1974), 137–59.

Caball, Marc, *Poets and politics: reaction and continuity in Irish poetry, 1558–1625* (Cork, 1998).

—, 'Providence and exile in early seventeenth-century Ireland', *Irish Historical Studies*, xxix (1994–5), 174–88.

Caerwyn Williams, J.E., and Ford, Patrick K., *The Irish literary tradition* (Cardiff, 1992).

Carey, John, 'Werewolves in medieval Ireland', *Cambrian Medieval Celtic Studies*, no. 44 (2002), 37–72.

Carney, James, *Studies in Irish literature and history* (Dublin, 1955).

—, *The Irish bardic poet* (Dublin, 1967).

—, 'Literature in Irish, 1169–1534' in A. Cosgrove (ed.), *A new history of Ireland, ii, medieval Ireland 1169–1534* (Oxford, 1987), 688–707.

Clanchy, M.T., 'Remembering the past and the good old law', *History*, lv (1970), 165–76.

Cosgrave, Art (ed.), *A new history of Ireland, ii: medieval Ireland, 1169–1534* (Oxford, 1987).

Cressy, David, *Travesties and transgressions in Tudor and Stuart England: tales of discord and dissension* (Oxford, 2000).

Cronin, Tadhg, 'The Elizabethan colony in Co. Roscommon' in Harman Murtagh (ed.), *Irish midland studies* (Athlone, 1980), 107–20.

Cunningham, Bernadette, 'Political and social change in the lordships of Clanricard and Thomond, 1569–1641', unpublished M.A. thesis, National University of Ireland, Galway (1979).

—, 'The composition of Connacht in the lordships of Clanricard and Thomond, 1577–1641', *Irish Historical Studies*, xxiv (1984–5), 1–14.

—, 'Native culture and political change in Ireland, 1580–1640' in Ciaran Brady and Raymond Gillespie (eds), *Natives and newcomers: essays on the making of Irish colonial society, 1534–1641* (Dublin, 1986), 148–70.

—, 'Natives and newcomers in Mayo, 1560–1603' in Raymond Gillespie and Gerard Moran (eds), *'A various country': essays in Mayo history, 1500–1900* (Westport, 1987), 24–43.

—, 'The historical annals of Maoilín Óg Mac Bruaideadha, 1588–1603', *The Other Clare*, xiii (1989), 21–4.

—, 'The culture and ideology of Irish Franciscan historians at Louvain, 1607–1650' in Ciarán Brady (ed.), *Ideology and the historians: Historical Studies xvii* (Dublin, 1991), 11–30, 222–7.

—, *The world of Geoffrey Keating: history, myth and religion in seventeenth-century Ireland* (Dublin, 2000).

Cunningham, Bernadette, and Gillespie, Raymond, '"The most adaptable of saints": the cult of St Patrick in the seventeenth century', *Archivium Hibernicum*, xlix (1995), 82–104.

— and —, 'An Ulster settler and his Irish manuscripts', *Éigse*, xxi (1986), 27–36.

— and —, 'Englishmen in sixteenth-century Irish annals', *Irish Economic and Social History*, xvii (1990), 5–21.

— and —, 'The purposes of patronage: Brian Maguire of Knockninny and his manuscripts', *Clogher Record*, xiii, no. 1 (1988), 38–49.

de Paor, Liam, *Saint Patrick's world: the Christian culture of Ireland's apostolic age* (Dublin, 1993).

Dillon, Myles, 'Laud 610', *Celtica*, vi (1963), 64–76.

Dillon, Myles (ed.), *Irish sagas* (Cork, 1968).

Dolley, Michael, and Mac Niocaill, Gearóid, 'Some coin names in Ceart Uí Néill',
    Studia Celtica, ii (1967), 19–24.

Duffy, Patrick J., Edwards, David, and FitzPatrick, Elizabeth (eds), *Gaelic Ireland: land,
    lordship and settlement, c.1250–c.1650* (Dublin, 2001).

Fletcher, Alan, 'Preaching in late-medieval Ireland: the English and the Latin tradition'
    in Alan Fletcher and Raymond Gillespie (eds), *Irish preaching, 700–1700* (Dublin,
    2001), 56–80.

Ford, Alan, *The protestant reformation in Ireland, 1590–1641* (Frankfurt am Main, 1985).

Geertz, Clifford, *Local knowledge: further essays in interpretative anthropology* (London, 1993).

Gillespie, Raymond, *Devoted people: belief and religion in early modern Ireland* (Manchester,
    1997).

—, 'The burning of Ellen Ní Gilwey, 1647: sidelight on popular belief in Meath',
    Ríocht na Midhe, x (1999), 71–7.

Grabowski, Kathryn, and Dumville, David, *Chronicles and annals of medieval Ireland and
    Wales: the Clonmacnoise-group texts* (Woodbridge, 1984).

Gwynn, Aubrey, *The medieval province of Armagh* (Dundalk, 1946).

—, 'The Annals of Connacht and the Abbey of Cong', *Journal of Galway Archaeological
    and Historical Society*, xxvii (1956–7), 1–9.

—, 'Cathal Mac Maghnusa and the Annals of Ulster', *Clogher Record*, ii, no. 2 (1958),
    230–43, no. 3 (1959), 370–84. Reprinted with a new introduction in Aubrey Gwynn,
    Cathal Óg Mac Maghnusa and the Annals of Ulster ed. Nollaig Ó Muraíle (Enniskillen,
    1998).

—, 'The cult of St Martin in Ireland', *Irish Ecclesiastical Record*, 5th ser, cv (1966), 353–64.

Gwynn, Edward, 'The manuscript known as the *Liber Flavus Fergusiorum*', *Proceedings of the
    Royal Irish Academy*, xxvi, sect. C (1906–7), 15–41.

Hamlin, Ann, 'The archaeology of early Christianity in the north of Ireland', unpub-
    lished Ph.D. thesis, Queen's University Belfast (1976).

Hardiman, James, *History of the town and county of the town of Galway* (Dublin, 1820).

Haren, Michael, and de Pontfarcy, Yolande, *The medieval pilgrimage to St Patrick's purgatory
    Lough Derg and the European tradition* (Enniskillen, 1988).

Hay, Denys, *Annalists and historians: western historiography from the eighth to the eighteenth centuries*
    (London, 1977).

Herbert, Máire, *Iona, Kells and Derry: the history and hagiography of the monastic familia of Columba*
    (Oxford, 1988; reprint Dublin, 1996).

—, 'The life of Martin of Tours: a view from twelfth-century Ireland' in Michael
    Richter and Jean-Michel Picard (eds), *Ogma: essays in Celtic studies* (Dublin, 2002),
    76–84.

Hunt, John, *Irish medieval figure sculpture* (2 vols, Shannon, 1974).

Jennings, Brendan, *Michael O Cleirigh chief of the Four Masters and his associates* (Dublin, 1936).

Kelly, Fergus, *A guide to early Irish law* (Dublin, 1988).

—, *Early Irish farming* (Dublin, 1997).

King, Heather A., 'Irish memorial brasses to 1700', *Proceedings of the Royal Irish Academy*, xciv, sect. C (1994), 111–40.

Kirk, G. S., *Myth: its meaning and functions in ancient and other cultures* (Cambridge, 1971).

Knox, H.T., *The history of the county of Mayo to the close of the sixteenth century* (Dublin, 1908).

Lambert, G.W., 'Sir Nicholas Malby and his associates', in *Journal of the Galway Archaeological and Historical Society*, xxiii (1948), 1–13.

Leerssen, J.T., *Mere Irish and Fíor Ghael: studies in the idea of nationality its development and literary expression prior to the nineteenth century* (Amsterdam and Philadelphia, 1986; 2nd ed. Cork, 1996).

Leslie, Shane, *Saint Patrick's Purgatory* (London, 1932).

Levi, Giovanni, 'On microhistory' in Peter Burke (ed.), *New perspectives on historical writing* (Oxford, 1991), 93–113.

Lowry-Corry, Dorothy, 'Ancient church sites and graveyards in Co. Fermanagh', *Journal of the Royal Society of Antiquaries of Ireland*, xlix (1920), 35–46.

Lucas, A.T., 'The plundering and burning of churches in Ireland, 7th to 16th century', in Etienne Rynne (ed.), *North Munster studies* (Limerick, 1967), 172–229.

Mac Airt, Seán, '*Filidecht* and *coimgne*', *Ériu*, xviii (1958), 139–52.

Macalister, R.A.S., 'Oidhe Chloinne Tuireann', *Béaloideas*, i (1927), 13–21.

Mac Aodha, Breandán, 'Tobarainmneacha i gContae Ros Comáin: réamhshuirbhé', *Journal of the Old Athlone Society*, ii (1978–85), 136–8.

Mac Cana, Proinsias, 'The rise of the later schools of *filidheacht*', *Ériu*, xxv (1974), 126–46.

McCarthy, D., 'The chronology of the Irish annals', *Proceedings of the Royal Irish Academy*, xcviii, sect. C (1998), 203–55.

McCarthy, D., and Breen, A., 'Astronomical observations in the Irish annals and their motivation', *Peritia*, xi (1997), 1–43.

McCone, Kim, *Pagan past and Christian present in early Irish literature* (Maynooth, 1990).

Mac Dermot, Dermot, *Mac Dermot of Moylurg: the story of a Connacht family* (Manorhamilton, 2000).

McDonnell-Garvey, Máire, *Mid-Connacht: the ancient territory of Sliabh Lugha* (Manorhamilton, 1995).

Mac Eoin, G., 'Poet and prince in medieval Ireland' in Evelyn Mullally and John Thompson (eds), *The court and cultural diversity: selected papers from the eighth triennial congress of the International Courtly Literature Society* (Woodbridge, 1997), 3–17.

McGrath, C., 'Í Eódhasa', *Clogher Record* ii, pt 1 (1957), 1–19.

MacHale, C., *Annals of the Clan Egan: an account of the Mac Egan bardic family of brehon lawyers* (Enniscrone, 1990).

McKenna, J.E., *Parishes of Clogher* (2 vols, Enniskillen, 1920–30).

Mackenzie, Alexander, *History of the Macleods with genealogies of the principal families of the name* (Inverness, 1889).

McLeod, William, 'The rhetorical geography of the late medieval Irish chronicles', *Cambrian Medieval Celtic Studies*, no. 40 (2000), 57–68.

Mac Niocaill, Gearóid, *The medieval Irish annals* (Dublin, 1975).

Martin, F.X., 'Confusion abounding: Bernard O'Higgins, OSA, bishop of Elphin, 1542–1561' in Art Cosgrove and Donal McCartney (eds), *Studies in Irish history presented to R. Dudley Edwards* (Dublin, 1979), 38–84.

Muir, Edward, and Ruggiero, Guido (eds), *Microhistory and the lost peoples of Europe* (Baltimore, 1991).

Nagy, Joseph Falaky, *Conversing with angels and ancients: literary myths of medieval Ireland* (Dublin, 1997).

Nic Eoin, Máirín, *B'ait leo bean: gnéithe en idé-eolaíocht inscne i dtradisiún liteartha na Gaeilge* (Dublin, 1998).

Nicholls, K.W., *Land, law and society in sixteenth-century Ireland* (NUI, O'Donnell lecture) (Dublin, 1976).

—, 'The Irish genealogies: their value and defects', *Irish Genealogist*, v (1975), 256–61.

Ó Buachalla, Breandán, '*Annála Ríoghachta Éireann* is *Foras Feasa ar Éirinn*: an comhthéacs comhaimseartha', *Studia Hibernica*, nos 22–3 (1982–3), 59–105.

Ó Caithnia, Liam P., *Apalóga na bhfilí, 1200–1650* (Baile Átha Cliath, 1984).

Ó Concheanainn, Tomás, 'The Book of Ballymote', *Celtica*, xiv (1981), 15–25.

O'Conor, Kieran, *The archaeology of medieval rural settlement in Ireland* (Dublin, 1998).

____. 'The moated site of Inishatiarra Island, Drumharlow Lough, Co. Roscommon', *County Roscommon Historical and Archaeological Society Journal*, vii (1998), 1–3.

Ó Corráin, Donnchadh, 'Irish origin legends and genealogy: recurrent aetiologies' in T. Nyberg et al. (eds), *History and heroic tale: a symposium* (Odense, 1985), 51–96.

—, 'Historical need and literary narrative' in D. Ellis Evans, et al. (eds), *Proceedings of the Seventh International Congress of Celtic Studies, Oxford, 1983* (Oxford, 1986), 141–58.

—, 'Legend as critic' in Tom Dunne (ed.), *The writer as witness: literature as historical evidence* (Cork, 1987), 23–38.

Ó Cróinín, Dáibhí, 'Early Irish annals from Easter-tables: a case restated', *Peritia*, ii (1983), 74–86.

Ó Cuív, Brian, 'Literary creation and Irish historical tradition', *Proceedings of the British Academy*, xlix (1963), 233–62.

—, *The Irish bardic duanaire or 'poem-book'* (Dublin, 1974).

—, 'The earl of Thomond and the poets, A.D. 1572', *Celtica*, xii (1977), 125–45.

—, 'Some Irish items relating to the MacDonnells of Antrim', *Celtica*, xvi (1984), 139–56.

Ó Dushláine, Tadhg, 'Lough Derg in native Irish poetry', *Clogher Record*, xiii (1988–9), 78–84.

Ó Fiannachta, Pádraig, 'Stair, finnscéal agus annála', *Léachtaí Cholm Cille*, ii (1971), 5–13.

Ó hÓgáin, Daithí, *The hero in Irish folk history* (Dublin, 1985).

O'Keefe, Peter, and Simington, Tom, *Irish stone bridges: history and heritage* (Dublin, 1991).

Ó Muraíle, Nollaig, 'The autograph manuscripts of the Annals of the Four Masters', *Celtica*, xix (1987), 75–95.

—, *The celebrated antiquary: Dubhaltach Mac Fhirbhisigh, c.1600–71: his lineage, life and learning* (Maynooth, 1996).

—, 'Court poets and historians in late medieval Connacht' in Evelyn Mullally and John Thompson (eds), *The court and cultural diversity: selected papers from the eighth triennial congress of the International Courtly Literature Society* (Woodbridge, 1997), 17–26.

—, 'Settlement and place-names' in P.J. Duffy, D. Edwards and E. FitzPatrick (eds), *Gaelic Ireland: land, lordship and settlement, c.1250–c.1650* (Dublin, 2001), 223–45.

O'Rahilly, T.F. (ed.), 'Irish poets, historians and judges in English documents, 1538–1615', *Proceedings of the Royal Irish Academy*, xxxvi, sect. C (1921–4), 86–120.

O'Rahilly, T.F., *Early Irish history and mythology* (Dublin, 1946).

Ó Riain, Pádraig, 'The "*crech ríg*" or "regal prey"', *Éigse*, xv (1973–7), 24–30.

—, 'The book of Glendalough or Rawlinson B. 502', *Éigse*, xviii (1981), 161–76.

—, 'Saints in the catalogue of bishops of the lost register of Clogher', *Clogher Record*, xvi, no. 2 (1992), 66–77.

—, '*Codex Salmanticensis*: a provenance *inter Anglos* or *inter Hibernos?*' in Toby Barnard, Dáibhí Ó Cróinín and Katharine Simms (eds), *A miracle of learning: studies in manuscripts and Irish learning* (Aldershot, 1998), 91–100.

Ó Súilleabháin, Seán, 'The feast of Saint Martin in Ireland' in W.E. Richmond (ed.), *Studies in folklore in honour of distinguished service: Professor Stith Thompson* (Indiana, 1957), 252–61.

O'Sullivan, Anne, 'Verses on honorific portions' in James Carney and David Greene (eds), *Celtic studies: essays in memory of Angus Matheson* (London, 1968), 118–23.

O'Sullivan, William, 'A Waterford origin for the *Codex Salmanticensis*', *Decies*, no. 54 (1998), 17–24.

Patterson, Nerys, 'Gaelic law and the Tudor conquest of Ireland: the social background of the sixteenth-century recensions of the pseudo-historical Prologue to the *Senchas már*', *Irish Historical Studies*, xxvii, no. 107 (1991), 193–215.

Price, Liam, 'Armed forces of the Irish chiefs', *Journal of the Royal Society of Antiquaries of Ireland*, lxii (1932), 201–7.

Quinn, D.B., *The Elizabethans and the Irish* (Ithaca, 1966).

Renehan, L.F., *Collections on Irish church history* (2 vols, Dublin, 1861–74).

Sharpe, Richard, *Medieval Irish saints lives: an introduction to* Vitae sanctorum Hiberniae (Oxford, 1991).

Simms, Katharine, 'Warfare in the medieval Gaelic lordships', *Irish Sword*, xii (1975), 98–108.

—, 'Gaelic lordships in Ulster in the later middle ages', unpublished Ph.D. thesis, University of Dublin (1976).

—, 'Guesting and feasting in Gaelic Ireland', *Journal of the Royal Society of Antiquaries of Ireland*, cviii (1978), 67–100.

—, *From kings to warlords: the changing political structure of Gaelic Ireland in the later middle ages* (Woodbridge, 1987).

—, 'The poet as chieftain's widow: bardic elegies' in Donnchadh Ó Corráin, Liam Breatnach, and Kim McCone (eds), *Sages, saints and storytellers* (Maynooth, 1989), 400–11.

—, 'Bards and barons: the Anglo-Irish aristocracy and the native culture' in Robert Bartlett and Angus Mackay (eds), *Medieval frontier societies* (Oxford, 1989, revised ed. 1992) 177–97.

—, 'Late medieval Donegal' in W. Nolan, L. Ronayne and M. Dunlevy (eds), *Donegal: history and society* (Dublin, 1995), 183–201.

—, 'Literary sources for the history of Gaelic Ireland in the post-Norman period' in Kim McCone and Katharine Simms (eds), *Progress in medieval Irish studies* (Maynooth, 1996), 207–15.

—, 'Literacy and the Irish bards' in Huw Pryce (ed.), *Literacy in medieval Celtic societies* (Cambridge, 1998), 238–58.

Strohm, Paul, *Hochon's arrow: the social imagination of fourteenth-century texts* (Princeton, 1992).

—, *Theory and the premodern text* (Minneapolis, 2000).

Szövérffy, Joseph, 'Manus O'Donnell and Irish folk tradition', *Éigse*, viii (1955–7), 108–32.

Walsh, Paul, *Gleanings from Irish manuscripts* (2nd ed., Dublin, 1933).

—, *The Ó Cléirigh family of Tír Conaill* (Dublin, 1938).

—, 'The Annals of Loch Cé', *Irish Ecclesiastical Record*, 5th ser, lvi (1940), 113–22.

—, 'The dating of the Irish annals', *Irish Historical Studies*, ii (1941–2), 355–75.

—, 'The learned family of Ó Maelchonaire', *Catholic Bulletin*, xxvi (1936), 835–42.

—, *Irish men of learning*, ed. Colm Ó Lochlainn (Dublin, 1947).

—, *Irish chiefs and leaders*, ed. Colm Ó Lochlainn (Dublin, 1960).

Whitelock, D., McKitterick, R., and Dumville, D. (eds), *Ireland in early medieval Europe: studies in memory of Kathleen Hughes* (Cambridge, 1982).

Wood, Juliette, 'Folkloristic patterns in Scottish chronicles' in S. Mapstone and J. Wood (eds), *The rose and the thistle: essays on the culture of late medieval and renaissance Scotland* (East Linton, 1998), 116–35.

Index

Index of first lines of poems cited